The Fraud Audit

The Fraud Audit

Responding to the Risk of Fraud in Core Business Systems

LEONARD W. VONA

WILEY

John Wiley & Sons, Inc.

Published by John Wiley & Sons, Inc., Hoboken, New Jersey.

Published simultaneously in Canada.

For general information on our other products and services or for technical support, please contact our Customer Care Department within the United States at (800) 762–2974, outside the United States at (317) 572–3993 or fax (317) 572–4002.

Wiley also publishes its books in a variety of electronic formats. Some content that appears in print may not be available in electronic books. For more information about Wiley products, visit our web site at www.wiley.com.

Library of Congress Cataloging-in-Publication Data:

Vona, Leonard W., 1955-

The fraud audit : responding to the risk of fraud in core business systems / Leonard W. Vona.

 p. cm. — (Wiley corporate f&a ; 16)

Includes index.

ISBN 978-0-470-64726-4 (cloth); ISBN 978-1-118-09370-2 (ebk); ISBN 978-1-118-09371-9 (ebk); ISBN 978-1-118-09372-6 (ebk)

 1. Fraud investigation—United States. 2. Forensic accounting—United States. 3. Fraud—United States—Prevention. I. Title.

HV8079.F7V66 2011

658.4'73—dc22

2011007524

Printed in the United States of America

10 9 8 7 6 5 4 3 2 1

*To my children: Amy, David, and Jeffrey.
Each of you, in your own way,
has contributed to this book.*

Contents

Preface   xi

Chapter 1: What Is a Fraud Audit?   1

Why Respond to Fraud Risk?   3
The Fraud Paradigm   4
Fraud Auditing   5
Fraud Defined   8
The Fraud Triangle   8
Responses to the Risk of Fraud   12
Summary   13

Chapter 2: Professional Standards   15

Overview   16
Fraud Audit Standards   18
Summary   25

Chapter 3: Fraud Scenarios   27

Key Definitions and Terms   28
Fraud Risk Structure   30
Classifying Fraud   32
Identifying Fraud Scenarios   41
Fraud Audit Considerations   46
Summary   51

Chapter 4: Brainstorming: The Implementation of Professional Standards   53

What Is Brainstorming?   54
When to Brainstorm   56
Summary   66

Chapter 5: Assessment of Fraud Likelihood   69

Preparing a Fraud Risk Assessment   69
Summary   81

Chapter 6: Building the Fraud Audit Program   83

Traditional Audit versus the Fraud Audit   84
Responding to the Risk of Fraud   84
A Fraud Audit Program   85
Testing Procedures   89
Fraud Concealment Effect on the Audit Response   97
Audit Evidence Issues   103
Fraud Scenario Examples   105
Summary   110

Chapter 7: Data Mining for Fraud   111

The Art and Science of Data Mining   112
Strategies for Data Mining   129
Limitations of Data Mining   131
Summary   132

Chapter 8: Fraud Audit Procedures   133

Basis of Fraud Audit Procedures   133
Levels of Fraud Audit Procedures   135
Design of Fraud Audit Procedures   138
Summary   145

Chapter 9: Document Analysis   147

Document Analysis and the Fraud Audit   148
Levels of Document Examination   148
Document Red Flags   150
Brainstorming Sessions and Document Red Flags   155
The Fraud Audit Program and Document Red Flags   156
Summary   156

Chapter 10: Disbursement Fraud 159

Fraud Risk Structure 159
Audit Approaches 166
Summary 178

Chapter 11: Procurement Fraud 179

Fraud Risk Structure 181
Audit Procedures 195
Summary 202

Chapter 12: Payroll Fraud 205

Fraud Risk Structure 206
Audit Procedures 212
Summary 222

Chapter 13: Revenue Misstatement 223

Fraud Risk Structure 224
Audit Approach 231
Summary 236

Chapter 14: Inventory Fraud 237

Fraud Risk Structure 238
Audit Procedures 243
Summary 249

Chapter 15: Journal Entry Fraud 251

Fraud Risk Structure 252
Audit Procedures 261
Summary 266

Chapter 16: Program Management Fraud 269

Fraud Risk Structure 270
Audit Approach 277
Summary 282

Chapter 17: Quantifying Fraud 283

Conveying the Impact to Management 284
Role of Evidence in Calculating a Fraud Loss 287
Impact on the Fraud Audit 289
Options for Management 292
Case Studies 293
Summary 296

Appendixes   297

Appendix A   298
Appendix B   311
Appendix C   325
Appendix D   339
Appendix E   347
Appendix F   360
Appendix G   363

About the Author   365

Index   367

Preface

S OMEDAY, I WOULD LIKE professional studies to indicate that auditing is the number one reason for fraud detection; I believe this goal can be accomplished. However, I also believe that we need to recognize that fraud auditing is different from traditional auditing by using all the methodologies of traditional auditing, but just applying them differently.

Fraud auditing is a methodology to respond to the risk of fraud in core business systems. It is a combination of risk assessment, data mining, and audit procedures designed to locate and identify fraud scenarios. It is based on the theory of fraud, which recognizes that fraud is committed with the intent to conceal the truth. It incorporates into the audit process the concept of red flags linked to the fraud scenario concealment strategy associated with data, documents, internal controls, and behavior.

To illustrate the "different" concept, fraud auditing recognizes that the greatest audit procedure in the world will not detect fraud if the sample does not include one fraudulent transaction. Data mining is the audit tool to build a sample. Fraud audit procedures use the authenticity principle versus the evidence principle for designing test procedures. These fraud audit procedures acknowledge the varying degrees of fraud concealment sophistication that the perpetrator intends to commit in the fraud scenario.

My book is intended to share my professional experiences in studying and performing fraud audits. I hope this is the first of many books in the industry to discuss methodologies for responding to the risk of fraud within the professional practice of auditing.

The Fraud Audit

CHAPTER ONE

What Is a Fraud Audit?

T HE DEBATE IS OVER; auditors have a responsibility to respond to the risk of fraud. The stockholders, board of directors, and management of organizations are looking to their internal auditors to detect fraud before it undermines the vital operations that are referred to herein as the core business systems. Auditing standards now require auditors to respond to the risk of fraud. Phrases such as *professional skepticism, identified fraud risk, fraud risk assessment,* and *fraud audit procedures* are now found in use within organizations of all types to meet the current standards. Unfortunately, this change seems to be an agonizing effort for all involved. Just say the very word *fraud* and everyone seems to react as though someone has contracted the bubonic plague. Therefore, all parties involved in the effective, efficient, and healthy operation of an organization, such as the aforementioned auditors and various stakeholders, need to recognize what fraud is, where it is found, and how it is found. So, when we speak of fraud in the context of auditing, it denotes a distinct body of knowledge, the mastery of which is needed to address the risk of fraud. The title of auditor does not immediately confer knowledge regarding fraud, and it certainly doesn't infer the mastery of identifying the risk. Auditors need to possess this specialized knowledge to solve the difficulties in addressing fraud that perplex the profession. So, fear no more, because you, the auditor, aren't facing a steep climb up a mountain of knowledge all alone. No, the purpose of this book is to give you the guidance, strategy, and tools you'll need to make a safe trip.

The Awareness Theory Methodology (ATM) approach to fraud auditing is at the heart of our discussion of the fraud audit. The objective of "ATM" is to provide a conceptual framework for the fraud audit. Fraud theory (the "T" in ATM) asserts that fraud is a body of knowledge. Understanding the how, why, and where of fraud are critical elements of this body of knowledge. Knowing "how" fraud occurs is dependent upon a logical, rule-based system whereby the auditor identifies the fraud scenarios facing an organization. Consequently, a process must be provided for describing the fraud scenarios inherent to the core business system. The process is commonly referred to as the fraud identification stage. The "why" fraud occurs involves the reasons individuals commit fraudulent acts against an organization. Referring to the quintessential fraud triangle, the reasons for committing fraud relate to pressure and rationalization factors. Knowledge of the typical underlying reasons of why fraud is committed is critical to both building the control environment and enhancing an auditor's awareness to the likelihood of fraud. Last, the question of "where" fraud occurs is the premise of this book, namely, the core business systems. These systems are identified herein as procurement, disbursements, payroll, financial statement reporting, inventories, and journal entries.

The auditor needs a methodology (the "M" in ATM) for building a response to detect fraudulent transactions. The fraud response starts in the planning stage with the brainstorming session and continues with the assessment of fraud likelihood and fraud significance. Included in the response are the steps of audit procedures that will reveal the true nature of the transaction (referred to as building a sample of transactions; also known as data mining), implementation of fraud audit procedures, and the final step of evaluating the audit evidence for qualitative and quantitative considerations. These steps are all essential parts of the overall audit response to the fraud risk.

Finally, there is the awareness (the "A" in ATM) required by the fraud audit approach discussed in this book. The auditor needs to be able to recognize fraud scenario potential among the millions of transactions that exist in today's business systems. Knowing the red flags of fraud and recognizing the potential for fraud scenarios inherent to specific organizational structures is critical to the overall process of finding fraud.

WHY RESPOND TO FRAUD RISK?

There are many reasons to detect and uncover fraud. The obvious reasons are the substantial monetary sums and industry-wide and international reputations at stake. There are many studies that have been done projecting the cost of fraud to organizations. The range of results is extreme, with some instances resulting in the cost being minimal to those cases where fraud is found to be so rampant that it causes the destruction of an organization. Organizations like Barring Bank and Enron do not exist today because of the fraudulent actions of their employees. The cost of corruption in public contracts has been estimated to exceed one trillion dollars. Examples abound, too, with large companies still in operation, like the fraudulent allegations regarding numerous Fortune 500 companies. Just pick up a newspaper on any given day and in all likelihood there will be a story concerning fraud. The overriding fact is that fraud costs organizations significant monetary amounts and reputation-harmful publicity each year.

However, organizations do not have to accept fraud as a cost of doing business, and they should not live in a state of denial that their existing internal controls will protect them from fraud. Organizations need to realize that a proactive audit approach is necessary in the detection of fraud. Whether this task is embedded in an internal audit or outsourced to an audit firm is a matter of corporate style and, therefore, should not compromise the overall purpose of finding fraud. Therefore, the primary result of rooting out fraud should be both an increase to the bottom line through financial recoveries and the stopping of future losses.

Professionally, the standards are requiring auditors to respond to the risk of fraud within their audit scope. Consequently, not having a response to fraud is a violation of standards. Other than fear, what is preventing the standards from being followed? As with any standards, regulations, policies, and so on, it comes down to interpretation. What continues to be debated is the breadth of the audit response to the fraud risk. Is a questionnaire sufficient to evaluate fraud propensity? Is the awareness of red flags the right approach? Should auditors search for fraud when no overt internal control red flags are evident? Is a site visit to validate the existence of a customer an audit or investigation procedure? These are all good questions that are being debated in the profession. The answers in all probability will eventually be derived from a combination of three things: the actual attempts at applying the audit standards, customer expectations of the auditors' efforts in finding fraud, and the desire of the auditor to detect fraud.

In light of such speculation, this book will focus on the first of these three things, specifically, the techniques that have been tried and proven effective in the detection of fraud. However, given the relevance of the professional audit standards to this discussion, Chapter 2 of this book will provide an overview of the professional audit standards so that the reader can correlate the standards to the processes being discussed.

 ## THE FRAUD PARADIGM

Times have changed. Old problems such as fraud have taken on new attributes because of the technological sophistication of our society. The ease of doing business because of continual technological advances presents opportunities that audit methodologies have not kept up with. We need to think differently about fraud in order to develop a realistic audit approach to fraud risk. There are essential questions that are needed to be asked to close this ever-growing gap.

For example, what is fraud? A simple question, but we still need to be on the same page. As auditors, we need to distinguish the difference between fraud in a legal sense and fraud from an auditor's perspective. We also need to understand the difference between a violation of law and a fraudulent act. From a legal perspective, the act of embezzlement, although a violation of law, is not necessarily a fraudulent act; however, most auditors would consider such an act as fraudulent. Therefore, auditors need a fraud definition that is consistent with the audit process, not the legal system. Words like *fraud scenario, intent, concealment,* and *damages* should be defined from an audit perspective versus a legal perspective. In order to find fraud, auditors must know what fraud is within the boundaries of the systems they are working in and not those of the law per se.

Should auditors prove fraud? The answer is no. Auditors are not the trier of fact. From a legal perspective, judges and juries are responsible for making the decision. Internally, the decision rests with management or the audit committee, depending on the organization's policies. Auditors are responsible for conducting audits that identify activity that may violate laws or internal policies. The activity should then be referred to the appropriate investigative body. For an analogy, the audit process is like a grand jury. The opinion of the grand jury and the auditor is that sufficient evidence exists to warrant an investigation. Whether the investigation is conducted by the same person is not relevant; however, it is important to note that there is a distinction between the fraud audit process and the legal investigative process.

Can auditors detect inherent fraud schemes within the audit process? Perhaps the answer is not a simple yes or no. Two critical points center on the sophistication of the fraud concealment strategy and the inherent fraud scheme. For example, the revenue-skimming fraud scheme is the diversion of revenue before the revenue transaction is recorded. By the nature of the scheme, there is no record trail. Therefore, the examination of the books and records will not detect the fraud scheme. The sophistication of the concealment is how the individual hides his or her actions, which can be rated as low, medium, and high. If the person uses his home address for his shell corporation, the audit process should be able to detect that scheme. If the individual uses a series of shell corporations using post office boxes, the audit process may not be able to detect the fraud scenario. Understanding what fraud scenarios are detectable within the audit process is critical to planning the fraud audit. Additionally, if the nature of the fraud scenario is not detectable within the audit process, then logically, the organization needs to strengthen internal controls or rely on allegations of the fraud scenario.

Can you have a complex fraud scheme inherent to an organization? No. Most inherent fraud schemes are fairly simple to understand. It is how individuals conceals their actions and shield themselves from the action that may be complex or difficult to detect. Some might say this is a game of words. Maybe so, but the difference between the action and the concealment strategy is an important distinction to know.

 ## FRAUD AUDITING

A fraud audit is the process of responding to the risk of fraud within the context of an audit. It may be conducted as part of an audit, or the entire audit may focus on detecting fraud. It may also be performed because of an allegation or the desire to detect fraudulent activity in core business systems. For our discussion purposes, this book will focus on the detection of fraud when there is no specific allegation of fraud.

Fraud auditing is the application of audit procedures designed to increase the chances of detecting fraud in core business systems. The four steps of the fraud audit process are:

1. **Fraud risk identification.** The process starts with identifying the inherent fraud schemes and customizing the inherent fraud scheme into a fraud scenario. Fraud scenarios in this context will be discussed in Chapter 3.

2. **Fraud risk assessment.** Fraud risk assessment is the linking of internal controls to the fraud scenario. The assessment of fraud likelihood is discussed in Chapter 5. Also involved is the use of data mining search routines to determine if transactions exist that are consistent with the fraud scenario data profile. While data mining is highlighted in Chapter 7, it is a relevant part of our discussion throughout the book.

3. **Fraud audit procedure.** The audit procedure focuses on gathering audit evidence that is outside the point of the fraud opportunity. Specific procedures will be discussed in Chapter 8 and have relevance in subsequent chapters.

4. **Fraud conclusion.** The conclusion is an either/or outcome, requiring either referral of the transaction to investigation or the determination that no relevant red flags exist. Chapters 3 through 9 contain relevant discussion of this step.

Traditional Audits versus Fraud Audits

As stated previously, but worth repeating, auditors today have a responsibility to respond to the risk of fraud. What continues to be debated is how to respond to that risk. The discussion centers around the difference between audit procedures performed in a traditional audit versus those performed in a fraud audit. To understand the differences, we first need to define each audit approach, then compare the two. A traditional audit typically focuses on the adequacy and effectiveness of the internal controls. The process is commonly referred to as a test of internal controls. A Generally Accepted Audit Standards (GAAS) audit of the financial statements would also include substantive tests of the financial accounts comprising them. In contrast, a fraud audit is the application of specific audit procedures to increase the likelihood of detecting fraud in core business systems. It is a proactive approach to detecting fraud, unlike a fraud investigation, which takes a reactive approach. The fraud audit does not test controls, but rather independently affirms the authenticity of the transaction by gathering evidence external to the perpetrator.

The two types of audits can also be compared in terms of the differences in sampling methodology, audit procedures, and the qualitative aspects of audit evidence as follows.

The traditional audit requires selecting a sample using random and unbiased sampling procedures in order to opine on the effectiveness of the internal controls. The fraud audit requires selecting a sample using a nonrandom and bias sampling methodology, based on the fraud data profile, to detect fraudulent transactions. The sampling approach for fraud auditing is commonly referred to as discovery sampling.

In a traditional audit, the audit response is to test controls and examine documentary evidence to verify that the control procedure is operating as designed by management. The resulting conclusion is that controls are or are not operating as management intended. In a fraud audit, the audit response is to perform fraud audit procedures designed to gather evidence independent of company documents. An example can be found by looking at testing in the cash disbursement cycle where the inherent fraud scheme is the use of a fictitious company billing for services not performed. A traditional audit of the cash disbursement cycle relies on the vendor invoice and authorized approval signature. Depending on the controls in place, purchase orders or two levels of approval may be required. The fraud audit does not focus on the controls, but rather on the authenticity of the transaction. In a fraud audit, the auditor will either perform procedures to independently verify if the company exists in the truest business sense or employ a procedure to ensure the vendor is conducting business consistent with that described on the invoice.

Fraud Audit versus Fraud Investigation

The primary distinction between the fraud audit and the fraud investigation is the standards for performing the engagement and the intent of the engagement. The fraud audit is performed under the auditing standards. Whereas fraud investigations are performed using the criminal or civil standards applicable to the jurisdiction, fraud auditing is intended to identify transactions that warrant an investigation. The intent is not to prove fraud, but rather identify the transactions as suspicious. In other words, the transaction has unresolved red flags. The decision tree analysis in Chapter 8 will further elaborate on the concept of a suspicious transaction. Fraud investigation is intended to refute or corroborate the suspicion of fraudulent acts. The law becomes the basis for the methodology and standards. Criminal and civil procedure, rules of evidence, statutes, and burdens of proof are critical element of the investigative process. Even in the fraud investigation, the purpose is not to prove fraud, that obligation is the responsibility of the trier of fact, specifically, either the judge or the jury.

In reality, a fraud audit and a fraud investigation do use many of the same procedures, such as document examination, interviews, and report issuance. In terms of responding to an allegation of fraud, the difference between fraud audit and fraud investigation rests with the eventual Trier of Facts standards. While in regard to the responding to the risk of fraud with no specific allegation of fraud, the difference between audit and investigation seems to balance on the perceived responsibility of the auditor to detect fraud within their audit process.

 ## FRAUD DEFINED

By defining fraud, we hope to establish the scope of the fraud response from an audit perspective. This means that the auditor may adopt the definition as written, or exclude those aspects not relevant to the scope of their audit. However, intent and concealment should never be excluded from the definition. What we are essentially doing in defining fraud from an audit perspective is describing the characteristics of fraudulent acts that differentiate them from similar or like acts. Specifically:

1. Acts committed on the organization or by the organization or for the organization. The first part of the definition focuses on the primary and secondary classifications of fraud, which will be discussed in Chapter 3.
2. Acts committed by an internal or external source. The focus is on the primary party committing the fraudulent act. Obviously, the scenario may include both parties.
3. The acts are intentional and concealed. The intent of the act and how the fraud is concealed differentiate fraud risk from control risk.
4. The acts are typically illegal or denote wrongdoing, such as in the cases of financial misstatement, policy violation, ethical lapse, or a perception issue. The purpose is to distinguish between the illegal act and the act that is not illegal, but conducted with intent and to conceal.
5. The acts cause a loss of company funds, company value, or company reputation, or any unauthorized benefit whether received personally or by others. Fraud by its nature is associated with financial gain.

 ## THE FRAUD TRIANGLE

The fraud triangle explains why people commit fraud. The theory behind it is simple: those with opportunity either rationalize their illicit behavior or are motivated by the pressures to commit the fraudulent behavior. Statement of Auditing Standard 99 requires auditors to understand the fraud risk factors as part of planning their audit response to the risk of misstatement. Understanding the concept is easy; however, applying the concept in the fraud audit is more of a challenge. The following sections describe the components of the fraud triangle, along with the challenges in the practical application of it.

Opportunity to Commit Fraud

Opportunity is an individual's ability to commit a fraud scenario and his or her related experience in committing the scenario. In the audit planning stage, the fraud opportunity should be viewed absent of any internal controls. The goal is to identify all parties that logically have the opportunity to commit the fraud scenario. The parties can be identified through job title or function; for example, from an internal control perspective, it is a person's job duties that provide an opportunity to commit fraud rather than the level of operation presenting an opportunity to commit fraud. Also, the actual opportunity is either direct or indirect. In Chapter 3 we will further discuss fraud opportunity in context of the permutation analysis.

Opportunity also correlates to one's experience in committing the fraud scenario. We have identified four categories of fraud perpetrators and experience levels as follows:

1. There is the first-time offender, where the pressures and rationalization cause the person to commit the fraudulent act. Remember that opportunity pertains to the ability to commit the fraudulent act and not the cause. There are many theories regarding first-time offenders. Typically, their fraud starts from nothing, as when the perpetrator learns of a control weakness and becomes tempted. Then it grows with each subsequent successful attempt. Consequently, these frauds are usually detected within a few years.
2. The repeat offender is a person who has committed a fraud scenario in more than one organization or committed fraudulent acts numerous times, but in different areas of the company without detection each time. This description indicates that opportunity is the critical factor involved with the intent to commit fraud a multiple of times, with the causes of pressures and rationalization being less significant factors.
3. The organized crime category pertains to a group of people external to the organization who are dedicated to committing the fraudulent act. Again, pressures and rationalization are not as critical as is opportunity. Often,

individuals in this category will extort or bribe employees to participate in the fraudulent act, or members of the organized crime group will seek employment within the organization to commit the act.

4. For the benefit of the company category, the individuals involved typically see their action as benefiting the organization; therefore, rationalization is typically the cause. These individuals are characteristically high-ranking employees in the organization. While they benefit from their actions as individuals, they also believe their actions are for the good of the organization.

Knowing these categories is useful in understanding how the fraud triangle theory correlates to the tendency for committing fraud. Also, they highlight why internal controls sometimes fail to stop a motivated person from committing the fraudulent activity. Within the fraud audit, the opportunity to commit fraud is the critical consideration, as seen with the experience factors just described. For example, the control owner has the primary opportunity to commit the fraud scenario. Consequently, linking the inherent fraud scheme to the person with the opportunity becomes the basis for identifying the fraud scenarios related to a particular business system. Using the fraud permutation analysis will also bring to light other fraud opportunities that are not considered in a more traditional, control-based audit. Clearly, understanding the fraud opportunities and linking them to an inherent fraud scheme is a critical first step before an audit response can be planned and executed.

Pressures Affecting People or Organizations

The identification of pressures will vary with the nature of the primary classification of fraud. Typically, the pressure is associated with financial reasons. For example, pressures are evident in financial reporting's meeting investors' expectations of more income, leading to asset misappropriations, a primary fraud classification. The key is to understand which pressures correlate to which primary fraud classification, but more on that in Chapter 3. For now, you have to know that an audit, by its nature, generally does not have procedures to accurately gather information that would disclose these issues with any certainty. However, the audit process can create an awareness of behaviors in the workplace indicative of a lifestyle-maintenance issue creating pressure. It is interesting to note that in a subsequent investigation, private investigators would collect information to be used regarding behaviors that relate to vices or other lifestyle anomalies.

Rationalization of Fraudulent Behavior

People rationalize their behaviors. The reasons vary from person to person, but a justification always exists. Fundamentally, rationalization is a conscious decision by the perpetrator to place his or her needs above the needs of others. Even though the ethical decision-making process varies by individual, culture, and experience, rationalization is present. The concept is important in the understanding of why people commit fraud. You can put two employees in the same job duties with the same opportunity to commit fraud. One will take the opportunity and the other will not. How the one who does take the opportunity rationalizes the fraud speaks to the cause and not the opportunity. Therefore, when you think of the practicality of using the rationalization concept to identify fraud, you are limited to being observant to lifestyle behaviors.

Fear of Detection

The reasons for not committing fraud are numerous. Personal integrity, family values, and religious beliefs are just a few of them. One reason, outside the area of virtues, morals, and character, is the fear of detection. There we go talking about fear again, but the fear of being detected is a very significant factor in discussing fraudulent behavior. From an internal control perspective, once pressure and rationalization exceed the fear of detection, people are more prone to committing a fraudulent act. This condition is important to understand, especially when auditors place too much reliance on an internal control's ability to mitigate a fraud risk. This does not mean that internal controls are to be ignored. They are one of the important defenses in preventing fraud. However, in assessing the likelihood of fraud, the fear of detection, or the lack thereof, is an intangible; that is, it is difficult to assess, and therefore is not a part of our discussion of factors mitigating risk in a fraud audit.

Fraud Triangle Premises

The body of knowledge surrounding the fraud triangle is critical to the fraud auditor. The ATM approach to a fraud audit relies on the concepts denoted by the fraud triangle. The triangle as a whole is critical in the planning phase for the recognition of the tendency for fraud within the core business system. In particular, designing the methodology for the data mining, audit procedures, and evidence considerations relies on the fraud opportunity. The following summarizes key considerations regarding the fraud triangle:

1. The three elements of fraud—rationalization, pressure, and opportunity—coexist at different levels per individual.
2. The three elements of fraud will vary based on personal circumstances of the individual.
3. The strength of one element may cause an individual to commit a fraudulent act.
4. The strength of one element may eliminate the worry of fraud detection.
5. Identifying the three elements is easier than measuring the three elements.
6. The fraud risk factors may originate from internal or external sources.
7. Fraud opportunity is the one aspect of the fraud triangle that is easily identifiable.
8. The fraud audit is based on the opportunity to commit an inherent fraud scheme.

RESPONSES TO THE RISK OF FRAUD

There are two fundamental approaches to responding to the risk of fraud. The first approach is to test internal controls and be alert to the red flags of fraud. The second approach is to actively search for the existence of fraud scenarios that are occurring in the core business systems and not rely on internal controls. The approach used is dependent on the purpose of the audit and the applicable audit standards.

The methodology for responding to the risk of fraud will vary depending on the professional standards and the purpose of the audit, that is, financial statement audits will apply Generally Accepted Audit Standards. In particular, Statement of Auditing Standards 99 provides guidance to responding to fraud risk in a financial statement audit. The overall purposes can be categorized in the following four groups:

1. Reliance on internal controls for purposes of a financial statement audit. In the financial statement audit, the auditor will test internal controls and be alert to the red flags.
2. Provide an opinion on the operating effectiveness of the internal controls regarding fraud minimization. The internal controls are tested and alert to the red flags.
3. Provide an opinion on the existence of fraud in core business systems. In the fraud audit, the auditor does not rely on internal controls and instead actively searches for fraud. The internal controls are considered to

control avoidance strategies, circumvention strategies, and inhibitor considerations.

4. Respond to an allegation of fraud. The investigation by design is intended to refute or corroborate the allegations. The existence or avoidance of internal controls may be relevant to establishing intent.

The types of methodologies to responding to the risk of fraud are the following:

1. **Red flag approach.** The purpose is to test the effectiveness of internal controls and be alert to the red flags that are consistent with the fraud scenario. In a financial statement audit, the purpose is to determine the reliance on internal controls as part of the decision process on substantive testing procedures. Internal auditors test internal controls to determine the effectiveness of the internal control. Understanding the red flags is critical to both the awareness and the methodology of the fraud response.
2. **Integrate a fraud audit procedure into an audit program.** The purpose is to respond to a specific fraud scenario. Does the identified fraud scenario result from a perceived risk within the risk assessment or a mandatory fraud risk such as revenue recognition as required by SAS 99?
3. **Fraud audit.** The purpose of the fraud audit is to uncover fraud in the core business systems and be alert to internal control weaknesses regarding fraud opportunity.
4. **Fraud allegation response.** The purpose is to refute or corroborate the allegation of fraudulent activity

 **SUMMARY**

Although the methodology for conducting a fraud audit is different from traditional auditing, the auditor employs many of the same skills and tools. Therefore, fraud audits are a blend of new methodologies and traditional audit tools. Instead of debating whether the procedure is a traditional audit, fraud audit, or fraud investigation, this book will direct its efforts toward what the auditor can do to uncover fraud in the places it is most often found: the core business systems.

CHAPTER TWO

Professional Standards

E VERY PROFESSIONAL FOOTBALL TEAM uses a playbook filled with intricately designed plays made up of X's and O's with arrows and such. No matter how refined or how numerous the plays in the book, it is the execution of them that determines a team's success. As unbelievable as it may first sound, the same can be said of fraud auditing. Without standards, the playbook, as it were, directed at fraud, causes successful results to be happenstance, and who wants to watch a team constantly calling an audible anyway? The standards may seem too broad for practical implementation. How can every possible situation be taken into account? However, like our plays, there needs to be room to adjust to the distinctiveness of the situation, and the tools provided by these standards allow for successful outcomes if executed properly.

The accounting scandals of the past few decades, as well as the recent economic downturn, have left a cloud over the auditing profession. It became apparent that the traditional standards of control testing and the overview of financial statements were not effective in detecting fraud. As a result, some old audit standards were revised and new ones were created. These "playbooks" offer the auditor guidelines, tools, and a solid basis for devising "a game plan" for addressing the risk of fraud.

 **OVERVIEW**

Like a professional football team's game plan, whereby a playbook is revised to match a certain opponent, the focus of this chapter's discussion is not on one set of standards, but on standards provided by the Institute of Internal Auditors (IIA), the American Institute of Certified Public Accountants (AICPA), the U.S. Government Accountability Office (GAO), and the International Auditing and Assurance Standards Board (IAASB). Each of these organizations have similarities with regard to fraud audit standards, but the major differences between them is whether the auditors are internal or external; whether the organization is governmental in nature or receiving government funding; or if the organization is international.

For example, the IIA defines fraud as

[a]ny illegal act characterized by deceit, concealment, or violation of trust. These acts are not dependent upon the threat of violence or physical force. Frauds are perpetrated by parties and organizations to obtain money, property, or services; to avoid payment or loss of services; or to secure personal or business advantage.

The IIA addresses how boards of directors and senior management may deter fraud. The standards put forth by the IIA provide approaches for management via their annual plans to respond to the risk of fraud. Specifically, these approaches entail management controls over fraud and testing areas prone to fraud. Essentially, information is provided on how organizations can establish their own risk management program, whereby entities need to determine risk management needs based on size and circumstances.

In addition to the standards provided by IIA for internal auditing, the AICPA issued the Statement of Auditing Standards 99 or SAS 99 entitled "Consideration of Fraud in a Financial Statement Audit." Within this statement fraud is defined as

an intentional act that results in a material misstatement in financial statements that are subject of an audit.

However, it also distinguishes between intentional and unintentional errors. With regard to intentional acts, there are two types of fraud considered: misstatements arising from fraudulent reporting and misstatements from the misappropriation of assets. SAS 99 also incorporates the use of professional skepticism; addresses the fraud triangle elements of pressure, rationalization, and opportunity; and acknowledges the use of interviewing to uncover fraud.

The federal government also issued standards with regard to fraud. The Generally Accepted Government Auditing Standards (GAGAS), or as it is more commonly referred to, the "Yellow Book," is published by the U.S. Government Accountability Office (GAO). These standards are used to audit government entities or entities that receive government funding. For example, Section 4.10 of GAGAS states that

> [a]uditors should design the audit to provide reasonable assurance of detecting misstatements that result from violations of provisions of contracts or grant agreements and could have a direct and material effect on the determination of financial statement amounts or other financial data significant to the audit objectives.

The standards are a combination of those from the AICPA and those that the GAO created specifically for government entities; therefore, it is not uncommon for nongovernmental auditors or organizations to use them as well.

Expanding beyond a national level, the IAASB issued a standard entitled: "The Auditor's Responsibilities Relating to Fraud in an Audit of Financial Statements," which defines fraud as

> "[a]n intentional act by one or more individuals among management, those charged with governance, employees, or third parties involving the use of deception to obtain an unjust or illegal advantage."

Three primary objectives are targeted by the standard:

1. To identify and assess the risks of material misstatement of the financial statements due to fraud.
2. To obtain sufficient appropriate audit evidence regarding the assessed risks of material misstatement due to fraud, through designing and implementing appropriate responses.
3. To respond appropriately to fraud or suspected fraud identified during the audit.

FRAUD AUDIT STANDARDS

As reviewed previously, there are four standard-creating entities for fraud auditing, and the following is an explanation of the fraud-auditing standards by each one.

The Institute of Internal Auditors (IIA) and Fraud

Since the IIA is an organization that primarily focuses on the work of internal auditors, it recognizes that an internal auditor's failure to detect fraud can have an irreparable effect on the financial health of an organization. That being said, the IIA is consistently evolving its audit standards to help internal auditors build a "strong fraud program that includes awareness, prevention, and detection programs, as well as a fraud risk assessment process to identify fraud risks within the organization."

Guidelines Regarding Fraud

The IIA has developed two sets of guidelines in an effort to furnish internal auditors with an updated fraud-auditing methodology. The first set of these guidelines, called "Internal Auditing and Fraud," provides the internal auditor with guidance in building an audit approach to respond to inherent fraud schemes, while the second set, entitled "Fraud Prevention and Detection in an Automated World," outlines fraud risk and prevention as it relates to Information Technology (IT). The fraud triangle elements of pressure, rationalization, and opportunity are recognized in these guidelines, providing a basis for designing an effective fraud management program to be used by internal auditors.

A Fraud Management Program   Specifically, a fraud management program consists of several steps or segments, the first of which requires management is to establish a "tone at the top" with a formalized company ethics policy. Given that subordinates tend to mimic the behavior of management, a top-down approach to creating an ethical work environment is needed. Similarly, the establishment of a fraud awareness policy is recommended in order for an organization to understand the nature, causes, and characteristics of fraud. The objective of such a policy is to have fraud awareness become a part of an organization's culture to the extent that everyone, knowing what fraud is, will also realize the risk of pursuing fraudulent behavior.

With clear and cogent policies in place, a step needs to be made to perform a comprehensive and coherent fraud risk assessment. With such an assessment, management gains insight into the overall types of fraud their organization is susceptible to and therefore the fraud schemes inherent to the workings of the organization, and what controls need to be implemented or, in the case of existing controls, strengthened, to prevent occurrences of fraud.

With these major segments in place, the next step in a fraud management program is to initiate ongoing reviews of audit activity within the organization. Are audit procedures being performed based on the fraud risk? If so, then efforts are directed to the prevention and detection of fraud, whereby the organization's culture and its internal controls limit the opportunities for fraud and aid in the detection of fraud, respectively. Such efforts persuade employees to avoid committing fraudulent acts as the chances of detection are high.

The last segment of investigation is composed of practices and resources to fully investigate a potential fraud situation. Having these procedures in place allows internal auditors to respond quickly and efficiently if and when fraud is detected.

IPPF Standards The IIA's International Professional Practices Framework (IPPF) describes the standards by which an auditor can detect, prevent, and monitor fraud risks while addressing those risks in audits and investigations. These standards are:

- **IIA Standard 1210.A2: Proficiency and Due Professional Care.** Internal auditors are required to have a level of knowledge that is adequate in being able to understand and respond to the risk of fraud. However, this knowledge is not expected to be on a level of someone who is a forensic auditor.
- **IIA Standard 1220.A1: Due Professional Care.** Internal auditors must demonstrate professional responsibility by considering the following:
  - The amount of work needed to achieve the audit's objectives.
  - How assurance procedures are applied to significance of matters, related complexity, or materiality.
  - Adequacy and effectiveness of governance, risk management, and control processes.
  - The likelihood of significant errors, fraud, or noncompliance.
  - Cost of assurance in relation to potential benefits.
- **IIA Standard 2060: Reporting to Senior Management and the Board.** The chief audit executive (CAE) must periodically notify senior

management and the board of directors on the internal audit activity overall performance, specifically, providing a report on significant risk exposures and control issues, fraud risks in general, governance issues, and any other matters deemed necessary and appropriate.

▪ **IIA Standard 2120.A2: Risk Management.** The internal audit program must be set up in a fashion that evaluates the potential of fraud occurring and how the organization manages this risk.

▪ **IIA Standard 2210.A2: Engagement Objectives.** When developing engagement objectives, internal auditors must consider the following: probability of significant errors, fraud, noncompliance, and other exposures.

Recognition of Fraud

Clearly, the aforementioned standards provide a needed basis for internal auditors in addressing fraud within their auditing duties. However, the ultimate responsibility for fraud deterrence is in the hands of management and the board of directors. The role of the internal auditor with regard to this responsibility is critical in establishing whether the organization's controls are adequate. This determination can be made based on the fraud management program and the IPPF standards.

Consideration of Fraud via SAS 99

AICPA standards with regard to auditing and fraud have certainly evolved over the past few decades as evidenced by the breadth of SAS 99 in relation to previous standards in place to assist the auditor in responding to the risk of fraud. SAS 99 states, "The auditor has a responsibility to plan and perform the audit to obtain reasonable assurance about whether the financial statements are free of material misstatement, whether caused by error or by fraud." Most commonly, these material misstatements are the result of fraudulent financial reporting or the misappropriation of assets. The most recent SAS update at the end of 2002 took into consideration the fraud triangle, thereby clarifying the auditor's responsibility in detecting and reporting fraud. Simply stated, knowing the pressures, opportunities, and rationalization underlying the committing of a fraudulent act, an auditor can implement a professional skepticism about findings that on the surface appear benign.

The importance of professional skepticism is actually addressed in paragraph 13 of SAS 99. Fraud can occur because of the pressures facing a person, such as financial hardship or because of what the person interprets as an easy opportunity to commit fraud. Whatever the reason of the perpetrator, the auditor needs a professional skepticism that maybe all is not what it seems. Regard must be given to pressures, opportunity, and rationalization. Is there something here that would indicate the existence of an environment that would support these fraud triangle elements?

A question arises as to how an auditor develops this professional skepticism if the auditor has experience with only traditional auditing. SAS 99 provides tools, for example, as paragraph 14 states: "Prior to or in conjunction with the information-gathering procedures . . . members of the audit team should discuss the potential for material misstatement due to fraud." This discussion "should include" brainstorming of ideas and the importance of maintaining the proper mind-set throughout the audit. Chapter 4 of this book provides an in-depth discussion on the use of brainstorming sessions as a manner of information sharing about the client, the industry, past audit findings, and inherent fraud schemes. The general hope is that all the engaged auditors will come out of this meeting with a skeptical mind-set in regard to how the audit is to be approached.

Another tool provided is interviewing. Specifically, at the beginning of the audit, SAS 99 guides the auditor to obtain the information needed to identify the risks of material misstatement due to fraud. This process typically begins with the auditor's inquiring of management and others in the organization what their views are on the risks of fraud. Obviously, the types of answers one does not want to hear are: "Oh, we can't have any problems with fraud here" or "I've personally hired everyone who works here and can vouch for them" or "We have the highest hiring standards of any company, so we don't have those kinds of people here." In light of such responses, or given that managers or those responsible for the financial reporting will provide false information and deflect such questions if they are involved in a fraud scheme, it is just as important for the auditors to question personnel who are not in management roles or those not involved in financial reporting.

In addition to using interviews in obtaining the information needed to identify the risks of material misstatement due to fraud, SAS 99 directs auditors to consider unusual or unexpected relationships that have come to light using specific analytical procedures. These analytical procedures are part of the planning process, whereby the unusual or unexpected can be identified pertaining to either events, amounts, ratios, trends, revenue, or other items that relate to financial statements. The auditor is also to consider fraud risk factors, specifically, the elements of the fraud triangle. Going back to the interviewing process, an auditor may formulate questions to ascertain pressures, opportunity, or rationalization, but also to uncover revenue recognition, management overrides, and so on. For example, in order to assess any pressure to commit fraud on the part of an employee in a sales department, an auditor may ask: "What impact will your competition have on meeting your goals?" Or if investigating revenue recognition, the auditor may ask the same person: "What type of practice is followed regarding approval or sales?"

Concerning when or if risk is identified, SAS 99 directs the auditor to identify any risk that could lead to material misstatements. To do this identification, a risk assessment must be performed. The question that must be answered by the risk assessment is: "Does this risk associate with a specific account, transaction, or the financial statement as a whole?" It is also important for the auditor to consider the possibility of management overrides of internal controls during this process. After taking into account an organization's programs and controls that pertain to the identified risks, the auditor must question whether the internal controls mitigate the identified risks of material misstatement due to fraud.

Upon arriving at the results of the risk assessment, SAS 99 prescribes that a response be devised. There is no overall response, but rather a collection of them, such as:

- A response that has an overall effect on how the audit is conducted.
- A response to identified risks involving the nature, timing, and extent of audit procedures.
- Application of professional skepticism in response to the identified risks.
- A response to address management override of controls.
- A response to the risks associated with revenue recognition.

As the fieldwork progresses and evidence is collected, the focus should be on situations where there are discrepancies in the accounting records, conflicting or missing evidential matter, or problematic or unusual relationships between the auditor and management. Specifically, discrepancies of accounting records can be transactions that were not properly recorded, records that do not reconcile to the general ledger, or unsupported balances or transactions. Conflicting or missing evidential matter is a distinct situation with missing or altered documents and unexplained reconciling items. Last, problematic or unusual relationships between the auditor and management can result from undue pressure during the audit process, complaints by the management about audit procedures and inquiries, and the management's attempt to control the auditor's access to records.

The extent of SAS 99 continues with the auditor's responsibility to communicate possible fraud to management or an audit committee. If the auditor has determined that there is evidence of fraud, the matter should be brought to the appropriate level of management. In situations of material misstatement, the financial statements should be brought to the attention of the audit committee or the highest level of management. It is important to note that if there is only a slight risk of fraud occurring, the auditor should use his or her professional judgment as to whether to report this risk factor. If the fraud involves potential misappropriation of assets or if the fraud is on a large scale, the auditor should consider consulting with legal counsel before bringing the matter to management. The disclosure of fraud to parties other than management is not part of the auditor's responsibility unless required to comply with certain legal and regulatory requirements, discussions with the entity's previous auditors, subpoenas, or specific rules that apply to organizations that receive federal funding.

The seriousness of these communications, in all cases, makes the SAS 99 requirements on documentation all that more important. Paragraph .83 states the auditor should document the following:

- The audit team discussion during the planning process regarding the susceptibility of the entity's financial statements to material misstatement due to fraud.
- The procedures performed to obtain information to identify and assess fraud risk.
- The specific risks identified.
- Supporting reasons why the auditor has not identified improper revenue recognition as fraud.
- The results of the procedures performed to address the risk of management overrides.
- Other conditions and analytical relationships that resulted in additional auditing procedures being performed.
- The nature of communications about fraud to management, those charged with governance, and others.

Clearly, the audit team must record all of their work throughout the process, and these records must be detailed in regard to notes, findings, and general observations.

When compared to previous sets of standards, like SAS 82, SAS 99 provides noteworthy recommendations about fraud detection and prevention.

For example, the section of SAS 99 that requires the audit team to have a brainstorming session helps auditors approach the audit with the necessary professional skepticism. Another addition in SAS 99, interviewing, gets the auditor away from the one-dimensionality of the numbers by providing a tool, whereby communicating with numerous people in an organization may lead to where the numbers do not result in the identification of fraud. These two additions, as well as the general fundamentals of SAS 99, clearly provide much-needed direction to the auditor in their duties of detecting and resolving issues of fraud.

Government Standards for Fraud Auditing

The GAO's Yellow Book provides a section called "Ethical Principles in Government Auditing," which sets a tone for ethical behavior throughout the organization by outlining acceptable behavior and expectations for each employee. These ethical principles also provide a foundation, discipline, and structure, as well as the climate influencing the application of Generally Accepted Government Auditing Standards or GAGAS. The standards themselves provide guidance on how to perform financial audits and attestation engagements. They are meant to establish a foundation for the credibility of an auditor's work. Specifically, they emphasize the importance of the independence of the audit organization and its individual auditors, the professional competence of the auditors, and overall audit quality control.

The Yellow Book also provides fieldwork standards for financial audits and attestation engagements. The standards adopted here are those of SAS 99 unless otherwise specified. For example, one of the SAS 99 standards adopted concerns how the auditors must adequately plan for the upcoming audit in order to have sufficient understanding of the entity and its environment. As with the fieldwork standards, reporting standards are those of SAS 99 unless they have been excluded or modified for GAGAS—for example, the requirement that audits must state whether the financial statements are in accordance with GAAP and identifying when GAAP has not been consistently implemented. Although these government standards are SAS 99–reliant, they are modified with those standards created by GAGAS for the auditing of government entities. One example of this modification is the consideration of an entity's previous audits. Auditors can use the information provided by previous audits to determine the nature, timing, and extent of the upcoming audit work; thus, the auditors can see if findings and recommendations from previous audits have been addressed.

Government-specific standards also exist for financial reporting, and, just like the fieldwork standards, they are a combination of modified SAS 99 standards and those specifically created to audit government entities. An example of this specificity occurs when there are deficiencies in internal controls, fraud, illegal acts, violations of provisions of contracts or grant agreements, or abuse, and auditors are then required to obtain and report the views of responsible officials concerning the findings, conclusions, recommendations, and planned corrective actions.

Another section of the Yellow Book pertains to fieldwork and financial reporting standards. It should be noted that, unlike the other sections of GAGAS that are derived from SAS 99, the "Performance Audits" section is exclusive to government auditing. The fieldwork standards for performance audits relate to planning the audit; supervising staff; obtaining sufficient, appropriate evidence; and preparing audit documentation; while the reporting standards for performance audits relate to the form of the report, the report contents, and report issuance and distribution.

International Standards of Auditing (ISAs) and Fraud

Many of the standards set by the IAASB may appear similar with those set by the IIA, AICPA, and GAO in that the auditor is required to have a professional skepticism, that there is discussion between audit team members, risk assessment procedures are required, and interviewing is used. On the audit level, using the ISAs, the auditor conducting an engagement is required to obtain reasonable assurance that the financial statements are free from material misstatement, whether caused by fraud or error. ISAs are in place to recognize that there is an inherent risk of fraud not being detected even though the audit is properly planned and performed.

 SUMMARY

Each of the four groups' standards discussed offers a definition or description of fraud as it relates to the professional requirements. The fraud definitions adopted by the four organizations are similar in intent, with the notable difference being the realm of practice. The external auditors focus on those intentional acts resulting in the misstatement of the financial statements, while the internal auditors focus on illegal acts. Obviously, this is not intended as an all-or-nothing statement, but rather a generality. The concepts of intentional acts and concealment of acts are the basis of the standards, regardless of their origin.

As pointed out, many similarities are shared between the standards issued by the various governing organizations, such as brainstorming sessions during the audit planning, communication requirements regarding the likelihood of fraud occurring, creating a methodology for fraud detecting and prevention, and the value of a fraud risk assessment process. Yes, there are differences, too. SAS 99 and International Standards on Auditing focus on the primary fraud categories (see Chapter 3 for a discussion of these classifications) of asset misappropriation and financial reporting. The IIAs are broader in nature by offering examples of the type of fraud that may occur within an organization, while the Yellow Book, being comparable to SAS 99, has a distinct focus on violations of provisions of contracts and includes the concept of material abuse either quantitatively or qualitatively. SAS 99 differs from the IAABS standards with its focus on performing an audit with a methodology directed on fraud risk, whereas the latter group's direction is toward preventing and detecting the fraud in the workplace. For example, SAS 99 relates to the fraud triangle by relying heavily on the auditor's ability to assess what fraud risks exist and how to find them. Conversely, IIA standard 2060 provides guidelines on how the internal audit department is responsible for evaluating internal control weaknesses and presenting that information to management and the board of directors.

Regardless of the similarities or differences in these standards, auditors and organizations need a strategy to respond to the risk of fraud. Clearly, external auditors and internal auditors have differing roles by the nature of their job titles. External auditors focus on the misstatement of the financial statements, whereas internal auditors tend to focus on detecting, preventing, and monitoring fraud risks. However, this distinction is a generalization of responsibilities given that within the context of the standards, every auditor has a responsibility to respond to the risk of fraud. The standards bespeak of the distinctiveness of fraud auditing as a method to proactively identify fraud in financial statements and, thereby, the core business systems.

3

Fraud Scenarios

C AN WE BE BLUNT? Long before you do anything regarding fraud within the context of an audit program, you must understand fraud scenarios. A fraud audit program isn't just a traditional audit structure that consists of doing a risk assessment, then sampling and testing. It isn't just the labeling of these traditional audit concepts and steps as the "fraud assessment," "fraud sampling," or "fraud testing." Sure, you can paint some stripes on a donkey to make it look like a zebra, but it's not the same animal, is it? So, too, a fraud red flag isn't just a red flag, a fraud risk assessment isn't just a risk assessment, and certainly a fraud audit program isn't just an audit program.

Developing a comprehensive list of the fraud scenarios consistent with the organization under audit is our objective in addressing fraud via the audit mechanism. The question of why this development is so imperative will be answered in the discussion that follows. For now, understand that the two most common responses to fraud risk are the fraud risk assessment and the design of a fraud audit program. We tend to think of them as distinct animals like our donkey–zebra analogy. However, by building a fraud risk structure, the vital connection between the fraud risk assessment and the fraud audit program is made. Specifically, this connection occurs through identification of the inherent fraud scheme, the fraud scenarios, the fraud concealment strategies, and the fraud conversion point. Therefore, understanding how an inherent fraud scheme occurs within a business system of a particular organization is vital to the fraud risk assessment, just as understanding how the fraud is concealed is vital to the fraud audit program and understanding the fraud conversion is critical to the fraud investigation.

KEY DEFINITIONS AND TERMS

Before we embark on our discussion of the process of determining fraud scenarios, we need to be on the same page as to what exactly we mean when we say things like *inherent fraud scheme, fraud scenario, conversion,* and *concealment.*

Inherent Fraud Schemes

An inherent fraud scheme will correspond to a secondary fraud classification, whereby each secondary fraud classification will have one or more inherent fraud schemes. In turn, each inherent fraud scheme typically has two components. One component involves the direct linking of each business transaction to an entity, such as an employee, vendor, or customer. The entity structure used by the perpetrator of the fraud scenario is either a real or fictitious entity. In the case of a real entity, it is either knowingly complicit or is unknowingly involved. In the case of a fictitious entity, the entity is either a created or an assumed entity structure. The other component of the inherent fraud scheme is the action that occurs, such as billing for services never provided. The action will depend on the core business system. In terms of building a fraud risk structure, the inherent fraud scheme provides the auditor with a starting point to identify and describe the fraud scenarios facing a business system. Therefore, the key principles of an inherent fraud scheme are the following:

- Each business system has a finite and predictable list of inherent fraud schemes.
- Each inherent fraud scheme has a finite and predictable list of fraud permutations.
- How the inherent scheme occurs will be influenced by the business processes and internal controls.
- Each fraud scheme permutation creates a finite and predictable list of fraud scenarios.

The key points to remember are that fraud is predictable with regard to the schemes that occur, and there is a finite number of schemes that can occur in a given business system. Through a permutation process, the potential number of scenarios facing an organization can be identified and computed with mathematical precision.

Fraud Scenarios

A fraud scenario is the unique way the inherent fraud scheme occurs at the audited entity. Statement of Auditing Standards 99 refers to a fraud scenario as an "identified fraud risk." Therefore, for the purposes of our discussion, a fraud scenario describes how the inherent fraud risk will occur under specific circumstances. Upon identification, a specific fraud scenario becomes the basis for the fraud risk assessment and the fraud audit program.

Fraud Concealment

Fraud concealment involves the strategies used by the perpetrator of the fraud scenario to conceal the true intent of the transaction. Common concealment strategies include false documents, false representations, false approvals, avoiding or circumventing control levels, internal control inhibitors, blocking the access to information, geographic distance between documents and controls, and both real and perceived pressure. An important aspect of fraud concealment pertains to the level of sophistication used by the perpetrator. Further discussion of concealment strategies has been left for Chapter 6, but for now, please note that unlike fraud scenarios, understanding fraud concealment is not required for developing a fraud risk assessment. However, it is a critical element for the development of a fraud audit program. Regardless, the connection between concealment strategies and fraud scenarios is essential in any discussion of fraud risk structure.

Fraud Conversion

Fraud conversion refers to the converting of the fraudulent act to an economic gain for the perpetrator. The fraud conversion is otherwise known as the money trail. Fundamentally, the conversion cycle occurs in an "on the book" or "off-the-book" mode. When the conversion occurs directly between organizations or "on the books," the audit function can establish the perpetrator's receiving the funds. When the transfer occurs off the organization's books, the audit is not able to gather direct evidence of the conversion cycle. Fraud occurring through a company purchasing card is an example of an "on the book" conversion, whereas a bribe is an example of an "off-the-book" conversion.

 ## FRAUD RISK STRUCTURE

In its most simplest of definitions, the fraud risk structure is a comprehensive technique used to identify all the possible fraud schemes facing an organization. Fraud is complicated, and we want to make its identification as effortless as possible; however, its complexity tends to be caused by layering and overlapping. Therefore, we have broken down the schemes into two levels denoted herein as primary and secondary. We need to be as exact as possible in identifying the proper schemes in order to develop a fraud risk assessment that leads us down the right path. By "right path" we mean that with the proper fraud risk assessment being performed, a fraud audit program can be developed that directly addresses fraud concealment and fraud conversion.

Now, please note that we don't use the terms *fraud scheme* and *fraud scenario* interchangeably. They are not the same thing. A fraud scheme may be thought of as the identified fraud risk associated with an organization typically found in the business systems that prevail in that organization. Just how a fraud scheme occurs may differ with each type of organization, for example, schemes that can occur in health care provider reimbursement systems are not going to be exactly the same for the billing department in a large construction company. Would you ever dare to compare what a cardiologist does to what a plumber does? These differences are referred to as the inherent fraud risk and, subsequently, as the inherent fraud schemes. So, how does an inherent fraud scheme become a fraud scenario, you ask?

Each core business system in an organization has inherent fraud schemes associated with them. Basically, we are talking about a specific opportunity for fraud to occur. These inherent schemes will have permutations, and each permutation creates a fraud scenario. Again, by scheme variation, we mean that each fraud scheme occurs differently in each industry, business, or organization. Think of it as the taxonomist and the process of binomial nomenclature or scientific naming. On second thought, you better not think of it that way. However, the analogy does apply, so think back to your high

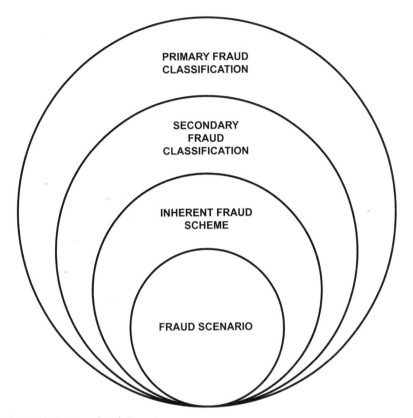

FIGURE 3.1   Fraud Risk Structure

school biology class. No, not the dissections, but the hierarchy of biological classifications with its eight major taxonomic ranks from largest to smallest: kingdom, phylum, class, order, family, genus, and species. With this succession in mind, Figure 3.1 will hopefully allow you to follow our fraud hierarchy.

What follows is a discussion on each of these levels and the process it takes to go from primary fraud classification to fraud scenario. Other items that we will discuss as they relate to this hierarchy, and fraud schemes and scenarios in particular, include that each fraud scheme has unique characteristics, especially with regard to concealment strategies; that each fraud scheme has a unique data profile; and that the objective of each fraud scheme is the conversion whereby the perpetrator converts the scheme to personal gain.

CLASSIFYING FRAUD

As we discussed, a fraud risk structure is needed to be built to ultimately identify the fraud scenarios that are possible in the existing environment. To get to that point, we are beginning by understanding the primary and secondary levels, or classifications, or categories of fraud.

Primary Fraud Classifications

These classifications are referred to as primary because they are applicable to almost all organizations. There are differing opinions concerning which classifications should be called "primary." For example, as explained in Chapter 2, SAS 99 has both asset misappropriation and financial reporting as primary, whereas an operational audit performed under the Yellow Book standards would focus on fraud in operational performance reporting. Remember, we are trying to arrive at a definitive scope in our search for fraud and not be all things fraud. The following is a list of the primary classifications of fraud as we see them. Along with a description, we also provide internally occurring and externally occurring fraud examples that fall under each classification.

Asset Misappropriation

Asset misappropriation is the wrongful taking possession or use of monetary funds or tangible assets. An internal example would be when an accounts payable clerk of an organization, by means of false billing, puts an invoice through the payment system and takes possession of the disbursement check. An external example would be when a vendor doing business with an organization takes possession of unearned funds by means of overbilling. Now, the false billing in the internal example and the overbilling in the external example are the methods by which the fraud, asset misappropriation, takes place. We tend to refer to them as the action elements, that is, the point at which the personal gain or benefit occurs.

Corruption

Corruption is the abuse of power, position, authority, or knowledge with the intent to give illegal or improper advantage or benefit. Also, corruption can be a fiduciary's or official's use of a station or office to procure some benefit, either personally or for others, contrary to the rights of others. For example, an employee of an organization bribes his manager to falsify documentation for overtime hours by promising a kickback of the overtime pay the employee receives. This scheme would occur internally, considering it is between employee and supervisor, and it involves an organization's payroll system. Corruption can and often does occur with outside agents. For example, a customer extorts a sales representative of an organization by using information regarding favored terms other customers have received inappropriately. This external example is interesting in that it doesn't involve a core business system per se. Instead, it involves extortion based on information that highlights fraudulent actions of an employee.

Financial Reporting

Financial reporting fraud is the improper reporting of the financial statements, budget processes, or program activities. Typically, the reporting is improper because it involves improper recognition, misclassification, or false assertions of any item attributed to the reporting. This improper reporting can occur when an executive manager of an organization falsifies documentation and then uses influence to capitalize items that should be expensed, resulting in a misstatement on the financial statements. Most financial reporting manipulation occurs internally and at a high level of an organization typically due to pressures to display the organization in good light for outsiders, such as investors and the board of directors. That is not to say it can't happen externally—for example, an external valuation firm purposefully provides incorrect calculations, resulting in financial reports being misstated. Such firms are often used in order for large bond issuances to take place, as well as with impending sale of the organization or one of its components.

Revenue Obtained Improperly

Revenue obtained improperly pertains to revenue earned through false representations either to the customer or the organization. An internal example is when an organization falsely advertises the capabilities of its product, which leads an additional 5,000 customers to purchase it under false pretense. Externally, it can happen when a customer purchases an organization's product with the intention of returning the product after the period close. In both examples, it is the purchasing system that is being targeted for fraud, but in the internal example, it is the organization that is receiving the benefit, while in the external example, the organization is the victim of the fraud.

Avoidance Strategies

Typically when we speak of avoidance strategies, they pertain to either expense avoidance or government regulation avoidance. Expense avoidance is the act of evading financial obligations to employees, customers, or vendors through false representations or outright avoidance. An internal example is when a manager of an organization alters hourly employee timecards, manipulating them so that the employees received fewer hours paid. An external example is when a vendor does not provide a warranty to the organization when one was guaranteed as part of the contract.

Government regulations avoidance is the act of evading government regulations applicable to the industry and organization. For example, an organization does not pay minimum wage to all employees of the organization. Again, this is a situation where the organization avoids the regulation. An example where an organization is victimized by government regulation avoidance is when a customer identifies themselves as sales tax exempt for the products or services the organization provides when they are not.

Informational Manipulation and Misuse

Information manipulation and misuse is the act of obtaining information outside proper channels for improper uses or the purposeful loss of information. An internal example would be a business development associate of an organization using confidential intangible information from a client project to benefit his or her personal business. An external example would be when outside agents take possession of an organization's client information and, by means of identity theft, use it for their own benefit.

Technological Manipulation and Misuse

Technological manipulation and misuse is the act of using computers and other technological devices to deceive, misrepresent, destroy, steal information, or cause harm to others by accessing information through deceptive and illegal means. Although the topic has relevance to our discussion of fraud schemes and scenarios, the specialization of the manipulation is beyond the scope of this book. We will provide you with two examples, however. The first occurs internally and involves the theft of a human resource department employee's computer password in order to change performance and salary information for personal benefit. An external example would be the case of a competitor misusing an organization's web site, causing glitches in any online ordering processes.

Management Override

Management override is the use of position, authority, responsibilities, and/or reputation by senior management of the organization to perform any illegal acts or policy violations. Senior management includes, at a minimum, the board of directors, chief executive officer, and chief financial officer. An internal example would be an executive manager's influencing the internal audit team to not report negative audit findings. An external example would be when the management of a vendor contacts another organization's employee in order to use that employee's position and reputation to get the organization to make payment for goods that have been returned. Collusion is a key element in both these types of schemes.

False Program Reporting

False program reporting refers to improper reporting that occurs with regard to specific programs involving the program's financial reporting or program accomplishments. Typically, the reporting is false through improper recognition, misclassification, or false assertions of any item attributed to the reporting. An internal example is when an executive manager directs staff to charge expenses to unrelated projects, resulting in project reporting being incorrect. An external example would be when a subcontractor misallocates overhead expenses to a project of the organization that are not allowable by the terms of the contract.

Secondary Fraud Classifications

The secondary fraud classifications are subclassifications of the previously listed primary fraud classifications. Therefore, we aren't just repeating ourselves and don't mean to confuse you on purpose by listing the primary fraud classifications all over again. However, to maintain some sort of consistency with our groupings, we have decided to discuss the secondary fraud classifications using the same titles as listed for the primary fraud classifications. Think of the subclasses as the action points of the fraud schemes.

Asset Misappropriation

Includes the following:

- **Embezzlement of funds.** The act of taking monetary or monetary equivalent funds entrusted to one's care.
- **Theft of tangible assets.** The act of taking tangible property of an organization for personal use or resale on the open market.
- **Misuse of assets.** The conversion of the organization's assets for personal or nonbusiness use without theft of the asset.
- **Lack of business purpose.** The use of organizational funds to acquire assets that are not intended to benefit an organization or when the quality of the asset exceeds its organizational use.
- **Conflict of interest.** An undisclosed legal ownership or beneficial interest in a related entity of an organization (vendor, customer, or employee).
- **Unauthorized asset disposal/acquisition that is below/above fair market value.** Specifically, when an asset is acquired above the fair market value or the disposal of an asset below the fair market value. In either situation, a relationship often exists between the seller and the buyer where each will benefit by the difference.

Corruption

Corruption can occur in all business cycles, but is typically associated with purchasing, employment, and the revenue cycle as follows:

- **Favored status.** An entity (employee, vendor, or customer) is given an unfair advantage through the structuring of a business process by an employee of an organization. The entity has a personal relationship with the employee, prior employment or previous dealings with the organization, or has an extended business relationship with the organization. The favored status does not involve illegal activities per se, but rather there is a violation of organization policies.
- **Nepotism/discrimination.** Nepotism is a type of favoritism shown or patronage granted to relatives defined as individuals who are related by blood, marriage, or adoption. These relationships include spouse, child,

step-children, parent, step-parent, grandparent, grandchild, brother, sister, half-brother, half-sister, aunt, uncle, niece, nephew, parent-in-law, daughter-in-law, son-in-law, brother-in-law, and sister-in-law. Discrimination refers to the treatment or consideration of, or making a distinction in favor of or against, a person or thing based on the group, class, or category to which that person or thing belongs rather than on individual merit.

- **Conflict of interest.** An undisclosed legal ownership or beneficial interest by an employee of an organization in a related entity (e.g., vendor, customer, or employee).
- **Bribery/extortion/kickbacks.** A payment made, monetary or nonmonetary, or information used to obtain an unauthorized benefit.
- **Bid rigging.** The process of entities, such as vendors, customers, or employees, deciding among themselves which entity will submit the best response to be ultimately selected.

Financial Reporting

Includes the following:

- **Fictitious or sham transactions.** The creation and recording of false transactions in the accounting records.
- **Improper recognition.** Recording an actual or "real" transaction in an improper period.
- **Journal-entry schemes.** The use of journal entries to create false assertions, improper recognition of a recorded transaction, or the misclassification of a transaction. The entry is either recorded in the general ledger or is considered a top-sided entry.
- **Misclassification.** The classification of actual assets, liabilities, equity, revenue, and expenses through the reporting process.
- **Improper disclosure.** The failure to disclose or false disclosure of pertinent terms and conditions or information.
- **Improper interpretation of GAAP.** The intentional misapplication of fundamental principles of GAAP or an FASB standard.
- **Improper interpretation of GAAP standards.** The intentional misapplication of fundamental principles of GAAP regarding false assertions, transactions, accounts, or presentation and disclosure.
- **Manipulation of budgets.** The falsification or misclassification of budgetary information.

Revenue Obtained Improperly

When we are dealing with schemes involving revenue obtained improperly, we need to distinguish them as to who is benefitted, the organization or an individual. This difference is important to note because the opportunities to obtain revenue improperly on an organizational level are of a wider scope, of course, but also pose a detriment to a wider population. For example, when a company's policy promotes sales strategies to deceive consumers, it is that population of consumers that are affected, whereas when an individual commits this type of fraud scheme, it is the organization that is victimized as well.

For Organizational Benefit   When it involves the organization as a whole, then the following techniques are commonly found:

- Overbilling of customers
- Improper fees or charges
- Deceptive advertising
- Nondisclosure of known defects or hazards
- Market manipulation

For Individual Benefit   When pertaining to an individual benefitting, the same techniques apply; however, the element of collusion typically exists as well. The core business system that the individual works with also dictates the fraud scenario, while the duties and responsibilities of the individual dictate the opportunities for fraudulent behavior within that core business system. For example, an overbilling scheme where revenue is obtained improperly would consist of: a real vendor colluding with an employee, whereby the vendor overcharges the company, and the employee, an accounts payable manager, approves the invoice for payment. This is just one method; others include fictitious charges on fictitious invoices, charging for a higher quantity than delivered, charging for goods and services that are not needed, and false or inflated charges on real invoices.

Avoidance Strategies

Again we highlight two areas: expense avoidance and government regulation avoidance. For expense avoidance, the inherent scheme will vary by the nature of the organization and the expense account. To illustrate:

- Warranty avoidance
- Tax evasion
- Certification to contract work not performed to specification

Government regulations avoidance can be defined as the disregard or improper interpretation of the pertinent regulations that apply to an organization and industry. To illustrate:

- Anti-Money laundering
- Foreign Practices Act
- Price fixing

Informational Manipulation and Misuse

Includes the following:

- **Identity theft.** The taking of an entity's information and using this information to gain benefit.
- **Espionage.** The act of spying on an organization, its vendors, customers, or employees in order to obtain information to be used for benefit.
- **Intellectual property.** The taking of intellectual property for personal use or for resale.

Technological Manipulation and Misuse

Technological manipulation and misuse, as discussed previously, pertains to the use of computers and other technological devices as a means to manipulate or misuse information. Computer fraud schemes are beyond the scope of this book.

Management Override

There are two distinct areas of fraud when discussing management override. The first concerns conflict-of-interest situations, and the second involves those situations when managers use their position, authority, responsibility, and reputation to override controls and processes. Conflict-of-interest situations arise when a manager has an undisclosed legal ownership or beneficial interest in a related entity to an organization, such as a vendor, customer, or employee. Some examples include:

- Often a conflict-of-interest relationship exists between the seller and the buyer of an asset that enables the acquisition of an asset from an organization below the fair market value, thereby providing an unauthorized benefit to the parties.
- Disguised real estate leases, whereby the manager, without any disclosure, owns a building that the organization leases.
- Undisclosed loans, whereby an organization provides a loan to an entity in which a manager has an undisclosed interest.

The other area of fraud occurs when managers use their position, authority, responsibility, and reputation to override controls and processes. Some examples include:

- Disguised compensation: When a manager provides him- or herself through misrepresentation with compensation that he or she is not entitled to.
- Disguised benefits: When a manager of an organization provides him- or herself benefits through hidden perks.
- Stock option manipulation: This situation arises when there is manipulation of stock option dates in order to receive early benefit.
- Misuse of assets: The conversion of the organization's assets for personal or nonbusiness use without theft of the asset.

False Program Reporting

The situations surrounding false program reporting may seem identical to those listed under the secondary classification of financial reporting; however, we want you to think of the following list as being found on a program or project level versus the financial reporting that occurs for the organization as a whole.

- Fictitious or sham transactions: The creation and recording of false transactions in the project or program accounting records.
- Improper recognition: The recording of an actual transaction of the project or program in an improper reporting period.
- Improper reporting of program achievement or status of program.
- Improper reporting of program results.
- Program has failed to comply with laws, regulations, or pertinent terms and conditions of the contract.
- Improper disclosure: The failure to disclose or false disclosure of pertinent terms and conditions or information of the project or program.

TABLE 3.1 Comparison of Corruption in Core Business Systems

Primary Classification	Secondary Classification	Procurement Functions	Recruitment Functions
Corruption (Internal)	Favored Status	Favored Vendor	Favored Recruitment
Corruption (Internal)	Nepotism/ Discrimination	Family Vendor	Family Candidate
Corruption (Internal)	Conflict of Interest	Interest in Vendor	Interest in Candidate
Corruption (Internal)	Bribery/ Extortion/ Kickbacks	Bribery/Extortion/Kickbacks for Selection of Vendor	Bribery/Extortion/ Kickbacks for Employment
Corruption (External)	Bid Rigging	Vendor Bid Rigging	Applicant Fraud

- Manipulation of budgets: The falsification or misclassification of budgetary information of the project or program.

Business System Considerations

Now having circumnavigated you through the primary and secondary levels of fraud, we continue on our path to fraud scenarios by explaining how the core business systems enter into the process. For example, if we compare corruption in the procurement systems or functions to corruption in the hiring processes, there is a similarity in the secondary classifications or subclasses that could occur, although just how the type of fraud will occur, meaning the fraud schemes and scenarios, will differ between the two business systems. Remember we are not just discussing one fraud scheme and one fraud scenario. There are variations within each that affect each. Table 3.1 gives examples of how a primary classification of fraud, such as corruption, can occur in differing ways depending on the subclass of fraud and on whether the procurement functions or recruitment functions have been corrupted.

IDENTIFYING FRAUD SCENARIOS

The auditor is responsible for developing a list of the fraud scenarios that can be customized from the inherent fraud scheme structure. There are specific decisions that an auditor needs to make in this identification process, there are definite steps to be taken, and there are guidelines to be followed in taking these steps. What follows is a discussion of the types of decisions needed to be made in identifying fraud scenarios.

Decisions

The process starts with identifying the permutations of the inherent scheme as they are merged with organization business process and internal controls. Therefore, there are four key decisions to be made by an auditor in identifying a fraud scenario:

1. **Determine the fraud risk structure.** Which primary classification of fraud is involved, what subclasses provide the opportunity for fraud, and what inherent fraud schemes are apparent given the systems involved?
2. **Determine the depth at which the fraud scenario is occurring in terms of the business system being affected.** The level at which the fraud scenario is dependent on the purpose of the audit and the auditor's judgment. The three levels for fraud scenario identification, from highest to lowest, include a business system level, a transaction class level, and a specific-to-criterion level that pertains to a general ledger account, entity type, person, or internal control.
3. **The extent of "drilling down" to take place during the permutation process.** This extent is up to the auditor; however, there are considerations that need to be made for both opportunity and entity. An opportunity must directly tie to job duties, and it must be decided if the entity involved is real or false.
4. **A decision must be made concerning the intended use for identifying the fraud scenarios.** The two primary uses for identifying fraud scenarios are to conduct a fraud risk assessment and to develop a fraud audit program. Remember that concealment and conversion are aspects of the fraud scenario that need to be taken into account when performing a fraud audit program.

Steps

Once the pertinent decisions have been made, there are distinct steps to be taken in order to identify the fraud scenario. These steps are as follows:

1. Establish the scope of the fraud assignment through the development of a fraud risk structure.

2. Determine the extent of the drill-down process from the broadest level, such as system-wide, to the narrowest level, such as person specific.
3. Obtain an understanding of the business processes and internal controls.
4. Identify the permutations of opportunity, entity, and transaction codes.
5. Merge business process knowledge with the results of the permutation analysis.
6. Describe the fraud scenario that becomes apparent in the merger process.
7. Identify the relevant concealment strategies and conversion method associated with the fraud scenario.

Hints

We have bandied around terms and concepts like *fraud risk structure, drill-down process, business processes and internal controls, permutation analysis,* and *fraud opportunity* as if they were used every day by everyone. So, now we need to talk about them all in the context of fraud auditing because that's where they are found and we all need to be on the same page understanding-wise to make any use of this discussion.

Fraud Risk Structure

The fraud risk structure is a tool, and it is used to establish the scope of the fraud project. In a sequential manner, it entails the primary classification of fraud, the secondary classification or subclass of fraud, the inherent fraud schemes, and last, the fraud scenarios. Arriving at the primary and secondary levels of fraud is pretty obvious; however, for deciding on the inherent fraud scheme, typically a good starting point is to begin by determining whether an entity is real or false. If the decision relies solely on the auditor's judgment, then focusing on the "on the book" conversion schemes is a good starting point.

The Drill-Down Process

The drill-down process is used to determine at what level, from broadest to narrowest, the fraud scenarios are existing. Relevant to fraud detection, the following guidelines should be considered:

- There is a direct correlation between the extent of the drill-down and the visibility of a fraudulent transaction. Is the apple rotten just on the skin or from the core out?

- The level of drill-down affects the number of scenarios; for example, the business process level will have the most scenarios, while the specific criteria will have the smallest number of scenarios.
- The level of drill-down will have minimal effect on the number of entity permutations.
- A specific criterion is used, depending on whether there is an allegation of wrongdoing or a suspicious transaction has been identified.
- The class of transactions level is most suited for fraud auditing because of the homogeneous nature of the pool of transactions.

Business Processes and Internal Controls

An understanding of an organization's business processes and the internal controls related to those processes is necessary to recognize how an inherent fraud scheme would occur in a specific business environment. Obviously, for purposes of performing a fraud risk assessment, the linking of the internal control to the fraud scenario is a critical step.

Permutation Analysis

Analysis of the permutations of fraud opportunity, as it pertains to specific organization, entity, and transaction codes, is a necessary operation in the identification of fraud scenarios. Knowing what entity and transactions codes are specific to the business processes and how they are arranged within those processes is key to separating scenario possibilities. The breadth of the analysis extends from the organizational-specific as with entity codes, down to the process-specific as with transaction codes:

- **Entity analysis.** Entity analysis is used to recognize that transactions are connected to employee, vendor, or customer. Entity may also relate to other structures, depending on the nature of the business system, such as an inventory code number. Whatever the condition, an entity is either fictitious or real. In the case of a real entity, it is either knowingly complicit or is unknowingly involved in the fraud scenario. In the case of a false entity, it is either created by the perpetrator or the perpetrator assumes the identity of a real entity. The assumed entity is either already in the company's database or it is external and is added to the database.
- **Transaction analysis.** Transaction types correlate specifically to a specific business system by way of specific codes or actions within the

business system. For example, a transaction code would be the active or inactive identifying number for a vendor or a customer.

Fraud Opportunity

Fraud opportunity is a person's ability to commit a specific fraud scenario. The fraud opportunity may occur with just internal employees, or there could be a connection between internal employees and individuals external to an organization (aka outside agents). External fraud opportunity may exist to vendors or customers who do business with an organization, or there may be no relationship whatsoever. This book will primarily focus on internal fraud opportunity and externally related entities, such as vendors or customers. Typically, an internal fraud opportunity arises through an individual's job duties or through the failure of another person in performance of his or her respective job duties. In some instances, the opportunity is not related to job duties at all, as in the case of fraud scenarios associated with theft, where the opportunity is created by access to an asset.

When we speak of fraud opportunity, it does not mean that the person will be successful or go undetected; it simply means the person's job duties, security clearance, asset access, and so on, create a chance to commit the fraud scenario. It also does not mean that the existence of internal controls will prevent the action or mitigate the risk. Identifying an opportunity for fraud goes hand-in-hand with identifying a fraud scenario, as they say: Where there is smoke, there is fire. There are really two types of fraud opportunities: one being created through a function of job duties and the other involving internal controls.

For job duty opportunities, a person's job creates either a direct or indirect opportunity to commit a fraud scenario. The direct opportunity is easy to understand and indentify because an individual, with approval authority, is given a chance to falsely approve a transaction. An indirect job duty opportunity is created when a person's job duty causes someone else to perform the act. That is, an operations manager cannot directly add a new vendor to the master file; however, by submitting a vendor invoice, approved within the operations manager's authority level, accounts payable adds the new vendor to the master file.

Internal control inhibitor opportunities arise when a person's actions cause an internal control to fail. The typical considerations include management override, logical collusion, and nonperformance of an internal control procedure where the individual has indicated performance of the procedure. Of course, there are also opportunities present when there are no controls in place.

Common Mistakes Made with Fraud Scenarios

The process of building a fraud risk structure to arrive at the appropriate fraud scenario seems overtly intense and full of steps that appear to go nowhere. However, if you don't understand them and follow them in a rational manner, you sadly will go nowhere and the fraud will go undetected. If the process is not followed and mistakes are made, the listing of fraud scenarios we are seeking may not be appropriate or comprehensive given the specific needs of the organization. Some of the common mistakes that are made include:

- **Mitigating the scenario.** We want to identify the scenarios that could occur, regardless of whether the organization currently has mitigating controls or processes in place. Our focus is on identifying scenarios, not on mitigating controls. The internal controls are part of the assessment phase.
- **Focusing on the conversion cycle.** Audit instinct at times will pull toward looking at the conversion cycle or, in other words, how a perpetrator gains benefit. Remember, a scenario is not based on the conversion cycle, but rather the conversion cycle is based on the scenario. If we were to look at the conversion cycle rather than the scenario, there is a chance that we would miss those scenarios that use other conversion techniques.
- **Focusing on the concealment strategies.** Concealment, although an integral piece of the fraud audit program, will not help you build a comprehensive listing of fraud scenarios. The concealment is how the perpetrator hides the fraud to make it look like an actual business transaction; thus, it is based on the scenario.
- **Ignoring industry considerations.** Each industry has unique characteristics that could make the businesses within that industry susceptible to specific fraud scenarios. Knowing what scenarios are industry-specific is an important filtering process.

FRAUD AUDIT CONSIDERATIONS

One audit size does not fit all fraud risk. The audit approach must be tailored to the fraud risk structure because it is at that point, when we have identified the inherent fraud schemes, that we can go forward in developing the appropriate fraud audit program. The following discussion entails three major fraud types: financial reporting fraud, asset misappropriation fraud, and the ever-popular duo of bribery and corruption.

Financial Reporting

Fraud in financial reporting is at home in the financial statements, the management reporting process, and the budgetary process. Both fraud in financial statements and management reporting process are similar, whereas the budgetary process may have false representations for the need of the funds or expenditures that do not match the fiscal year in which the funds are expended or encumbered.

Fraud is predictable as to "how" the fraud will occur in the financial statements, in terms of the location, rather than "will" fraud occur, pertaining to the act of fraud. This is a common theme throughout the book. We favor looking at the predictability of "how" transactions are recorded and "how" companies are evaluated by external sources. No, the connection of external evaluation and fraud doesn't just jump off the page, does it? Companies are typically evaluated on key operating statistics within an industry by external sources. Those sources may be bond rating agencies, banks, investment brokers, or a potential purchaser of the business. Not all the sources use the same statistics in making their evaluations. We need to know how an organization is evaluated by these outside sources, in particular what measurements (i.e., statistics) are employed.

Typically, operating statistics correspond to the general ledger accounts, so it follows that the most predictable location for fraudulent reporting is in the key operating accounts. At the account level, consideration of whether an overstatement or understatement has taken place must be made, requiring an auditor's judgment. However, a careful evaluation of the fraud risk factors, a concept outlined in SAS 99, should provide a logical basis for predicting the direction of the misstatement.

Finding the location of the fraudulent activity begins with the financial statement as it links to the general ledger. Transactions within the general ledger are derived by entries from a source journal or a general journal entry. An exception is top-sided journal entries, which occur between the financial statements and the general ledger. Items to look for include entries within the source journal that are either false or recorded in the wrong accounting period, adjusting journal entries not recorded or that record an incorrect amount, and entries that reclassify an amount are moved from one section to another section of the financial statements. When looking at the materiality of the fraudulent amounts, the use of data analysis or data mining is to be employed regardless of location.

The shaded box is a bit of what we call practical guidance. The intent is to illustrate the detection of financial fraud by going through the layers of primary fraud classification, secondary fraud classification, inherent fraud scheme, and fraud scenario. The goal of these practical guidance sections is to aid the auditor in the understanding of the concepts presented in the chapter.

PRACTICAL**GUIDANCE**

A Company Is Experiencing Extraordinary Sales Growth and Profitability, Especially When Compared to Similar Companies in the Industry

Primary fraud classification: Financial Statement Reporting
Secondary fraud classification: Improper Revenue Recognition by way of overstatement
Inherent fraud scheme: Recognition of revenue when a right to return exists
Fraud scenario: Sales management makes oral promises to customers to induce sales by stating that the customers can return the product if they are not happy.

Asset Misappropriation

When building a fraud risk structure involving asset misappropriation fraud, there are six secondary classification or subclasses of asset misappropriation to be aware of because each secondary classification requires an audit approach specifically designed for it. For example, embezzlement schemes, which result in the diversion of monetary funds from an organization, provide an "on the book" audit trail, which means this type of fraud scheme can be detected with a degree of certainty. However, the skimming of cash receipts or revenues is an exception. The ability to detect skimming depends on whether the source providing the cash receipts is identifiable and willing to cooperate. So, the degree of certainty for skimming depends on the auditor's ability to obtain cooperation from the external parties.

Another subclass pertains to theft schemes that involve the removal of an asset from the organization for personal use or for resale of the asset for personal benefit. An audit can ascertain the loss by the very nature of the scheme; however, an after-fact audit cannot directly link the theft to the individual. Linking the theft to an individual requires a confession, catching the person in the act of the theft or in the possession of the asset, or establishing that the asset was sold. The financial gain aspect of the theft typically requires an investigative approach. Prior to starting the audit, a decision should be made as whether to link the theft to the individual or just establish the loss.

Misuse of asset schemes depend on whether there are records indicating that an individual has possession of the asset, and if those records indicate a date, time, and place of use that can be correlated to a nonbusiness use. When no records are available, the process will require an investigative approach.

A lack of business purpose scheme typically provides a complete audit trail to the asset. The audit approach should focus on establishing a reasonable business standard for the organization. The testing should not focus on the internal authorization process. Considering that these schemes result in negative publicity to an organization when they are uncovered, a good test would be determining how the organization would respond if the expenditure were made public through publication in an internationally recognized newspaper. Also, to be noted is when the expenditure is from government sources, whereby any fraudulent act may result in a loss of funds to the organization.

The disposal of an asset below fair market or acquisition of an asset above fair market value requires the auditor to establish the fair market value; thus, the use of outside experts may be required.

PRACTICAL**GUIDANCE**

A Company Automobile Shows Visual Signs of Excessive Use that Corresponds with a High Mileage Reading When Compared to Other Company Vehicles

Primary fraud classification: Asset Misappropriation
Secondary fraud classification: Misuse of Assets
Inherent fraud scheme: Personal use of company assets
Fraud scenario: The employee to whom this vehicle is assigned is using it for
    personal reasons.

Bribery and Corruption

Corruption by its nature is the act of providing an entity with an unfair advantage. The unfair advantage is either an overt or covert type of action. The overt action is typically an event that is observable through direct evidence, whereas the covert action is observable circumstantially through the one event or series of events.

The fraud audit approach for corruption should start with the direct evidence because the documents and records are available to the auditor. If they are not available, then circumstantial records would be the second place for examination. An overall attempt should be made to gather evidence that would make it more probable than not that the event occurred. Obviously, the degree of certainty becomes the critical factor in determining the successful uncovering of the corruption and in the convincing of management that the corruption has actually occurred.

The second apparent aspect to corruption is that the individual providing the advantage expects a benefit. However, since the benefit is an "off-the-book" activity, the transfer of wealth is observable through circumstantial evidence versus direct evidence that the event took place.

The difference between a fraud audit and a fraud investigation can be seen in situations where there is the payment of a bribe or a kickback. The bribe is from the person receiving the benefit to the person providing the unfair advantage. The transaction is an "off-the-book" one because bribes occur when the person receiving the benefit pays the person providing the unfair advantage. Therefore, for the auditor, only circumstantial evidence of the bribe can be obtained, whereas a fraud investigation enables access to the books and records of both individuals, thereby giving the fraud auditor the ability to locate direct evidence of the bribe.

PRACTICAL**GUIDANCE**

A Purchasing Agent and a Vendor Collude to Ensure the Vendor Receives a Certain Purchase, Whereby the Purchasing Agent Receives a Monetary Gift for Awarding It to the Vendor

Primary fraud classification: Corruption/Extortion
Secondary fraud classification: Employee in Collusion with a Vendor
Inherent fraud scheme: Favored vendor through bid avoidance
Fraud scenario: A purchasing manager issues a purchase order to a vendor
    that is below the control threshold because of the bidding process
    requirement in place.

SUMMARY

Our objective is clear: Find the fraud scenario. To reach the goal, we have to go through the fraud hierarchy, the first layer of which is the primary fraud classification that pertains to the type of fraud (e.g., asset misappropriation, corruption, financial reporting, revenue obtained improperly, avoidance strategies, informational manipulation and misuse, management override, and false program reporting). These types of fraud can occur either internally within an organization or accompanied by an external agent acting with or without a member of an organization.

The next layer is the secondary classification of fraud where we address the action of the fraud (e.g., embezzlement, theft, misuse, conflict of interest, bribery, bid rigging, improper recognition, improper disclosure, manipulation, improper reporting, overbilling, deceptive practices, disguised transactions, avoidance and misuse). Think of the primary classification as the noun and the secondary the verb—for example, corruption fraud occurs through the act of bribery.

The next layer is the inherent fraud scheme where we determine in which core business system the opportunity for fraud exists and in what manner (e.g., corruption occurs with bid rigging through the procurement system). Having gotten this far, we then, through a series of key decisions and defined steps involving obtaining a knowledge of the core business systems and merging it with the permutations of opportunity, arrive at the fraud scenario.

CHAPTER FOUR

Brainstorming: The Implementation of Professional Standards

UDIT INDUSTRY STANDARDS HAVE made professional skepticism the cornerstone in detecting fraud. The concept of the questioning mind is reiterated throughout the professional literature. Maintaining the appropriate mind-set is critical to the application of audit procedures. Being skeptical facilitates the asking of the right questions, thereby helping the auditor to analyze audit evidence in such a way as to detect red flags that may not have been originally intended by the audit procedure. As highlighted in Chapter 1, the "A" in the ATM approach pertains to awareness. Therefore, it can be said that professional skepticism is the awareness factor, because it combines an auditor's experience and ability to see red flags of fraud.

A brainstorming session is part of the planning process to assist in identifying the relevant fraud risks to the audit scope. The brainstorming session allows sharing between senior members of the audit team and the entry-level auditors, thereby establishing a cohesiveness of skepticism between all involved in an audit. This mutual understanding is important because the standards bestow the auditor with the ultimate responsibility of setting the proper tone regarding both the maintenance of the questioning mind-set throughout the audit and the critical evaluation of the audit evidence.

WHAT IS BRAINSTORMING?

The purpose of brainstorming is to open a dialog among the audit team members regarding the susceptibility of fraud within the audit scope. It is hoped that this discussion will facilitate an exchange of ideas that will result in a cohesive mind-set among the members. The application of the brainstorming outcomes will depend on the relevant audit standards under which the audit is conducted. However, regardless of the standards, there are *three major discussion points* to be addressed:

1. What fraud risks are relevant to the audit scope?
2. How could fraud be perpetrated and concealed from the auditor?
3. What type of audit procedures might detect the fraud risk?

The Free-Flow Approach to Brainstorming

The general approach to brainstorming is referred to as the *free-flow approach*, whereby the auditors are encouraged to present any ideas at any time. From a perspective of auditing financial statements, discussion would typically focus on how and where the financial statements might be susceptible to material misstatement due to fraud or how assets could be misappropriated. However, in the case of an internal audit, discussion might focus on how internal controls could fail, thereby causing asset misappropriation or a failure to meet program objectives.

For a fraud audit, there is still a free flow of ideas; however, the inherent fraud scheme is the focal point of the discussion. By focusing on the use of inherent schemes, the ensuing discussion will be relevant to the company or business process. Therefore, the three major questions listed previously will pertain to the inherent fraud scheme. Two examples are presented next to illustrate the differences between the discussions points followed per audit approach:

Example 1: Fraud Discussion Points Using a Free-Flow Approach

- At the financial statement level: What would suggest that management is recording false revenue?
- At the account level: What would be normal change in the level of accrued revenue?
- At a transaction-specific level: What would cause you to believe that the controller is recording false journal entries to inflate revenue?

- The red flags: What indicators would suggest that management is recording false revenue?

Example 2: Discussion Points Using the Inherent Fraud Scheme Approach

- At the financial statement level: Of the inherent revenue fraud schemes, which would be most likely occur within our client's business?
- At the inherent fraud scheme level: How would management conceal the fact that revenue was shipped to customers who did not order the product?
- At the revenue assertion level: Since the customer did not order the product, how will management provide the illusion to satisfy the realization principle?
- The red flags or false realization: How and what indicators are observed signifying management is falsifying the subsequent cash test?

Leading the Brainstorming Session

For a brainstorming session to be successful, the lead auditor will not only need to have good facilitation skills, but clearly demonstrate a belief in the process. The following general guidelines apply:

- **Follow the "no such thing as a stupid idea" rule.** All team members need to be encouraged to participate regardless of their professional experience. The lead auditor needs to effectively build off the most unrefined idea by asking relevant questions of the group.
- **No hierarchy.** All staff levels should have equal opportunity to participate and offer ideas. The audit leader must not allow office politics to form a hidden agenda.
- **No ownership.** The concept is to avoid arguments caused by an individual that thinks his or her way is best. The audit leader must engage in team building.
- **Set time limits.** There is a careful balance an audit leader must maintain between stifling ideas and belaboring the issue.

Some examples of mistakes commonly made:

- **Mistake 1.** A lack of agreement on the boundaries of the fraud audit project or the audit scope will cause parties to discuss fraud schemes that are not relevant to the fraud project.

- **Remedy.** Start the discussion with the primary fraud classifications that are to be included with the audit scope. Then, upon a consensus, move to the relevant secondary classes.
- **Mistake 2.** A lack of common definitions will cause the group to view the same issue differently.
- **Remedy.** Start the discussion with the definition of the inherent fraud scheme. Outline the scheme on a white board. After all questions about the scheme have been addressed, and it is felt that a mutual understanding has been reached by polling the team, the discussion should proceed to the three major discussion points.

 ## WHEN TO BRAINSTORM

A brainstorming session is performed as part of the audit planning process. Whether the session should be held at the beginning of the planning process or at the end will be dictated by many items, including but not limited to audit experience with the client, audit experience of the team, and manner of audit style. For the fraud audit, the session can be viewed as having the following three steps.

Step 1: Establish the Audit Scope

The fraud risk structure provides a framework in guiding any discussion regarding audit scope. First, the primary classification of fraud must be identified. This primary fraud risk category becomes the focal point of the fraud discussions. A GAAS audit would include asset misappropriation and financial reporting as primary fraud risks; an internal audit of accounts payable might focus on asset misappropriation and corruption; and a program audit might focus on false reporting of program results.

Once the primary classification is identified and understood, the discussion should focus on the secondary classifications of fraud risk, with any further discussion addressing:

- Which secondary fraud risks are included in the audit scope?
- How do the secondary fraud risks relate to this business environment?
- What are the inherent fraud schemes associated with the secondary fraud risks?
- How would the inherent fraud scheme occur in this business environment?

Step 2: Fraud Scenario Boundaries

The second step of the brainstorming session is to understand the boundaries for identifying the fraud scenarios that are consistent within the audit scope. The business system level (overall, class of transactions or specific point analysis) and applicable fraud risk structure for that level should be the guidelines of this discussion, whereby the starting point is to understand the business process level at which the assignment will occur and the implications of conducting the fraud audit at that level. The following guidelines apply:

- Overall business system. Adheres to an internal control perspective of the overall business system.
  - Fraud risk identification occurs at the inherent fraud scheme level.
  - Opportunity permutation analysis identifies scenarios at the direct access or missing internal controls.
  - Entity permutation analysis identifies scenarios using the false or real structure.
  - Transaction permutation analysis focuses on transactions that do not adhere to the key internal controls due to the nature of the transaction.
  - Typically used in internal control audits or financial statement audits.
- Class of transaction(s) pertains to the fraud scenarios that are unique to the specific class of transactions and focuses on the fraud opportunity unique to the class of transactions.
  - The number of permutations will correlate to the specific class of transactions in the business system and the auditor's business knowledge of the class of transactions.
  - Opportunity permutation analysis identifies fraud scenarios at the direct and indirect access level.
  - Entity permutation analysis identifies all variations of the entity structure.
  - Transaction permutation analysis focuses on the codes used within the computerized system to create scenarios, that is active or inactive vendor code.
  - Typically used to conduct fraud audits.
- Specific point analysis: general ledger account, a person, or an entity.
  - Fraud identification is limited to the specific point analysis.
  - All permutations must be identified.
  - Typically used in responding to allegations or responding to a specific identified risk.

Step 3: The Fraud Audit Approach

In order to have an effective brainstorming session, discussion must take place concerning red flags, in particular the red flags associated with fraud.

Understanding Red Flags

A red flag is an indicator suggesting that a fraud scenario may be occurring. Unfortunately, the same indicator can also be associated with a nonfraudulent transaction. For example, a P.O. box can be a red flag indicating a false vendor. However, it is also used by most corporations as a lockbox for banking activities. So, how effective is this particular red flag as a fraud audit tool? It all depends on how the tool is used by the auditor.

In another example, if a purchasing agent has a close personal relationship with a vendor, most auditors would argue that relationship is a behavioral red flag of a vendor overbilling scheme resulting in a kickback to the purchasing agent. It would also be a fact pattern of two individuals who have a business relationship with common personal interests. The challenge becomes the development of a methodology to arrive at a conclusion regarding the behavioral red flag.

Any discussion regarding the purchasing agent example would first have to result in the recognition that the scheme involves asset misappropriation under the category of embezzlement, in particular, an overbilling inherent fraud scheme. Then the second discussion point would concern the type of overbilling scheme, such as price, quantity, and so on, that most likely occur based on the goods or service provided by the vendor. The third discussion point that would follow pertains to the red flags associated with each overbilling scheme.

Clearly, the correct use of the red flags requires a methodology for the new auditor to follow and the experienced auditor to help shape.

The results of this brainstorming session are then categorized into the four different categories of red flags and evaluated. Table 4.1 at the end of this chapter shows a matrix of red flags used as considerations for the fraud response to this construction project.

Red Flags Defined

A fraud red flag is an observable event that links to a fraud concealment strategy that is associated with a fraud scenario. Red flags are used by management to build fraud detection controls and by the auditor in the context of conducting an audit as an alert to the possibility of fraudulent activity.

Case Study: The Role of Brainstorming Sessions in the Uncovering of a Corruption Scheme

Overview

A small, historic city in the Midwest has experienced rapid growth in the past decade. The area's low cost of living, good schools, and low unemployment rate have lured many professionals into relocating to this city and its surrounding suburbs. As a result of this sudden influx of new residents, a commuting nightmare developed. Roadways that were originally built to serve a city of 300,000 residents were now congested on a daily basis as 500,000 local residents commuted to and from work. There was no public transportation system to help alleviate the traffic congestion.

The local government appropriated $500 million dollars and received another $300 million in grants from state and federal agencies to fix the problem. This $800 million total was to be used in expanding the highways going in and out of the city, as well as setting up a public transportation system through the use of bus stations. The project was expected to be completed within five years.

When finally completed, this construction project cost over $1.2 billion and took eight years to complete. The local community demanded answers, so a team of auditors was hired to evaluate why the project went over budget and time expectations.

Use of a Brainstorming Session by Audit Team

The team's senior members were specifically selected for this project because of their previous experience in auditing construction projects. A brainstorming session was held at the beginning of the audit process that included the senior auditors and all members of the audit team. To establish the audit scope, two primary categories of fraud were discussed: asset misappropriation and corruption. Having performed similar fraud audits, the senior auditors decided that a procurement fraud scheme was a very likely scenario in this situation. Some secondary concerns were the risk of unfair or illegal labor practices, theft of materials, and management override.

Having isolated a procurement scheme, the team evaluated the scenario boundaries. Since the auditors determined that the audit will focus on corruption in the procurement process, they began to discuss how this core business system in this particular situation could be corrupted to allow a vendor to be awarded a contract, and yet provide the illusion of a competitive bidding process. The team then concentrated on identifying potential red flags. The first and most obvious red flag was that the project cost exceeded the original estimate by 150%.

(continued)

(continued)

The Fraud Risk Structure

A result of the brainstorming session was the team's arriving at a collection of fraud scenarios that are common in procurement corruption schemes. These scenarios were ranked as follows:

1. Primary Fraud Classification: Corruption
2. Secondary Fraud Classification: Bribery/extortion/kickbacks
3. Inherent Fraud Scheme: Bid avoidance through a false representation regarding sole source capacity in the local marketplace
4. Fraud Scenario:
   a. Opportunity: The procurement manager's job duties provide the opportunity to determine the best approach for obtaining the right price balancing all other factors.
   b. Vendor, customer, or staff member entity: A vendor that was involved in the infrastructure project is known to have a close relationship to the procurement manager.
   c. Transaction type: Sole source justification for vendor selection.
   d. Unique issues: The procurement manager's past experience and relationship with the selected vendor raised concerns.

For the red flag to be an effective audit tool, the event must be observable and must be incorporated into the fraud audit program. Red flags by their nature cause an increased sensitivity to the likelihood of a fraud scenario's occurring. Not all red flags have the same weight with regard to fraud susceptibility. The weight of a fraud red flag correlates to the predictability of a fraud occurrence. Therefore, the auditor needs to interpret the importance of the red flag to the fraud scenario and be able to arrive at a conclusion regarding the occurrence of the fraud scenario.

Four Categories of Red Flags

There are four categories of red flags: data, documents, internal controls, and behavior. The categories are intended to aid the auditor in identifying the red flags in an orderly fashion, whereby the auditor should not view the process as a right or wrong exercise, but instead know that certain items can occur in multiple categories. For example, a vendor invoice number can be a data category of red flag observed through the use of data mining or a document category of red flag observed through the application of audit testing procedures.

Data Red Flags Data red flags are used as the basis of the sample selection process. Any discussion will, therefore, concern what data elements an auditor highlights when selecting a transaction for audit, starting with which data fields are chosen and then the specific criteria regarding those fields. Stating you are looking for a nondescriptive vendor name may sound good, but it provides no direction as to what constitutes a nondescriptive name. Therefore, avoid descriptions that merely sound good; they may prove useless. You can realize usefulness by stripping from the vendor name field the "Inc.," special symbols, and vowels to result in a name field equaling or less than five consonants. At this point, the brainstorming session can focus discussion on the pros and cons of the data description of the red flag.

PRACTICAL**GUIDANCE**

Fraud Scenario of a Favored Vendor in Collusion with the Procurement Supervisor Receiving a Kickback

A judgmental sample would be identified by the auditor by reviewing the vendor master file data and transaction data (purchase orders, invoices, and disbursements).

The data red flags are:

1. A pattern of invoices to a specific vendor that are within 10% of a key approval control.
2. A low invoice number range (i.e., invoices that start with 100, 1,000, etc.), which would indicate a recently founded company.
3. A recent vendor creation date.

Document Red Flags Document red flags are the basis of the fraud audit-testing procedures. The red flag discussions should identify the key control documents and discuss document condition, for example, either paper or electronic, industry or company standards for document information, and key identifying information.

From a practical point of view, the ability to use the document red flags effectively directly correlates to the level at which the audit is being performed. For example, at the business process level, with the sheer diversity of the populations, there is a generic use; that is, the description is vague. At the account or person-specific level, the types of documents are limited and specific to a fact situation; therefore, the ability to identify specific red flags becomes easier.

PRACTICAL**GUIDANCE**

Fraud Scenario of a Favored Vendor in Collusion with the Procurement Supervisor Receiving a Kickback

The documents for a particular vendor are irregular when compared to the other bid documents.
The document red flags are:

1. Files are disorganized, missing, or unavailable.
2. Files are under control of one person.
3. Signature line appears to be forged or contains a stamped signature or a set of initials.
4. Commonality of bid documents as to paper type, font size, and style and document organization.
5. Vague explanations for the sole reason of justification.

Internal Control Red Flags   Internal control red flags correlate to the adequacy of internal control design and the effectiveness of the internal control in the business environment. Specifically, the adequacy of design directly correlates to the opportunity for fraud occurring, which is a critical part of developing the opportunity permutations. The internal control effectiveness is a direct red flag to the occurrence of a fraud scenario. For example, a lack of segregation of duties between the person issuing a check and the person reconciling the bank account clearly creates the opportunity to issue fraudulent disbursements without detection.

Behavioral Red Flags   Behavioral red flags become the basis of determining the creditability of a person being interviewed. For example, in the case of an overbilling scheme, the audit procedure would dictate interviewing the

PRACTICAL**GUIDANCE**

Fraud Scenario of a Favored Vendor in Collusion with the Procurement Supervisor Receiving a Kickback

A determination is made that a vendor, whose work quality and reputation are below industry standards, has been awarded a contract. The internal control red flags are:

1. Procurement manager's deviation from the company's quality requirements.
2. Documents suggest that the procurement manager avoided company's procurement policies. The manager made the sole decision of which bid to accept.
3. Sole source vendor selection did not have the second required approval.

person authorizing requisitions to obtain reasons for the occurrence, and then corroborate that person's account of the incident through at least one independent source.

PRACTICAL**GUIDANCE**

Fraud Scenario of a Favored Vendor in Collusion with the Procurement Supervisor Receiving a Kickback

D etails emerge during interviewing that suggests the procurement manager has a close relationship with the company owner whose bid was accepted.
The behavioral red flags are:

1. Unexplainable changes in the manager's behavior that is inconsistent with normal behavior of the manager.
2. The manager's attempt to control who the auditor interviews.
3. The manager takes unusual and frequent trips and has unexplained absences in the middle of some workdays.
4. Manager's pressure to drop audit issues.

Red Flag Development and Brainstorming Sessions

The following pertains to a methodology for developing fraud red flags, which is designed to facilitate a brainstorming session by providing discussion prompts. The purpose of these prompts is to keep the discussion focused and/or to ensure all relevant items are discussed:

Prompt 1: Be aware of the correlation of red flags to concealment. The concealment strategy is how the perpetrator hides the true nature of their actions. The red flags are how the auditor observes the true nature of the perpetrator's actions. Therefore, it is imperative that the auditor link together the concealment strategy, the associated red flag, and the audit procedure.

Placing red flags into the four categories outlined is necessary to establish an audit strategy that becomes the basis of the fraud audit program, a key component of which is the audit testing procedures. The category of red flags will vary depending on the audit approach, the stage of fraud identification, and the auditor's/investigator's background. The audit approaches are discussed throughout this book, and the auditor's/investigator's background is self-explanatory. However, the stage of the fraud identification occurs either via the audit or through an allegation. The source of the allegation, either whistleblower, management observation, or accident, is not relevant, but the allegation provides the strategy's starting point. The strategy used would vary depending on the fact and circumstances of the allegation.

A fraud audit strategy is distinguished from other audit strategies in that it is built on fraud data mining, whereby data red flags drive the sample selection process. The sample selection causes the auditor to examine documents associated with the sample selection. The examination of documents links to the internal control owner and the fraud opportunity point. The behavior aspect will be observed as the auditor interviews the control owner. This strategy is a departure from the long-standing generalization that investigators rely on behavior red flags, whereas auditors rely on internal control and document red flags.

Prompt 2: Determine whether the red flag is a trigger or awareness red flag. In addition to four categories of red flags, there are two types of red flags: trigger red flags and awareness red flags. With the trigger red flag, the event is sufficient enough to require the auditor to perform fraud audit procedures to determine if creditable evidence exists to suggest that the fraud scenario is occurring. As a guideline, there should be no more than five trigger red flags per category, and preferably only three trigger red flags per category. To the contrary, with awareness red flags, the event is not sufficient to require the auditor to perform fraud audit procedures. However, the totality of all the awareness red flags will require auditor's judgment on the need to perform fraud audit procedures. While both may lead to the performance of fraud audit procedures, the underlying reasons differ. As a guideline for internal control audits, a red flag that links to a fraud scenario via a key control is denoted as a trigger red flag, whereas a red flag that links to a fraud scenario via nonkey controls is denoted as an awareness red flag. A trigger red flag is similar to the traditional audit use of red flags, whereby when an internal control is not working it "triggers" a red flag. The use of trigger and awareness red flags will change in fraud audits or specific point analysis, whereas the link is directly associated with concealment strategy and the elements of the fraud scenario.

Prompt 3: Identify the pattern and frequency relevant to the fraud scenario. The auditor needs to be alert to the pattern and frequency of fraudulent activity. However, the application of the concept requires exercising judgment and formulating decisions that do not have absolute certainty in building the fraud audit program. Therefore, the brainstorming session should start with identifying the patterns followed by the frequency of the event. While the actual criteria for each red flag category will differ, the process remains the same. The pattern analysis requires the auditor to identify all applicable patterns associated with the red flag category. The frequency analysis requires the auditor to determine the number of times an event must occur for sample selection or the performance of fraud audit procedures. Yes, the frequency analysis is judgmental and not intended to be hard and fixed.

Prompt 4: Understand how the red flags correlate to the fraud opportunity. Fraud opportunity, by definition, is the opportunity to commit a fraud scenario. Therefore, correlating red flags to the opportunity is critical for understanding how a fraud audit program is structured. The brainstorming session should focus on the likely person to have caused the red flag.

Prompt 5: Link the red flag to the applicable section of the fraud audit program. It is given that red flags should be incorporated into the fraud audit program, but how a red flag impacts the sample selection process and the testing procedures should be discussed as part of the brainstorming session.

Outcomes from a Brainstorming Session

The essence of the discussion is to establish the fraud boundaries of the fraud audit scope. The key outcomes are:

- Consensus on the scope of the fraud project.
- General agreement on the fraud definitions for the inherent fraud scheme(s).
- Provide a starting point for building the fraud audit program.

PRACTICAL**GUIDANCE**

Fraud Scenario of a Favored Vendor in Collusion with the Procurement Supervisor Receiving a Kickback

In this example, the concealment strategy is a false representation via the sole source statement. The following illustrates the starting point for the audit program:

1. Examine the bid documents for signs of corruption associated with the sole source selection of the vendor:
   a. Specifications are too vague for proper estimates to be made.
   b. Lack of explanation for sole source selection.
   c. Awards made to contractors with a history of poor performance.
   d. Failure to update cost of pricing data after prices have decreased.
2. The auditor would research the marketplace to determine if other vendors were available that would meet the totality of the business needs.
   a. If the statement is true, no additional audit work is necessary.
   b. Assuming the sole source statement is false, continue to step 3.
3. Gather creditable evidence that the manager knew the statement was false.
   a. If no creditable evidence exists, no additional audit work is necessary.
   b. Assuming that creditable evidence does exist, continue to step 4.
4. Refer this matter to investigation.

 SUMMARY

In addition to the practical application of brainstorming sessions, this chapter included a discussion, at great length, about the importance of fraud red flags. Table 4.1 hopefully will illustrate just how red flags become a tool that helps the auditors develop their audit approach.

TABLE 4.1 Red Flag Matrix

Type of Red Flag	Statements of Work and Specifications	Evaluation of Bids and Proposals	Award of the Contract	Defective Pricing
Anomaly	Copies versus originals	A "loss" of a bid proposal from an outsider who wants to participate	Award to contractor who is not the lowest, responsive bidder	Persistent defective pricing
Vagueness	Lack of clear job requirements, sloppy and carelessly written contract	Lack of explanation for sole source selection	Disqualification of a qualified bidder and no explanation is documented	Failure to make complete disclosure of data known to responsible contractor
Restrictive	Designing specifications to fit the capabilities of only one contractor	Biased individuals on the evaluation panel	None	Failure to correct known deficiencies
Missing	Specifications don't include work site details	None	Awards made without adequate documentation	None
Illogical	Specifications are too vague for proper estimates to be made	Improperly disqualifying the bid or proposal of a contractor	Awards made to contractors with a history of poor performance	Purchase order date after invoice date
Frequency	None	Documents from competing firms contain similar or identical names, handwriting/ signatures, invoice numbers, telephone numbers	None	None
Range	None	None	None	None

(continued)

TABLE 4.1   *(Continued)*

Type of Red Flag	Statements of Work and Specifications	Evaluation of Bids and Proposals	Award of the Contract	Defective Pricing
Change	Format and style of a given bid contract shows irregularities	None	Material changes in the contract shortly after the award	Failure to update cost of pricing data after prices have decreased
Error	Excessive spelling or grammar mistakes	None	None	Recorded to improper account
Arithmetic	Charges do not total	No independent check of totals	None	None
Unusual	No typical add-on charges for industry	Handwritten additional charges	Allowing a low bidder to withdraw without justification	Handwritten special instructions

CHAPTER FIVE

Assessment of Fraud Likelihood

A FRAUD RISK ASSESSMENT is a critical tool for managing the cost of fraud to an organization. In its simplest form, the risk assessment is a listing of possible fraud risks to an organization. In its more advanced form, the document not only assesses the likelihood of fraud's occurring within an organization, but becomes an impact statement as well. From an audit perspective, the fraud risk assessment is the initiation point for the fraud audit program, as its substance is critical in the building of such a program. This substance should include the following:

- A comprehensive listing of all fraud risks facing an organization.
- A likelihood assessment of the fraud risk occurring.
- An understanding of the resulting impact.
- Ownership of the fraud risk for both control and audit responsibility.

 ## PREPARING A FRAUD RISK ASSESSMENT

The fraud risk assessment can be thought of as a fraud deterrence control for organizations in their managing the cost of fraud. It is also the document auditors rely upon to plan their response to the risk of fraud. The preparer of the fraud risk assessment should strive for the following attributes:

- The determination of the fraud likelihood assessment should be free from bias.
- Provides a consistent qualitative and quantitative calculation for assessing the fraud likelihood and the exposure identification.
- Ensures a complete identification of fraud risk based on the primary fraud classifications.
- Evaluates internal controls.

Fundamental Principles

Judging the likelihood of fraud's occurring is more difficult than understanding the impact fraud has on an organization. This reality is not intended to diminish the value of the risk assessment, but rather acknowledge the complexities in assessing the likelihood of a person's committing a fraudulent activity. It's pretty straightforward; everyone knows the harm fraud does, but like anything involving a judgmental factor, determining the likelihood of fraud is a difficult exercise given the knowledge required. Questions abound, such as: Is it fraud or just human error or something else? The fraud triangle indicates that individuals commit fraud because of opportunity, pressures, and rationalization. The opportunity aspect can be easily determined through understanding the internal controls in the core business processes. Unfortunately, determining the individual pressures or rationalizations in a fraud risk assessment is not as easy given the judgment of fraud likelihood necessary.

SAS 99 recommends the use of a fraud risk factor in understanding the environmental factors that contribute to material misstatement of the financial statements. While the process is useful to enhance awareness, it does not contribute a predictability factor that a specific fraud scenario is more or less likely to occur. So, we have fraud likelihood scoring and fraud-loss exposure scoring to aid in determining the predictability that a fraud scenario is likely to occur.

The fraud likelihood score, fraud-loss exposure score, and the resulting audit response have to be in direct relation to each other in order to ensure a proper design of a fraud audit program. By having this relationship in balance, the fraud audit response is linked to the fraud scenario. In the progression of these steps, the strength of each connection is critical to the overall strength of the fraud audit program being developed. Many audit departments prepare the risk assessment and the audit program as separate documents, and by doing so neglect to establish these critical links, which results in a less-than-effective fraud audit program.

Fraud risk assessment requires a structured methodology to identify fraud. It is easy for auditors to fall back on the familiar and take a haphazard approach to identifying fraud instead of taking the time and effort to follow a structured methodology. Instead, they may commingle the fraud components of concealment and conversion to describe a fraud scenario. Such action could result, for example, in the identification of a kickback scheme rather than an overbilling scheme resulting in a kickback. It sounds like we are being really picky here, but it is necessary in order to find out how the fraudulent behavior is being carried out and perhaps more importantly to determine what can be done to correct it. A well-defined, structured methodology avoids such haphazardness, as it allows for a clearer purpose leading to distinct results. As stated previously, a sound professional judgment is needed to assess the likelihood of fraud's occurring. Regardless of how structured the methodology becomes, the process requires the auditor's judgment and professional experience in its application. Therefore, please remember, the purpose of the methodology is not to be a substitute for professional judgment and experience, but to enhance a consistent qualitative determination.

Fraud risk by its nature is different from traditional control risk. The intent to deceive is a critical element of fraud risk. Therefore, an audit response to fraud risk must be prepared with this intent in mind.

Approaches for Assessing Fraud Likelihood

As stated previously, in its more advanced form, the fraud risk assessment document contains an assessment of the likelihood of fraud's occurring within an organization at some defined level. There are two approaches to be taken when assessing the likelihood of fraud in building the fraud audit program. Specifically, fraud likelihood can be determined through data analysis via data mining or in the more traditional manner of control identification.

Data mining is predicated on the absence or the occurrence of transactions that are consistent with the fraud data profile for a fraud scenario. Simply, if no transactions meet the fraud data profile, then the assessment states that the specific fraud scenario is not occurring. Further discussion of data mining as a fraud likelihood determination tool can be found in Chapter 7.

Control identification is based on the thought that properly designed internal controls will minimize the likelihood of fraud's occurring. The progress involves linking the internal control to the fraud risk, then assessing the adequacy of the fraud controls. Chapter 6 includes a discussion of the relationship between an organization's internal controls and the use of red flags links to detect the possibility of fraud's occurring.

The difference between the two approaches is simple. Data mining states the fraud scenario *did not occur* in the scope period or these transactions meet the profile of the scenario, whereas the internal control approach states that the fraud risk *should not occur.* From a fraud audit strategy standpoint, selecting the right approach for the organization is important.

Common to both approaches is the goal of identifying fraud scenarios and understanding how the fraud scenarios occur in the core business systems. Once identified and understood, the process of building the fraud audit program can commence. Both approaches have their respective strengths and weaknesses. Control identification is widely practiced and utilizes fraud auditing red flags. To the contrary, data mining is a new approach to assessing the likelihood of fraud risk and is presented here as an integral component of the fraud audit program. The approaches can operate simultaneously or separately and are chosen based on the intended use of the risk document.

Key Elements

The steps for building the fraud risk assessment are generally understood and agreed upon, but there are key elements in those steps that must be performed or recognized in actual practice. These items are listed next and a discussion of each element will follow.

- Identification of the fraud risks consistent with the intended use of the fraud risk assessment.
- Fraud risk identification occurs at:
  - Entity-wide level or macro level.
  - Core business system or micro level.
  - Fraud penetration level or mega-micro level.
- Identification of the internal controls that minimize the likelihood of the fraud scenario's occurring.
- Linking the internal controls to the fraud scenario.
- Calculate the likelihood of fraud's occurring score.
- Rank and categorize the fraud scenarios based on the likelihood score.
- Understand and identify both the monetary and nonmonetary exposures of the fraud scenario.
- Link the audit response to the fraud likelihood score.

Identification of the Fraud Risks

Identification of the fraud risks must be consistent with the intended use of the fraud risk assessment. The fraud risk structure outlined in Chapter 3 allows an organization to expand fraud identification efforts without re-creating the wheel. The users of the fraud risk assessment, either management or auditors, can tailor the fraud risk assessment to meet their needs.

The use of the fraud risk assessment is necessary in determining the organization level to operate on when trying to identify fraud. All organizations should use a macro level for assigning responsibility and authority for managing fraud risk. However, fraud identification at a micro level is sufficient for regulatory and auditing standards. The minimum level for fraud auditing is the micro level, preferably targeting a specific class of transactions. Fraud auditing testing procedures, for example, red flags functioning at the micro level, focus on the core business systems. The following general caveats have evolved through the actual practice of conducting fraud audits.

Caveats of Fraud Risk Identification   There is a direct correlation between managing the fraud risk and the organizational level designated for fraud risk identification. At the entity-wide level, the fraud identification has a high degree of understandability for management; however, the entity-wide level will not identify all scenarios facing an organization. The fraud penetration level will provide a comprehensive listing of all fraud scenarios, but the level of detail might be too exhaustive for management. This is, so to speak, the yin and yang of fraud risk identification.

The number of fraud scenarios facing an organization can be computed with mathematical precision using the counting principal (i.e., the number of fraud scenarios equals the product of four variables: the inherent scheme, opportunity, entity, and transaction). The value of each variable will vary based on the detail of the fraud risk assessment.

Designing the fraud audit program becomes easier to manage when the lowest possible level is used. For example, permutation analysis will indicate at least six categories of false entity structure. The data mining and audit procedures need to be tailored to the specific scenario; otherwise, the auditor will arrive at a false conclusion.

The lower the level of the risk identification, the greater the number of fraud scenarios. At the lowest permutation level, fraud scenarios will overlap other fraud scenarios at the same level. While the number of scenarios increases, a close scrutiny of how the fraud scenario occurs will reveal that the same internal control, data mining routine, and fraud audit procedures will address the multiple scenarios. Above all else, know that each scenario is being addressed.

Experience has shown that when a disagreement occurs among auditors regarding fraud auditing, it has more to do with the definition of the terms than any other reason. For example, the term *conflict of interest* would mean one thing to the fraud auditor if there is undisclosed ownership. Since the ownership of a privately held corporation is generally not part of a public record, the ability of fraud auditing to detect such a conflict is very difficult. However, many auditors define a conflict of interest within the context of a favored-vendor status scenario or overbilling scenario. Any such disagreements can be handled by making sure everyone on the audit team is on the same page with how conflict of interest is defined in the context of the audit. Clearly, fraud audit programs must have a fraud definition section as part of documenting the response to the risk of fraud.

Models for Risk Identification The previous discussion highlighted the relationship between organizational level and fraud risk identification. Listed in the following sections are several models for risk identification that can be applied to practical use.

Entity-Wide Level—Macro Level Identification of the primary and secondary fraud classifications and the inherent fraud schemes are the basis for an entity-wide fraud risk identification model. The critical decision with this model is which primary fraud classifications to include. At minimum, financial reporting, asset misappropriation, and corruption should be included. By responding to the risk of fraud at a macro level, you are establishing an organizational fraud risk structure and providing the basis for assigning responsibility and authority for managing and auditing the fraud risk.

Core Business Level—Micro Level The purpose of this model is to identify the fraud scenarios facing an organization. Each inherent fraud scheme is customized into a fraud scenario using the permutation analysis. Operating at a level of core business is considered micro in range, therefore, the minimum guidelines concerning the analysis are the following:

▪ Entity: Recognizes the difference between false and real entities.
▪ Opportunity: Recognizes fraud opportunity based on direct access associated with the job duties, title, and responsibilities.

▪ Transactional: Recognizes transactions based on internal controls. If all transactions are managed by the same control, then only one transaction type exists. If the transaction bypasses a control or uses a different control, then the permutation analysis would recognize the fraud scenario based on the irregularity.

The Fraud Penetration Risk Assessment Model—Mega-Micro Level The purpose of this model is to identify all permutations of a fraud scenario consistent with the drill-down decision based on business system, class of transactions, and the fraud specific. The scale is referred to as mega-micro, which sounds like a contradiction: How can something be mega, that is, it is large, and micro, yet small, at the same time? The scale is mega-micro given the low organizational level where the operation takes place; however, there is a complexity factor considering the breadth of the level encompassed, hence, a mega-micro risk level. The guidelines for fraud scenario identification are:

▪ Entity: Recognizes all permutations of the entity structure.
▪ Opportunity: Recognizes fraud opportunity based on no internal control, direct and indirect job opportunity, and the internal control inhibitors.
▪ Transactional: Recognizes that computer business systems are driven by data; transaction types; functions, for example, create, update, and delete; and security profiles that are built into access systems. A complete understanding of the transactional responsibilities bestowed on an individual or job title is critical to identifying the fraud opportunities.

Defining, Categorizing, and Criteria for Internal Controls

One purpose of a fraud risk assessment is to determine the likelihood of a fraud scenario's occurring in a business system. The assessment is judgmentally based on the adequacy of the internal controls linking to a fraud scenario. Therefore, a key element of the risk assessment is the identification of the internal controls that minimize the likelihood of the fraud scenario from occurring. To make this identification, we must define the internal controls, categorize them, and establish criteria upon which the likelihood of fraud risk can be scored based on the internal fraud controls.

Defining Internal Controls Clearly stated definitions of the internal control and assessment criteria are required. The risk assessment should provide definitions of the internal control terms in order to ensure a consistency in the evaluation criteria. For example, in the United States, the control model is COSO (Committee of Sponsoring Organizations), thereby providing a basis of uniformity.

Categorizing Internal Controls   Internal controls can be categorized in four areas, as follows:

1. **Fraud Prevention.** Controls designed to minimize the likelihood of a fraud scenario occurring. These controls are associated with the control activities section of the COSO Model.
2. **Fraud Detection.** Controls designed to alert management that a fraud is occurring. These controls are associated with the monitoring and supervision aspects provided in the COSO Model.
3. **Fraud Deterrence.** Controls that are designed to discourage individuals from committing a fraud scenario. These controls are associated with the control environment aspects of the COSO Model.
4. **Fraud Prosecution.** Controls designed to ensure that an investigation can establish with reasonable certainty that an individual committed a crime. These controls are associated with the entire model, but look to documentation standards, accountability, separation of duties, and the enforcement of internal controls.

Criteria for Internal Controls   To increase the consistency of risk likelihood scoring, it is best to establish criteria for each category of fraud controls. The criteria is judgmentally based on management's or the auditor's risk tolerance. The following list of criteria is generic and, therefore, in practice, the preparer will need to identify the appropriate criteria for an organization.

1. Fraud Prevention Criteria
   - Fraud prevention is performed by someone other than individual with the ability to initiate fraudulent transaction. The approval process is the typical control procedure.
   - The volume of transactions reviewed is reasonable for an individual to adequately review and approve.
2. Fraud Detection Criteria
   - Fraud monitoring should detect the fraudulent transaction within a specific time period.
   - Fraud monitoring is performed by someone other than individual with the ability to initiate fraudulent transaction.

■ The volume of activity is reasonable for someone to review and detect the fraud.

3. Fraud Deterrence Criterion
   ■ There is a correlation between the time period for the fraud deterrence procedures to commence and the level of risk tolerance for detecting the fraud scenario.

4. Fraud Prosecution Criteria
   ■ Documents to establish that the event has occurred are created and retained.
   ■ A direct accountability for creating the transaction can be recreated.

Linking the Internal Controls to the Fraud Scenario

By targeting a level of fraud risk (e.g., micro, macro, and mega-micro), the auditor is able to gather information to better understand how a fraud scenario will occur in the core business system. Therefore, the process of understanding how the system operates and how the fraud scenario operates should occur at the same time. This knowledge is obtained through the management interview process and the documenting of the business process and the internal controls.

During the management interview, the auditor should explain the concept of fraud prevention via internal controls and the criteria used to evaluate the fraud prevention capacity of the internal controls. A good starting point in the interview is with an explanation of the fraud scenario, then eliciting management's understanding of the internal controls.

Once the internal controls are identified and linked to the fraud scenario, the process of evaluating the likelihood of fraud can carry on. This process is procedural in that it involves the calculation of a fraud likelihood score.

Calculating a Fraud Likelihood Score   The calculation of the likelihood score should allow for a consistency in assessing the likelihood of fraud. The technique should be agreed to and understood by the users of the system. To achieve this goal, the following guidelines should be followed:

■ Keep the system simple.
■ Use a three-tier grading system.
■ The lower score correlates to a lower likelihood of the fraud scenario's occurring.
■ Provide definitions for each grade.

- The evaluation should occur at the fraud scenario level.
- The fraud likelihood score should be an aggregate score based on the fraud prevention, detection, and deterrence scores.

The definitions of the grading system should pertain to the fraud opportunity embedded in the fraud scenario. The following example illustrates a defined grading system:

1. The control design would reasonably minimize the occurrence of the fraud scenario, plus minimize the effect of internal control inhibitors.
2. The control design would reasonably minimize the occurrence of the fraud scenario.
3. The control design would not reasonably minimize the occurrence of the fraud scenario.

Rank and Categorize the Fraud Scenarios For the purpose of assessing fraud, the ranking and categorizing of the fraud scenarios add a helpful layer of organization. Some common ranking methods and categories are as follows:

- Rank the fraud scenarios by likelihood score, highest score to lowest score.
- Rank the fraud scenarios by the identified risk exposure.
- Categorize by business system using the likelihood score or identified risk exposure as a ranking within each category.
- Categorize fraud scenarios by conversion technique

Understand and Identify the Organizational Loss Exposure If a fraud scenario occurs, the organization will be facing both monetary and non-monetary loss exposure.

Step 1: The first step in determining this exposure is to identify and understand the type of exposure facing the organization based on the primary classifications of fraud. The primary classification will generally dictate the appropriate method for determining the resulting exposure. For example:

- **Primary Fraud Classification: Financial Misstatement.** There is no actual direct loss of funds to the organization. While eventual lawsuits or forensic accounting fees may occur, there is no realistic way to calculate the monetary cost to the organization. A company's stock may fall by reason of a loss in investor confidence (a nonmonetary event).

- **Primary Fraud Classification: Asset Misappropriation.** There is a direct loss of funds at time of the theft. The amount of the loss will depend on a variety of factors, including, but not limited to, the perpetrator's position in management, perception or fear of consequences from detection, and state of mind. It should be noted that the accompanying secondary risk category of misuse of assets will not result in a direct monetary loss.

- **Primary Fraud Classification: Corruption.** There may or may not be an actual loss of funds to the organization. If the corrupt act is a Foreign Corrupt Practices Act violation, the organization will incur legal fees. Once again there is no easy way to calculate the monetary loss without a lot of assumptions. If the corruption scenario resulted in bribery or kickbacks, then the loss calculation would be predicated on the increased costs.

- **Primary Fraud Classification: Revenue Obtained Improperly.** The exposure calculation would be similar to the corruption explanation, except the focus would be on the revenue cycle versus the expenditure cycle.

- **Primary Fraud Classification: Avoidance of Government Regulation.** Generally, the impact is codified in the statute that was avoided. The auditor can also look to the media to determine how the government has acted in regard to the regulation.

- **Primary Fraud Classification: Avoidance of Expense Obligations.** Can be determined if the avoidance is a clearly defined obligation. However, oftentimes the avoidance is a matter of interpretation. Therefore, both the calculation of the obligation and the analysis of the occurrence of the obligation are subjective.

Step 2:   The second step in determining monetary or nonmonetary loss exposure is to identify the type of exposure possible associated with the primary fraud classification. Adverse publicity, reputational risk, corporate criminal action, class action lawsuits, and a reduction in value of corporation stock are all examples of types of loss exposure. For example, the occurrence of asset misappropriation lends itself to a dollar-loss calculation. However, the amount of the loss calculated is arbitrary based on a variety factors. Therefore, associating the loss calculation to the likelihood score and creating arbitrary amounts or percentages consistent with organizational size would allow for an assigning of dollar-loss exposure to the fraud scenario. The first method of determining exposure operates off a preset dollar amount. The second method focuses on a percentage of the core business system. The methods are listed as follows:

Method 1:	
Likelihood Score	**Dollar Impact**
Two or Three	Less than $100,000
Four	Greater than $100,000 less than $1,000,000
Five and Six	Greater than $1,000,000

Method 2:	
Likelihood Score	**Dollar Impact**
Two or Three	5%
Four	3%
Five and Six	1%

Linking the Audit Response to the Fraud Likelihood Score   The fraud risk assessment becomes the basis for the auditor's response to the risk of fraud. Therefore, given the importance of the likelihood score as it provides a quantitative element to the overall assessment of fraud, it should directly link to the audit response. An example of this link is as follows:

Likelihood Score	**Audit Response**
Two or Three	Test the internal control using red flags.
Four	Optional—based on exposure score.
Five and Six	Test the authenticity of the transaction through the use of a fraud testing procedure.

Deriving a Total Control Score   Table 5.1 illustrates how the fraud likelihood scores for prevention and detection controls are tallied per each fraud scenario to arrive at a total control score.

TABLE 5.1 Fraud Risk Score

	Fraud Likelihood Score		
Fraud Scenario	Prevention Controls	Detection Controls	Total Control Score
False billing	2	1	3
Pass-through billing	2	2	4
Conflict of interest	2	3	5
Overbilling	2	3	5

 SUMMARY

There was a lot of linking going on in this chapter. The fraud audit response is linked to the fraud scenario, and the internal control links to the fraud risk, fraud scenario, and likelihood scores, and so on. The intent was not to confuse, but to highlight how interconnected these elements of a fraud risk assessment are. Therefore, the stronger you can make those connections, the more effective the fraud audit program will be. The most critical of these links are the fraud risk to the fraud scenario via the internal control identification and/or data mining approaches. The fraud scenario can then be linked to an appropriate fraud response by the development of a predictability factor that the fraud scenario is likely to occur. This predictability factor is comprised of the fraud likelihood score and the fraud exposure-loss score. Remember, "to link" means to establish a bond, and in any building project you have to bond things together, whether it is the nailing of boards or the taping of sheetrock. In our context of fraud auditing, all this linking is needed for our next step: building a fraud audit program.

CHAPTER SIX

Building the Fraud Audit Program

HISTORICALLY, THE RESPONSE TO fraud risk consisted of control testing or an overview of financial statement development procedures. This approach relied on the auditor's awareness of red flags indicating fraudulent activity. The standards traditionally addressed the need for professional skepticism in responding to the fraud risk. It could be said that these standards were enacted with the sole purpose of addressing the issue of fraud. Consequently, the audit profession was left with ambiguity concerning how to actually respond to fraud risk because such standards are not specific about providing a methodology for uncovering fraud in core business systems. Undoubtedly, to dispel this ambiguity, the response to the risk of fraud requires a methodology specifically designed for fraud risk. Imposing such a requirement is not to speak disapprovingly about the use of professional skepticism with regard to fraud risk; however, it should be pointed out that the mere tacking on of an undefined degree or direction of skepticism when reviewing controls during an audit lacks any manner of an effective methodology in responding to fraud.

TRADITIONAL AUDIT VERSUS THE FRAUD AUDIT

Considering that the traditional audit and the fraud audit both involve the exercise of auditing, there are similarities between the two. These similarities can be summarized as follows:

- The four phases of an audit are planning, sampling, testing, and reporting.
- The use of an audit program to document audit procedures performed on internal controls or key financial statement assertions.
- The examination of documents and records to formulate opinions.
- The issuance of a report containing opinions based on the objective of the audit.

The fraud audit differs from the traditional audit in several key aspects; some may be considered structural design differences, while others may be thought of as nuances to the traditional audit. Specifically, the differences are as follows:

1. The fraud audit program is designed to uncover fraud versus providing assurance on the effectiveness of the internal controls or the offering an opinion on the financial statements.
2. While the four audit phases are the same for both, the methodology in each phase is different, the fraud risk assessment being the key difference. With a traditional audit, the assessment is based on linking the internal controls to fraud risk, while with the fraud audit, the assessment directs data mining to be performed.
3. The sampling performed for a fraud audit is the most extensive process and typically is performed by the most senior auditor of the fraud audit team. The sampling is based on discovery sampling versus a random selection process.
4. The fraud audit focuses on the authenticity of the representations versus the evidence of an assertion.
5. The fraud audit relies on evidence external to the organization, whereas traditional auditing tends to rely on internal evidence.
6. The fraud audit opinion opines on the creditable evidence associated with the existence of fraud scenarios.

 RESPONDING TO THE RISK OF FRAUD

As just discussed, the two types of audits, the traditional and fraud, lend themselves to two approaches in responding to the risk of fraud. The first approach is designated the integrated fraud audit approach, while the second is simply termed the fraud audit approach.

The integrated fraud audit approach can be thought of as an interim approach between the traditional audit program and fraud audit program. As in a traditional audit, it is designed to offer an opinion on the effectiveness of internal controls or an opinion on the financial statements. However, while the integrated approach uses the framework of the traditional audit program, it includes audit steps that are designed to uncover fraud that is deemed material. An audit testing procedure under this approach is either linked to a specific control objective or to a specific fraud scenario. With this approach, the sampling tends to be either random or based on auditors' judgment. Overall, the integrated approach assumes the auditor will be sufficiently aware of the associated red flags.

Under the fraud audit approach, a fraud audit program is followed that essentially consists of two components: The first is structured to *locate* fraud, and the second is structured to *recognize* the type of fraud. Audit procedures are specifically designed to locate fraud in core business systems through a fraud sampling plan known as data mining. Data mining is used to search for transactions consistent with a fraud data profile. Upon locating the fraud, fraud audit testing procedures are engaged to recognize the fraudulent transaction. These procedures are known as either red flag testing procedures or fraud audit testing procedures and are designed to validate the authenticity of documents and the performance of internal controls. Detailed audit steps and specific red flags must be included in the overall fraud audit program planning.

 ## A FRAUD AUDIT PROGRAM

An entire chapter devoted to the data mining component of the fraud audit program is contained in this book. Therefore, in consideration of the divergence from the traditional response to fraud risk that the fraud audit program entails, the discussion that follows concentrates on the fraud audit procedure component and its objective to locate and recognize fraud risk.

Purpose

The purpose of the fraud audit program is to document the auditor's response to the risk of fraud. In one sense, the fraud audit is a mirror image of a traditional audit because both audit programs list audit procedures that are designed to gather evidence to support a conclusion. The traditional audit program opines on the effectiveness of internal controls, program objectives, or the financial statements. The fraud audit program is designed to opine on whether creditable evidence exists to suggest that a specific *fraud scenario* has occurred in the core business system. The fraud audit program does not opine on whether any and all fraud has occurred. There is a huge difference between a fraud scenario and fraud in its totality.

Key Concepts

In developing the fraud audit program, understanding the following concepts are critical to the success of its execution.

Linkage

The term *link* is used extensively throughout this chapter and the entire book because it aptly highlights the relationship between the various fraud audit program components and objectives. For example, the fraud audit program is built by linking the data mining, audit testing procedures, and audit evidence considerations to a given fraud scenario found in the risk assessment. At its core, the concept of linkage is a simple one; however, with the traditional audit program as a frame of reference, many auditors have difficulty grasping the idea that fraud audit procedures should be designed, and therefore linked, to a specific fraud scenario.

Inherent Limitations

Audits by their nature are limited to the organizations' books and certain available public records. To establish with a degree of certainty that a fraud has occurred, the auditor needs access to the books and records of other companies or individual personal records. In particular, the conversion cycle is oftentimes an off-the-book activity. For example, if a vendor has provided a kickback, the transfer of money is from the vendor to the employee. Therefore, the lack of access to vendor records will stymie auditors from being able to establish elements of the fraud scenario. Therefore, it is advisable that the auditor, prior to including scenarios into the audit scope, understands what can or cannot be established through available records.

Degree of Certainty

The degree of certainty concerning the finding of fraud will depend on the level of concealment sophistication and the on/off access to books and records. When the fraud is an on-the-book scheme and has a low level of sophistication, the auditor will be able to obtain a high degree of certainty that a fraud scenario has occurred. Consequently, with an off-the-book fraud scenario and high level of sophistication, the auditor will not achieve the same degree of certainty that a fraud scenario has occurred. Therefore, the auditor must recognize the degree of certainty differences when developing the fraud audit program.

The difficulty in ascertaining the degree of certainty directly influences the quality and quantity of evidence needed. If an auditor assumes a low level of certainty with regard to a fraud scenario's occurring, then the audit plan may not incorporate the gathering of creditable evidence at all. However, if an auditor is well versed in inherent fraud scenarios and, therefore, establishes some degree of certainty that a scenario has occurred, the audit plan needs to incorporate the obtaining of the appropriate amount and quality of evidence to justify that degree of certainty.

Specifically, as part of the fraud audit plan, it should first be determined what elements of proof will be necessary to recommend an investigation. Then a decision is needed to determine if the chosen elements are attainable in the context of a fraud audit based on the specific scenario, concealment sophistication, and access to books and records.

Creditable Evidence

In control testing, the conclusion is that internal controls are designed adequately and operating effectively. In fraud auditing, the conclusion is that there is creditable evidence to suggest that a specific fraud scenario has not occurred or that an investigation is necessary to resolve the red flags. The concept of stating whether there is creditable evidence to suggest that a fraud scenario has occurred tends to baffle auditors who are accustomed to control testing and financial statement opinions. This is why the use of a decision tree focusing on the red flags associated with a scenario can be instrumental in the process of establishing creditable evidence.

Whether evidence is creditable is determined by the extent necessary to establish an action. The action is either to recommend an investigation or that there are no overt red flags evident to recommend an investigation. The concept of credibility focuses on both the qualitative and quantitative aspects of the audit evidence that links to the fraud scenario. Practically speaking, once the event is identified, the question of whether there is enough evidence and if the quality of that evidence is sufficient needs to be addressed. With this understanding, the degree of certainty that fraud has occurred as discussed previously is directly linked to the concept of creditable evidence, with both concepts having a bearing on the quantitative and qualitative aspects of a fraud audit plan.

Overt Capacity

Overt capacity pertains to the ability to obtain information from external sources and that the external source may be aware the auditor is requesting the information. The concept behind fraud auditing is the corroboration of a representation through sources external to the organization. Therefore, by the nature of the process, the fraud audit procedures may create a more overt visibility of the audit process.

Steps

As stated in Chapter 1, there are four steps to building a fraud audit program: assess, identify, respond, and conclude.

The fraud audit program is initially formed from the fraud scenarios identified in the fraud risk *assessment*. The next step in building the fraud audit program is the linking of the concealment strategies associated with the fraud scenario to the associated red flags of the concealment strategy, thereby *identifying* a target area of fraud. In formation of a *response*, the data mining, the audit procedure, and the sufficiency of audit evidence are combined, constituting the overall the fraud audit program. Such a program provides a logical process for identifying events that constitute fraud indicators and also one for directly and effectively arriving at a *conclusion*.

The fraud audit program begins with the fraud scenario. The number of fraud scenarios to consider depends on a likelihood analysis as discussed in Chapter 5. The auditor should think of the fraud scenarios as audit objectives or control objectives. Although data mining and audit procedures specifically designed for each fraud are necessary, they will typically overlap each other.

Having a specific data mining plan ensures a link to the fraud data profile of the fraud scenario. The sampling is a judgmental selection in that it will be based on a visual examination of transactions or through the use of audit software. In either case, the selection process should be based on the data red flags associated with the fraud scenario. Remember, the purpose of the data mining component of the fraud audit program is to locate the fraud.

When considering the fraud audit procedure component of the fraud audit program, its design links the concealment strategies of the fraud scenario and the associated red flags. While the purpose of the fraud audit procedure is to recognize the fraud, its design must also allow the auditor to arrive at a conclusion regarding sufficiency of audit evidence regarding the fraud scenario.

 ## TESTING PROCEDURES

There are two fundamental testing procedures in response to the risk of fraud: the red flag testing procedure and the fraud audit testing procedure. The red flag procedure pertains to the integrated fraud audit approach mentioned previously. It is based on observing indicators in the internal documents and internal controls. In contrast, the fraud audit testing procedure, the basis of the fraud audit approach, verifies the authenticity of the documents and internal controls. The difference between the two may seem slight, because in building a fraud audit program, there are overall guidelines that take into consideration the testing procedures of each approach, with more specific guidelines used dependent on which approach is followed.

The following are the overall guidelines in testing:

- **Testing procedures must link to the fraud scenario.** On the surface, the concept appears simple; however, in practice it seems to be one of the more difficult tasks in responding to the risk of fraud. The first problem occurs when the auditor reverts back to the traditional audit standards, whereby there is no methodology and thus no linking to a fraud scenario. The second problem is when the auditor wants to expand the audit step beyond the stated fraud scenario. This is not to say that auditors should limit their thinking, but rather focus on taking greater care in describing the fraud scenario and linking the testing procedures to that fraud scenario.
- **Testing procedures must identify the concealment strategy and associated red flags.** There needs to be linkage between the perpetrator's concealment strategy and the testing procedures. Based on the specific scenario, the auditor should identify the concealment strategies used to hide the transaction. Once found, the auditor should then identify the observable events associated with the fraud concealment strategy.

  For example, if the perpetrator is creating false documents, then what observable event would cause the auditor to believe that the document was falsely created? As discussed in Chapter 4, these events will either be trigger red flags or awareness red flags under the red flag testing procedures and the elements of the fraud scenario in the fraud audit testing procedures.

▪ **The audit process must incorporate decision tree logic.** Use of decision tree logic aids in the process of identifying and resolving fraud red flags found during the audit. The process of identification and resolution is a dynamic, continually evolving one for an auditor. Because of this vacillation, the step-by-step method offered by a decision tree allows for a logical ending point for the auditor's work, thereby, negating chances of going in the wrong direction resulting incorrect conclusions or perhaps no conclusions at all.

▪ **The audit testing procedure must focus on the concealment strategy.** Once again, remember that the concealment strategy is the weak link of the perpetrators fraud plan. Once the concealment strategy is revealed, the fraud scenario becomes obvious. Therefore, the response to the fraud risk should be designed to pierce the concealment strategy. With red flag testing procedures, auditors should direct their testing to the question: what observable events would create a conclusion of impropriety? In contrast, with the fraud audit testing procedures, the question is: what external evidence could be gathered to show the falsity of the representation? With both testing areas, the concealment strategy is the target.

▪ **The audit process must be conclusion based.** Audit testing procedures should be designed to arrive at a logical conclusion based on the red flags associated with the concealment strategies. The basic assumption of any conclusion is that the audit program has identified the observable events. The logical conclusions for each of the two areas of procedures, that is, the red flag testing procedures and the fraud audit testing procedures, are presented under the appropriate areas discussed below.

▪ **The work papers should document the actual work performed by the auditor.** The audit program should include the trigger red flags and the awareness red flags that are the basis for the response to risk of fraud. The test of transactions should have a notation regarding the observation of the tick marks and the conclusion should be stated.

Red Flag Testing Procedures

Red flag testing procedures include the following:

▪ **Audit procedure focus on either the documents or internal controls.** By design, the red flag testing procedures examine documents as to their condition, information contained, industry standards, if they are missing in whole or part, and if there are overt signs of document alteration or document creation. The internal control test examines the documents for evidence of the performance of a procedure. The audit program should identify the trigger red flags and awareness red flags of each category that would result in added audit work. The program should also identify the additional audit work needed based on the observed condition.

■ **Observation of a red flag should be documented in the working papers.** The working papers should contain a notation regarding whether the trigger red flags were observed and a conclusion regarding whether the totality of the awareness red flags were sufficient to raise a fraud concern.

■ **No assumptions on likelihood of fraud risk.** The fraud risk assessment links the fraud scenario to the internal controls. With this link, an assessment of the likelihood of the occurrence of the fraud scenario is formulated. The risk ratings typically follow a high, medium, or low risk rating. While the risk rating has no immediate impact on the design of the red flag audit procedure, the rating may have an impact on sample sizes and whether fraud audit procedures are necessary. The response to the risk of fraud should consider the following guidelines:

  ■ A low risk rating may rely on the red flag testing procedure.
  ■ A medium risk rating would depend on the perceived fraud impact rating, where if the medium risk rating is linked to a high exposure, then a fraud audit testing procedure should be performed, otherwise the red flag testing procedure may suffice.
  ■ A high risk rating should necessitate the performance of a fraud audit testing procedure.

■ **The audit testing procedure and the veracity of the internal control or the document.** The audit testing procedure questions the veracity of the performance of the internal control or identifiable events in the document. An audit testing procedure by design should confirm the performance of an internal control and ensure that sufficient documents exist to support the internal control representation. The red flag testing procedure relies on the examination of internal controls and documents for either trigger or awareness red flags.

■ **Use of decision tree logic.** The decision tree logic is based on the trigger red flags observed or the totality of the awareness red flags. With red flag testing procedures, the decision tree begins with determining whether a trigger red flag has been observed in the audit. If an observation has occurred, then fraud audit testing procedures will be performed. If the answer is no, another determination must be made as to whether the totality of the awareness red flags is sufficient enough for the auditor to render fraud audit procedures necessary. If sufficient, the fraud audit testing procedures will be performed. If not, the auditor's work is complete.

Note that fraud audit procedures should be performed on any transaction:

▪ Where a trigger red flag has been observed, or
▪ Where the totality of the awareness red flags raises the auditor's professional skepticism.
▪ The outcome of the fraud audit procedures is either the red flag is resolved or the transaction is included in the audit report. Figure 6.1 shows a red flag flow chart.
▪ **Evidence is based on that found in the traditional audit.** As in the traditional audit, evidence relies exclusively on internally stored documents and documents that were created by external or internal sources.
▪ **Conclusion reached.** The working papers should provide an opinion as to the fraud scenario. The conclusion would correlate to the logical conclusions reached in the overall fraud audit guidelines. With this basis in mind, the following conclusions would apply for red flag testing procedures:
1. There are no observable trigger red flags.
2. The observable trigger red flags were resolved.
3. The totality of the awareness flags were not sufficient to suggest a fraud scenario is occurring.
4. The totality of the awareness flags were sufficient to suggest a fraud scenario is occurring.
5. The observable red flags were not resolved and a fraud audit was performed.
6. The conclusion defers to the fraud audit testing procedures conclusion.

Fraud Audit Testing Procedures

Fraud audit testing procedures include the following:

▪ **Focus is on the two parts of the inherent scheme structure.** The inherent scheme has two parts, the entity structure and the fraudulent

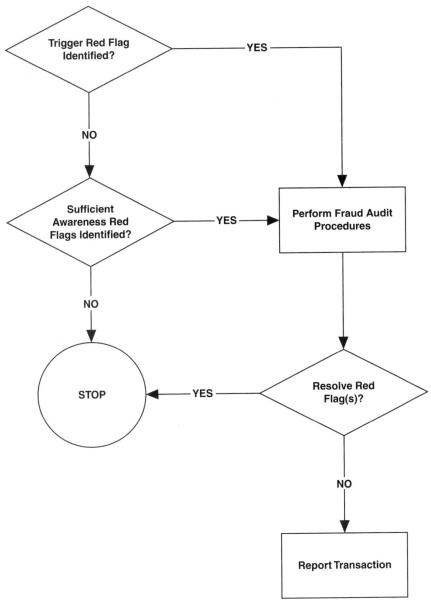

FIGURE 6.1 Red Flag Flow Chart

action; therefore, the fraud audit program should be designed to address both parts of the fraud scenario. The first step should be to determine whether the entity is a false entity or real entity. The entity determination focuses on the following:

1. **Legal capacity of the entity.** With legal capacity testing procedures, the auditor is establishing whether the vendor or customer has been legally created, the incorporation date, names and addresses associated with the entity, other business relationships, and any other information in the secretary of state files. The information obtained then needs to be correlated to internal databases containing name and address information and internal transactional databases.

2. **Physical existence of the entity.** This test is simple: Does the entity physically exist? The challenge becomes with the degree of certainty required in ensuring the entity exists. Caution should be exercised to remain within the context of an audit, not an investigation. So, within the context of an audit, the evidence could be telephone call, Google search, or an actual site visit. Another caution is advised with regard to the degree of sophistication as it closely related to the degree of certainty. For example, the perpetrator could be renting an office space and using a cell phone or an answering service, all to provide the illusion of physical entity existence.

3. **Capacity to provide the service based on the action description.** The nature of the audit procedure will vary greatly based on the core business function, fraud scenario, entity structure, and fraudulent action. The purpose is to ascertain whether the entity had the capability to provide or accept the goods or services identified in the associated document.

The conclusion of the entity testing will provide a predictability factor on the most likely inherent fraud scheme. In turn, the inherent fraud scheme will provide predictability on the most likely action, which typically will correlate to a service or a tangible good. In the end, the goods or service were either provided or not provided. As a starting point, the audit should focus on the most predictable fraud action, and then use a decision tree to determine other possible fraudulent actions.

▪ **Documentation needed in the working papers.** Criteria used to question the two parts of the inherent scheme should be documented in the working papers. The working papers should document the facts and circumstances surrounding the three false-entity criteria listed above, the documents supporting the transaction, and any interview statements.

Also to be documented is a conclusion regarding the transaction and the fraud scenarios.

- **The likelihood of fraud risk is rated as high.** As explained under the red flag testing procedure guidelines, a high risk rating should necessitate the performance of a fraud audit testing procedure. In addition, a fraud audit testing procedure should be performed if there is an unresolved red flag.
- **Fraud audit procedures question the veracity of the concealment strategy.** Remember, the concealment strategy is the weak link of the fraud scenario. Once the fraud audit procedures provide creditable evidence that the representations made via documents that internal control procedures are false, then the fraud scenario becomes obvious.
- **Use of decision tree logic.** Use of decision tree logic provides predictability on the inherent fraud scheme and a basis for fraud audit conclusions. The decision tree is designed to determine the logical order of fraud audit testing procedures and to provide the basis for the fraud audit conclusion as discussed earlier in the chapter. The decision tree starts with determining whether the entity is false or real. If the entity is determined false, an evaluation must be made as to whether the entity is fictitious or is a situation of stolen identity. The answer to this choice then links to a specific action associated with the inherent fraud scheme. Upon identification of the action, the question of what evidence standard is necessary to formulate a conclusion must be made, whereby the sufficiency and qualitative aspects of the audit evidence are determined. Figure 6.2 shows an example of a decision tree.
- **The audit evidence must be externally created and stored.** The basic assumption in the fraud audit testing procedure component of the fraud audit program is that any evidence either created by or retained by the control owner and, thereby, internally created and stored is not reliable in the formulation of a fraud conclusion. The term *control owner* in this sense is to be thought of in the broadest manner, meaning if the possibility of the control owner either directly or indirectly impacting the creditability of the evidence exists, then additional or expanded procedures should be employed to search for other evidence that is externally created and stored.
- **Confirms the authenticity of the documents or internal controls.** Confirming authenticity is the act of proving the genuineness of a representation. The concept for the purposes of distinguishing traditional auditing from fraud auditing is perhaps easier to illustrate than explain.

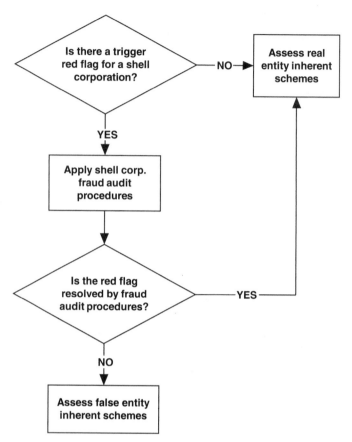

FIGURE 6.2 Entity Analysis Decision Tree Logic

For example, in control testing, the auditor looks for evidence of the approval signature on a document such as an invoice. If the signature is on the document, and it is the signature of the person authorized to sign such documents, then the internal control is thought to be working as intended. However, in fraud auditing, the auditor looks to ensure the approval signature is genuine. To do so, the auditor would compare the signature to known handwriting samples referred to as standards and/or verify the approver was in the office that day.

Using the vendor invoice in Figure 6.5 at the end of the chapter as an example, the invoice indicates that Atlantic Supply, Inc., is a corporation. The auditor verified that the new vendor procedures were performed by accounts payable. Therefore, the internal control inference is that the vendor is a corporation. The fraud audit testing procedures would confirm with the secretary of state incorporation records that the entity is a legally created entity in the state of New York. Therefore, gathering direct evidence that the corporation is a valid corporation.

▪ **Conclusion reached.** The conclusion would correlate to the logical conclusions in the overall fraud audit guidelines. With this basis in mind, the conclusions for the fraud audit testing procedure would be any of the following three outcomes:

1. There is no creditable evidence to suggest a fraud scenario is occurring.
2. There is creditable evidence to suggest a fraud scenario is occurring, and sufficient evidence could be gathered to allow a management response. (Note: This conclusion occurs when the fraud conversion can be directly linked to the fraud perpetrator, that is, travel expense scenario.)
3. There is creditable evidence to suggest a fraud scenario is occurring and a fraud investigation is necessary to resolve the fraud observation. (This conclusion occurs when the fraud conversion cannot be linked to the perpetrator or the sophistication of the concealment exceeds the audit capacity, that is, false billing scenario.)

FRAUD CONCEALMENT EFFECT ON THE AUDIT RESPONSE

True or false: Are audits designed to fail regarding fraud detection? The answer is true. The truth of the answer lies with how the fraud concealment impacts the auditor's ability to locate and detect fraud. The fraud audit program must take into consideration the fraud concealment strategies and their relationship with the fraud scenarios.

How a Fraud Scenario Is Concealed

Concealment can occur because of the nature of a business system or the actions of a perpetrator.

Items to consider with regard to the nature of business systems are the number of transactions, geographic distance between documents and the controls in place for those documents, use of electronic documents, the existence of more than one business entity, and management due diligence of the controls and personnel.

Actions of the perpetrator can involve the following areas:

- False entities
- False documents
- False information
- False representations
- False approvals
- Avoiding or circumventing control levels
- Management override
- Collusion
- Blocking the access to information
- Off-the-book transactions

Relationship between Concealment Strategy and the Red Flags

The concealment strategy applies to the perpetrator, whereas the red flag applies to the auditor. The red flag should link to the concealment strategy or should be an observable event related to the concealment strategy. However, it should be understood that not all concealment strategies have observable overt red flags.

Sophistication of the Concealment Strategy

Inherent fraud schemes aren't thought of in terms of complexity; rather, it is the level of sophistication used to conceal the fraud that is the focus for the fraud auditor. On its most simplistic level, without a concealment strategy, the inherent fraud scheme would be visible. The analogy that comes to mind is that of a baseball pitcher who has one pitch: a fastball with no movement. Everyone in the park knows what he is going to throw, including the batter, who will consequently probably hit it out.

Fraud concealment sophistication should be rated on both the perpetrator's ability to hide the transaction (our pitcher having several pitches besides that fastball) and the auditor's ability to detect the transaction (the batter being able to correctly figure out what pitch is coming). To aid in the determination of a level of sophistication applicable to a concealment strategy, a rating scale of low, medium, and high is used, as Figure 6.3 illustrates.

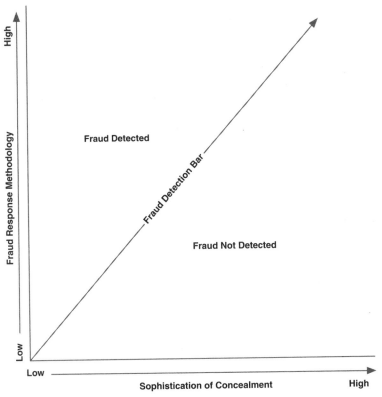

FIGURE 6.3 Fraud Sophistication Chart: Detection of Fraud

Relationship between Concealment Strategy Sophistication and Audit Detection

There is a correlation between fraud detection and the sophistication of the concealment strategy. When the perpetrator's concealment strategy is more sophisticated than the audit methodology, the fraud goes undetected. However, in addition to audit methodology, the auditor has the fraud detection tool of awareness. Figure 6.4 illustrates the relationship between the sophistication of the fraud concealment strategy and the combination of audit methodology and auditor awareness comprising audit detection. Fraud is revealed when the audit detection is as sophisticated as the concealment strategy, thereby resulting in a directly proportional relationship as shown in the figure.

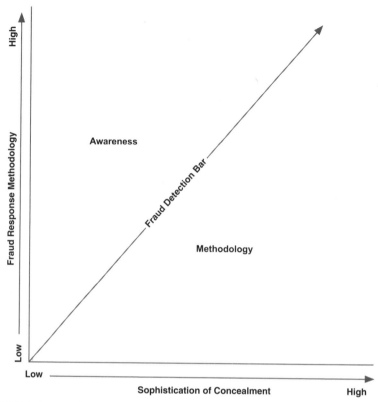

FIGURE 6.4 Fraud Sophistication Graph: Fraud Audit Response

An example of the level of sophistication and corresponding detection methodology and awareness levels can be found by contrasting the false entity concealment strategy at three different levels of sophistication. The degree of sophistication influences both the sample size and ability to locate the fraud scenario.

Typically, low sophistication concealment strategies are detectable with the use of data mining matching routines, whereas a high-sophistication concealment strategy requires the auditor to be able to interpret the data for red flags associated with the fraud scenario.

Concealment Strategy Sophistication and Audit Approaches

A Low-Level Sophistication of Concealment Example   A typical conceal-ment strategy with a low level of sophistication would be when a perpetrator, who is the approving manager or one working with the approving manager, uses his home address or personal bank account, then proceeds to use a software word processing template to create an invoice to be processed. In addition to the obviously homemade invoice document, the invoice is missing critical identifying information due to the lack of industry or accounting-savvy knowledge of the perpetrator.

In detecting this concealment strategy, a traditional audit would consider examination of the transaction (processing of the fake invoice) for evidence of internal control procedures. The transaction is supported by a properly approved vendor invoice, thereby supplying evidence of internal control. Through awareness, the auditor may detect that the vendor invoice was lacking vendor information, such as no telephone number, and thus could proceed to ask additional questions about the transaction.

Using the integrated fraud audit approach, an auditor could detect the fraudulent transaction, if the audit program included a step to compare the vendor address to the approving manager's home address or one to include the examination of the canceled check and thereby noting the identical endorsement signature, or a step included for comparison of the approving manager's bank account number to the bank account number on the back of the check.

With the fraud audit approach, data mining can detect the legality of the entity by matching the entity address or bank account to the employee database, or red flag testing procedures could show the invoice had one or more trigger red flags, thereby directing fraud audit testing procedures to be employed under the decision tree logistics. Consequently, the fraud audit testing procedure would focus on the entity structure by verifying the physical address. In this instance, the procedure would determine the address was a residence, not the location of a commercial building.

A Medium-Level Sophistication of Concealment Example   A fraud scenario with a medium-level of sophistication in concealment strategy is when a perpetrator obtains a post office box and a separate bank account for the entity. This scenario is at a level of medium sophistication because the post office box is in the same zip code as the perpetrator's residence and the fake corporate bank account is at the same bank where the perpetrator does his personal banking. Also, the perpetrator files the incorporation papers resulting in his name being on the documentation versus a legal representative's. Last, the invoice is created using a small business accounting software package.

Under the traditional audit procedures, the likelihood of detection is diminished unless the perpetrator makes a mistake that will be picked up during typical internal control testing.

With the integrated fraud audit approach, the audit procedures would focus on the action described on the invoice and ascertain whether there is creditable evidence that the event occurred.

Unlike the low-level sophistication example, the scenario would not be detected as easily with the fraud audit approach. The data mining would not be able to detect the fraud through data mining matching routines used in the low-level sophistication example. However, if the fraud audit procedure focused on a department or person, high-level matches would provide a smaller population for sampling purposes. For example, the vendor creation date would be a useful data element to identify vendors with a higher likelihood of being a false vendor. Therefore, the data mining would need to focus on the vendor invoice or purchase orders as to numbers, dates, and amounts searching for a pattern and frequency. In addition to the data mining component, the fraud audit testing procedures would focus on entity structure, whereby the secretary of state filing would reveal that the registrar of the corporation matched to an employee's name.

A High-Level Sophistication of Concealment Example   This is an example where the perpetrator, a false vendor, uses a corporate registration firm to incorporate the entity, thereby concealing the owner's real name. The false vendor has an office space in an office complex, and the post office box for payments is directly linked to a lockbox bank account, which is also located out of state. The false vendor's invoices are created by an accounting firm that specializes in small businesses.

The traditional audit approach would be the same as it was for the low- and medium-level sophistication examples, thus the likelihood of detection becomes less probable. Likewise, the integrated audit approach would also follow the same steps as in the previous examples. However, the fraud audit approach allows for detection abilities to be adaptable enough to meet the high-level sophistication presented in this example. Although the data mining procedures would be the same as in the medium-level example, the fraud audit procedures would direct the auditor to perform a comparison of the incorporation date to the first payment to the vendor. By doing this comparison, the fraud may be detected if the first payment date is in close proximity to the incorporation date.

Effects of Concealment Strategy Sophistication upon the Overall Audit Plan

A fraud audit by design is intended to pierce a concealment strategy, thereby revealing the true purpose of a transaction. As seen in the example from the previous section, low-sophistication schemes can typically be detected with standard audit procedures. When the scenario becomes increasingly more sophisticated, the ability of the auditor to locate and recognize the fraudulent transaction becomes more of a challenge. Therefore, in building the fraud audit program, the sophistication of the perpetrator becomes an important factor in planning both program components: data mining and fraud audit procedure.

As previously discussed, the ability to detect the fraud scenario despite of the level of sophistication of the concealment strategy employed is dependent upon methodology and awareness. A function of both of these detection tools concerns the sampling techniques used to locate fraud. When searching for fraud, auditors develop a sampling plan that is focused and biased toward a specific fraud scheme. This sampling is referred to as data mining because of the particular data, that is, transactions being sought and subsequently uncovered.

 ## AUDIT EVIDENCE ISSUES

A discussion of evidence takes place in Chapter 17 regarding loss calculations. Our discussion for this chapter is to place the concepts within the general context of a fraud audit program.

The Quality and Quantity of Evidence

An important factor in building the fraud audit program concerns the quantitative and qualitative aspects of the audit evidence. As discussed in a previous section herein, the degree of certainty and evidence creditability denote a key relationship with regard to qualitative and quantitative evidence aspects of the an audit program. Simply stated, if the degree of certainty is to be supported, it will necessitate the appropriate quantity and quality of evidence being sought. Therefore, the fraud audit program should establish the parameters of these aspects before commencing any audit processes and procedures. An auditor must be clear on her degree of certainty and the creditability of her intended evidence at the planning stage. If there is an imbalance between the two concepts, an occurrence of a fraud scenario may be overlooked, or a preponderance of evidence could result causing diminished creditability of that evidence.

The audit evidence should also link to the decision tree logic. In simple words, what evidence will the auditor accept to formulate a decision? That is, "Is the entity false or real?"

Trier of Fact

A second concern regarding evidence is the concept referred to in the legal community as the trier of fact. The trier of fact is the person or group of people who will read the fraud audit report, both the opinions and fact and circumstances, and then make a determination as to the next course of action. The key evidence questions are the following:

- **Sufficiency: Measure of quantity.** How much evidence is enough? This question concerns both the materiality level for the data mining search and the Trier of Fact requirements for surety.
- **Competency: Measure of quality.** In order to be competent, evidence must be valid and relevant to the fraud scenario. The competency question is at the heart of the creditable evidence conclusion. The very nature of the fraud scenario establishes that conversion be required. Another consideration is if the Trier of Fact will require absolute assurance or will reasonable assurance be sufficient. Remember the conclusion is not guilt, but rather sufficient and competent evidence to recommend an investigation.
- **Authenticity: The genuineness of the evidence.** Within the legal community, the authenticity standard is the first step taken by the court when considering the evidence. The fraud audit procedure is designed to verify the authenticity of the business transaction. A by-product of using external evidence to verify the transaction is that it usually will satisfy the standard. However, the question of authenticity is usually different for a legal matter versus a fraud audit comment.
- **Admissibility: The quality or state of being allowed to be entered into evidence in the legal arena..** From the fraud audit perspective, will the company support the fraud audit procedure to gather the evidence necessary? This question typically requires the auditor to collect evidence in a more overt manner.

▪ **Weight of Evidence: The evaluative significance assigned by the trier of fact.** From a legal perspective, determining this relevancy involves "weighing" the proof in the sense of determining that a reasonable person (acting as trier) could assign some weight to the evidence in deciding the point it is offered to prove.

 ## FRAUD SCENARIO EXAMPLES

The following examples consist of two fraud scenarios. In the first one, we are looking at the fraud triangle aspects, sampling strategies, and concealment strategies. Also, addressed are the audit approaches taken in consideration of slight variation in the fraud scenario. The second fraud scenario looks at a corruption scheme in terms of concealment strategies and red flags. With these examples we hope to tie together the concepts discussed in the prior chapters and by doing so show the capabilities of a fraud audit program in responding to the risk of fraud.

Fraud Scenario 1

Primary Fraud Classification: Asset Misappropriation
Secondary Fraud Classification: Embezzlement of Funds
Inherent Fraud Scheme: False vendor operating as a pass-through scheme
Fraud Scenario: A sales representative at a real manufacturer (called OK Corral Company), operating in collusion with a purchasing agent from a real company (called ABC, Inc.), set up a shell corporation (called Atlantic Supply Company). The sales representative sells to the shell corporation at a 10% discount. The shell corporation sells to the purchasing agent at a 5% discount. The sales representative and purchasing agent earn a 5% margin profit through the pass-through scheme.

Fraud Triangle Aspects

▪ The procurement supervisor was confident that no one within the organization would be able to identify the favoritism.
▪ The procurement supervisor's financial pressures were great enough to overcome the fear of detection.

Sampling Strategies

The following examples of how either a judgmental sample or a data mining search routine would be employed for the fraud scenario.

1. A judgmental sample would be identified by the auditor through review of the vendor master file data and transaction data, such as purchase orders, invoices, and disbursements for observable fraud red flags associated with the scenario. For example:
   - Split purchase orders for one transaction; purchase orders just below the dollar threshold for the bidding process, etc.
   - Sole source vendors: Vendors identified as the only vendor available to provide the goods and services in the amount or quality needed.
2. Data Mining: A data mining search routine would be developed that fits the fraud scenario profile, specifically, the data containing the fraud scenario red flags that are observable in the overall data found in the core business systems. For example:
   - Split purchase orders for one transaction; purchase orders just below the dollar control threshold, but no purchase orders.
   - Vendor record creation date within the scope period.
   - Payment to the vendor within 10 days of the invoice date.

Concealment Strategies

The following characteristics apply to the fraud scenario in two situations: when there is no effort to conceal and when there is a level of sophistication in concealment.

1. No effort to conceal the fraudulent act:
   - The procurement supervisor requests the use of the vendor through a new vendor process.
   - The procurement supervisor sets the vendor up as an active vendor in the procurement system.
   - The telephone number for the shell corporation is the same telephone number for the sales representative at the real manufacturer.
2. Sophisticated approach is used to conceal the fraudulent act.
   - The procurement supervisor has another staff member enter the vendor into the procurement system.

▪ The procurement supervisor split the bid or requisition so that each is below the dollar threshold for bid requirements, thereby not requiring additional bids from other vendors.

▪ The procurement supervisor has a different manager sign each of the purchase orders from the split.

▪ The procurement supervisor identifies the vendor as a sole source provider of goods or services in the local area.

This scenario carried out with these concealment techniques would be considered more sophisticated because the supervisor has used multiple levels in devising a concealment strategy.

Variation

In a variation of the same fraud scenario, the real manufacturer, OK Corral Company, ships directly to the purchasing agent's company, ABC, Inc., the shell corporation, Atlantic Supply, operates from a suite address, and the purchase orders were issued within three days of the incorporation date. All other conditions remain the same. Issues like materiality have been intentionally disregarded. The audit approach would include:

1. Examination of the invoice (see Figure 6.5) would alert the auditor to the red flags associated with the fraud scenario, specifically:
   ▪ Vague product description
   ▪ No vendor telephone number
   ▪ No apparent physical address

2. The awareness red flags would result in the auditor performing the following fraud audit procedures:
   ▪ Correlate the secretary of state incorporation date to the date of the first purchase order. The result is that the purchase date is November 21 and the incorporation date is November 20 of the same year.
   ▪ Examine the bill of lading documents to ascertain the shipping location of the supplies. The result of this examination is that the bill of lading indicates that the goods are being shipped from the OK Corral Company.

3. The transaction has red flags that cannot be resolved in an audit and, therefore, should be referred for an investigation. Remember the difference between a fraud audit and a fraud investigation.

INVOICE

Atlantic Supplies Inc.

INVOICE # 101

Date: March 29, 2011

Suite 401 Valatie, NY 12184

To   ABC Company, Inc.

381 Northern Blvd, STE 200

Albany, NY 12210

Customer ID 1000

Contact: Jane Smith

salesperson	Job	payment terms	due date
John Doe	F07181	30 days	November 21, 2010

qty	Description		unit price	line total
1	649-413-002		$9,172.00	$9,172.00
1	649-415-003		$16,644.00	$16,644.00
1	649-416-004 W/ SIGN ARM		$19,285.00	$19,285.00
1	649-425-203		$22,826	$22,826

			Subtotal	$87,212.00
Make all checks payable to Atlantic Supplies			Sales Tax	$6,104.84
Thank you for your business!			Total	$93,316.84

FIGURE 6.5   Vendor Invoice

Fraud Scenario 2

Primary Fraud Classification: Corruption
Secondary Fraud Classification: Vendor and Employee Collusion

Inherent Fraud Scheme: Sole source vendor

Fraud Scenario: A sales representative at a real company operates in collusion with a purchasing agent to inflate prices on invoices. The employee receives a bribe to do so.

Concealment Strategies

The following concealment strategies may be used by the perpetrator in this fraud scenario:

1. Purchasing goods from a real company that has conducted business in the marketplace for years and also has conducted business with your company for five years.
2. False documentation used as to the pricing on a bid for a lower amount. Once the bid is awarded, the vendor increases the price through change orders to the bid.
3. False documentation is used to create bids from competing vendors at higher pricing terms than the favored vendor.
4. Management override by the procurement supervisor by virtue of position, authority, and reputation. Staff members of the organization have an expectation that the procurement supervisor will select the vendor that offers the best value for the money score, thereby providing the greatest benefit to the organization. If the procurement supervisor dictates that a vendor is the best value for the money, then that vendor will be used.

Red Flags

1. The trigger red flags include:
   - Different vendor bids are similar in style, format, and paper type.
   - Vendors, whose bids were low, were consistently low by the same percentage.
   - Vendors who were requested or referred by the operations management were not requested to submit bids.
   - Questioned bids were not date and time stamp procedures according to company procedures.
2. The awareness red flags include:
   - Sole source vendors.
   - A pattern of vendors with purchase orders below the dollar control threshold.

- A significant number of known qualified bidders failing to make a bid.
- Dissimilar vendor bids.
- Bids that are missing key information or that are incomplete.
- Winning bid is not the lowest bid nor does it have the highest best value for the money score.
- Bids with close best value for the money scores are not put through the BAFO (best and final offer) process.
- Friendly relationship between vendor and procurement supervisor exists.

Fraud Audit Procedures

- Confirm authenticity of the bids on file by contacting the losing bidders.
- Determine reasons for ignoring vendors referred by operating management. Confirm the authenticity of the purchasing agent's reasons.

 ## SUMMARY

Obviously, after reading this chapter, you know that building a fraud audit program entails many concepts like linkage and degree of certainty. There are special testing procedures. It all seems foreign in relation to a traditional audit program, but there have to be differences, because with a fraud audit program, we are targeting fraud. Where we sampled and tested in the traditional audit, we now perform data mining searches to locate fraud and fraud audit procedures to recognize fraud. This recognition is done through the fraud red flag testing procedures and the fraud audit testing procedures. It is in the understanding of those differences that enable the auditor to build an effective fraud audit program.

CHAPTER SEVEN

Data Mining for Fraud

F RAUD AUDITING IS ABOUT locating and recognizing fraud, and data mining is the tool used in locating fraud. Data mining for fraud auditing purposes can be thought of as both a science and an art—a science because there is a discovery and exploration aspect to it. The art of it is derived through the auditor's ability to analyze the data from many perspectives to arrive at a summary of targeted information. Think of a painter who uses his tools, a brush and paint, to make numerous strokes into a recognizable pattern. If that analogy is a bit of a stretch for you, think of it as the auditor's ability to interpret the data to find the proverbial needle in the haystack. From a Las Vegas view, then, the odds are against the auditor in detecting a fraudulent transaction with visual judgmental or random selection. Obviously, databases are very large; that's why they are electronically stored. Business systems process millions of transactions on a daily basis with the dollar value of the transactions in the billions of dollars. What can an auditor do? As with any tool, the auditor needs to develop the skills to use the tool of data mining effectively.

Simply, auditors need the ability to group data into homogeneous groups in order for any anomalies to become apparent. Granted, the world's best audit program will not detect fraud if the sample, no matter how well organized for analysis, does not include a fraudulent transaction. Obviously, no method of searching for fraudulent transactions is useful if none exist. Then again, do auditors, as professionals, want to ignore the possibility of fraud when we know it to exist, and in many varieties of schemes? So, we have data mining, which, when used to its fullest, thereby becomes the heart and soul of a good fraud audit program.

 ## THE ART AND SCIENCE OF DATA MINING

As with any science, there is a nomenclature, sorry, terminology that is used specifically in discussing an item of science. There are also theories, definitions, assumptions, fundamentals, steps, and so on. So it is with our discussion of the science of data mining. The rest is art.

Data Mining Defined

What is data mining? Generally speaking, data mining is the process of analyzing selected data by finding patterns or anomalies in patterns, then organizing those resulting patterns or anomalies for interpretation. Going back to painting, for just a second, where does your eye focus when looking at a painting that is all in shades of gray except for one red stroke? That stroke can be thought of as our anomaly.

Data mining, although first used by researchers, has become extremely useful in the area of marketing. With the ever-evolving capacity to centralize data in data warehouses, companies were given the ability to use large amounts of data to analyze an almost endless supply of things like customer demographics, pricing, product sales, web site browsing, and many other parameters. The end result is that development of customer profiles has become a commonplace occurrence today. In fraud auditing there is profile development as well, making the use of data mining a natural fit.

The fraud auditing definition of data mining can be thought of as the process of organizing and analyzing transactional data and descriptive data that are consistent with a fraud scenario. The actual organizing and analyzing can be performed by visually reviewing a journal for transactions that appear suspicious or by using audit software to scrutinize the entire data file. In either case, the auditor has to define attributes for the data that match the fraud scenario.

The result of developing these attributes is the fraud data profile. Going back to the easel, you can think of it as the drawing of a picture of a fraud scenario using data rather than paint. The clarity of the picture depends on the availability and integrity of the information in the database. The fraud data profile will focus on the data in the master file description, the transaction description, or both. Given the size of databases, it helps to key on data that will identify fraud, much like the marketing director who will key on data that shows customer spending habits. So, in building the profile, it is useful to key in on the following data types in detecting fraud:

- Data that tends to conceal identity, for example, common names or lack of physical address.
- Data that controls access to the information, for example, no listed telephone number or contact name.
- Data designed to limit visibility (transparency) of a transaction, for example, structuring transactions below a control threshold or processing updates at off-time periods.

Terminology

To understand the process of data mining, an understanding of the terminology used in the process is helpful. The following is a list of often-used terms.

- Master file data: All data associated with the entity structure, for example, name, address, customer type, etc.
- Transactional data: All data associated with an event or action, for example, vendor invoice number, invoice date, invoice amount, etc.
- Pattern of data: A combination of qualities, acts, and tendencies forming a consistent or characteristic arrangement.
- Frequency of data: The number of occurrences of an event.
- Drill-down analysis: Drilling down is a concept analogous to data mining in that to work with large databases, they have to be broken down, not only into manageable parts, but perhaps down to the lowest level, that of the raw data, to get useful information.
- Transactional anomaly: A transaction containing the red flags of a fraud scenario.
- Entities: Can be vendors, customers, employees, or inanimate objects like inventory numbers.

Assumptions

Data mining is one of the key elements within the fraud auditing process. However, data mining also has logical limitations that need to be considered in the fraud audit plan. The data integrity will impact data mining effectiveness. The sophistication of the concealment strategy will determine the appropriate search routine and the resulting interpretation of the results. The discussions within this chapter are scenario-based versus simple data anomalies that exist any data file.

The Certainty Principle

We all know that nothing is certain in this world. So, true to this adage, nothing is certain in the results produced by data mining. In this case, to be certain of the results indicates that the data mining was predictive. While we want to scrub the data for problems and reduce the data to key in on fraud, we do not want to be predictive, thereby rendering useless results. Data mining allows the production of many informational reports, so to concentrate on obtaining one perfect report that will be guaranteed to find fraud is foolish. Remember, producing many reports allows a breadth of analysis whereby what may be missed in one report may be identified in another.

Data Mining Routines

Data mining routines must be derived from the fraud scenario identified in the fraud risk assessment. A fraud risk assessment addresses the likelihood of fraud *from* occurring, meaning that the design of internal control is sufficient to mitigate the fraud risk from occurring. However, within the fraud audit, data mining routines are developed to measure the likelihood of whether fraud *is* occurring. The difference between the likelihood of fraud from occurring and the likelihood that it is occurring isn't just semantics. It is important to note that saying the likelihood fraud is occurring is dependent upon the identification of events that are consistent with a fraud scenario and, therefore, a fraud data profile.

Just how a data mining routine measures fraud risk, thereby "assessing" risk is best shown through examples like the following:

Example 1: Low Risk. If no transactions are identified, then the risk of the scenario's occurring within the scope period is deemed low; therefore, no fraud auditing testing procedures are required because no transactions exist to be tested. For example, a type of fraud scenario involves an entity structure being created by the changing of a dormant-entity address to one controlled by the perpetrator. A data mining routine is developed with the purpose of searching for a dormant vendor with a change of address. Since the data mining routine did not detect a dormant vendor with an address change, the assumption is arrived at that the fraud scenario has not occurred in the scope period. This result doesn't mean other scenarios may be occurring within the audit scope; it's just the dormant vendor scenario is not occurring.

Example 2: High Risk. If a data mining routine results in transactions being identified that directly match, then the risk of the fraud scenario's occurring within the scope period is deemed high. All transactions identified must then be tested for evidence of the scenario. To illustrate: The data mining routine matches a vendor address to an employee's address. All matches identified must be tested.

Given the one-dimensionality of data in general, an auditor's interpretation of it is needed in using data mining routines. For example, a data mining routine is searching for false vendors based on a vendor invoice date of Saturday or Sunday. In reviewing the summary list, the auditor observes known vendors that operate in a 24/7 environment, so those vendors generally would not be selected. However, the auditor also observes a vendor with a nondescriptive name in which all vendor invoices have a Saturday or Sunday date. Given the anomaly, that transaction is selected for fraud auditing testing procedures.

So, if transactions are identified through auditor interpretation, the risk of the fraud scenario's occurring must be determined through fraud audit testing procedures. As the example shows, the choosing of that particular vendor is a judgment based on the auditor's professional experience; therefore, the risk rating would depend on the auditor's judgment as to low, medium, or high.

Remember, the preceding examples show the risk level of a fraud scenario's occurring and not the level of risk occurring. The distinction is critical to understanding how data mining routines relate to measuring fraud risk.

Data Mining Effectiveness

For data mining to be effective, audit software search features need to be adapted to coincide with the fraud scenario. Therefore, the starting point is the identification of a fraud scenario followed by the building of a fraud data profile.

The data mining routine is then constructed by scrubbing the data of problems and reducing it into a homogeneous population of transactions. A data mining search routine is then performed on this selected data to uncover any red flags associated with the fraud scenario.

Data mining effectiveness is directly correlated to the integrity or availability of the data residing in the database, which makes the preparation of the data an imperative step. The details of this preparation are interspersed throughout the sections that follow.

Number of Transactions

There is a direct correlation between the degree of sophistication of the concealment strategy and the number of transactions meeting the data profile requirements. Highly sophisticated concealment strategies tend to have a larger number of transactions required, whereas data mining routines that search for direct matches use a smaller number of transactions. The characteristics of the relationship between the number of fraudulent transactions and the sophistication level of the concealment strategy include the following.

Low sophistication:

- Direct matches of the fraudulent entity structure to another entity structure.
- Entity identifying information links to the perpetrator's known identifying information, for example, a specific street address.
- Fraudulent activity is linked to one or a few entity structures.
- Data mining routine searches key on data matching.
- Overall sample size is determined by the number of transactions that match the data profile. The sample size can range from zero to a large number.

Medium sophistication:

- Direct matching routines are less effective. Data interpretation skills are more crucial.
- Filtering techniques like drill-down analysis are effective in reducing the number of transactions fitting the data profile, thus allowing data interpretation to be more effective.
- Entity-identifying information relates to some aspect of the perpetrator's known identifying information, for example, a zip code location versus a physical street address.

- Sample selection relies on data interpretation skills and scenario-specific data mining routines.
- Sample size tends to be judgmentally determined versus the use of all transactions meeting the matching criteria.

High sophistication:

- Direct matches seldom occur.
- Fraudulent activity may be linked to multiple entities or smaller dollar transactions.
- Entity-identifying information has no relationship with the perpetrator's known identifying information.
- Entity-identifying information may relate to a mailbox service or an out-of-area address that has a mail-back feature.
- Sample selection relies on data interpretation skills.
- The population for deriving a sample is larger because the selection criterion identifies all transactions in a group versus a specific transaction.
- Sample size tends to be judgmentally determined versus the use of all transactions meeting the matching criteria.

The Fundamentals

There are certain fundamentals or ground rules to follow in using data mining to locate fraud. They may be considered as the eight steps needed for effective data mining, although following them in a sequence is not necessary:

1. Understanding the "what," "where," and "how much" of data.
2. Mapping the data fields to the fraud scenario.
3. Understanding the integrity of the data.
4. Applying inclusion/exclusion theory.
5. Understanding false positives.
6. Understanding the "norm" of the data.
7. Data correlations.
8. Entity structures and search routines.

Understanding the "What," "Where," and "How Much" of Data

The auditor needs to know "what" data fields exist in the database, then determine if a field is to be used, which may be accomplished by building a listing of the data required and working with the data administrator to identify the name of the data element in the table. Start with a generic listing of the type of data that will be necessary for the audit objectives. For example, in a payroll audit, consider name, employee number, gross compensation, and so on. Once the auditor has determined the type of data to be searched, the generic list should be referenced to the data names in the tables. Reviewing the tables identifies additional data that will assist in the audit. Such a review can also cause confusion as to the existence of data or what data exists in a particular heading. A good example is the general ledger code. The expenditure table may list the accounts payable or inventory code, whereas the purchase order file may indicate the expenditure or budget code. Most likely both tables will use a table heading of general ledger code.

The auditor needs to know "where" the tables with the needed data field are located and how the primary and foreign keys link the tables. This determination requires locating the data element in the applicable table. Care must be taken in ensuring that the extracted data is in fact the data that relates to the fraud scenario. Data tables capture information for a variety of purposes—in some cases, calculations, and in other cases, reporting. The field may be an accumulation field, total overtime for the year, or a rate field. Once the data is extracted, select a few transactions and verify that the extracted data is the actual data needed for interpretation.

The auditor needs to know "how much" data is being worked with through counting, by data element, the number of records that are actually populated. This is an important procedure because it will determine whether the selected fields are populated or, in essence, the availability of the data. It is common for columns not to be used or to be sparingly used.

Mapping the Data Fields to the Fraud Scenario

Data mapping is the process of connecting the data to the fraud scenario. The process starts with the fraud scenario, then each data element is linked to the fraud scenario. The mapping process includes the identified patterns that would exist in each data element and what type of data exists in each field.

Understanding the Integrity of the Data

In the real world, data in a database contains errors, blanks, and inconsistency caused by data input or system changes, and data, although accurate, may cause a red flag. So, part of the prep for a data mining routine is cleaning up or scrubbing the data. The auditor needs to identify the data inconsistencies, then develop strategies to fix, group, isolate, or eliminate them. If the problems with the data cannot be fixed, then a decision should be made on how to resolve them within the context of the search routine. For example, a problem occurs when a transaction is entered incorrectly, then it is reversed, and later entered correctly. From a frequency perspective, the one event will have a count of three transactions. Since the number of transactions is inflated, the average will be distorted. To clean this mess, a direct match on the reversals needs to be performed for the purpose of excluding the reversal or place all the reversals into one grouping for purposes of pattern, frequency, and analysis.

Frequently, errors occur due to a data input error. Informational fields, such as order number or date are prone to these types of errors. For date errors, the search routine would count the number of records that contain a date outside of the expected date range. If the date field is critical to the search routine, then transactions should be grouped into two groups, one group having dates within accepted range and the other group having dates out of expected range. If the number of transactions with the error is low, the date could be corrected in the database. Most likely, the number of errors will be too large to fix. Therefore, analyzing the date error transactions in a separate group will not distort the primary purpose of the search routine.

Another problem area is with control numbers that may contain alpha characters or special symbols. These characters may be part of the original document or added by the data input process. For example, vendor invoice numbers on documents vary from a sequential numbering system, no number, a date format, project number, and so on. The various invoice number formats will create false positives or data anomalies that appear to be an error or fraud indicator. Often the data mining will identify problems with control numbers that may not have been evident otherwise. In one company, it was noticed that 2009 expenditures were supported by vendor invoice date field of 1925. Obviously, the company did not have a reasonability check of the invoice date field.

Applying Inclusion/Exclusion Theory

The inclusion portion of the theory starts with a database of transactions where the data is categorized into like groups. The purpose of doing this categorization is twofold. For one, examining a smaller database is easier, and for another, an anomaly is easier to spot when all the transactions are in common. The grouping of data is dependent on the fraud scenario. Some logical groupings are the following:

- Geographical business divisions or territories.
- Dollar value of the account or transaction.
- Transactional codes.
- Major category of revenue or expenditure.
- Those with or without control documents.
- Company anomalies, house accounts, overrides, or one account number used by multientities are all often temporary vendors or one-time vendors.
- Active entity versus inactive entity.
- False entity or real entity.
- Class of transactions.
- Specific to a person, entity, or account.

Understanding False Positives

A false positive transaction is one that meets the fraud data profile, but is not in and of itself a fraudulent transaction. These false positives occur for a variety of reasons, some of the more common ones include the following:

- Data integrity issues such as the ones described earlier will create false positives.
- A data file will appear to contain all the same data, but in reality it will actually have different meanings. The address field is a common example of this data anomaly. The address field may represent a physical address, lockbox address, and outsource provider address. An example is a false entity scheme in which perpetrator assumes the identity of the real vendor. The fraud scenario can be identified by looking for inconsistencies in the vendor data. One routine compares the vendor address in the database to the physical address corresponding to the telephone area code. Since the vendor address may be the lockbox of a bank versus the physical address of the vendor, the search routine would flag the vendor as meeting the fraud scenario fraud data profile.
- The merging of different company databases into one database. It is common in these situations to have a duplicate number in the vendor number field. The problem becomes acute in areas like duplicate address checking, where the address will appear more than once. Depending on how

the name was originally entered into the system, the duplicate address may appear with the same name or a different name.

- Societal changes. Area codes once corresponded to a geographic area; however, with the telephone portability act, they no longer do so.
- Two entities sharing a common address or bank account. In terms of employees, this sharing is understandable for a variety of reasons, but in the case of vendor or customer, it should be considered a data anomaly.

Understanding the "Norm" of the Data

The word *anomaly* is defined as an extreme deviation from the norm, an outlier. Therefore, one should understand the norm before proceeding to the anomaly. In particular, we need to understand the volume of activity as to dollars and number of records. A report providing statistical information by entity structure as to the entity creation date, number of transactions, aggregate dollar value of transactions, maximum dollar value of a transaction, minimum dollar value of a transaction, and average dollar amount is a useful one to have in understanding the norm from the anomaly.

Data Correlations

Data correlation is an important aspect to developing effective search routines and analyzing the results of those routines. It is the process of making a connection between the fraud data profile and either an entity or an individual. While there are no absolutes, the key in data mining is correlating the data pattern to an entity structure and the related dollars. Correlation of the data can be considered a four-tier process as described next.

First-Tier Analysis   When correlating the fraud scenario pattern of activity to the internal entity structure, the master file fields are used. Data from the master file fields can be broken down into five areas: missing data, duplicate data, matched data, changed, and nondescriptive data.

1. **Missing.** When a data field in the primary database is blank or populated in a manner that renders the data field as nonfunctioning. Blank fields are sometimes populated with zeros or some other data string. Sorting the field low to high will detect the zero population, while counting high to low will detect the predefined data string. Therefore, missing data may have three or more counts, blank, zero, or a predefined data string.

PRACTICAL**GUIDANCE**

Using Databases for Data Mining Search Routines When Data Is Missing

Example: The telephone number of an entity is missing. A data mining search routine can be developed using the accounts payable database to search for entities that have a blank field where telephone numbers are stored. The lack of a telephone number may indicate any of the following conditions:

- Accounts payable is not a control function, but rather a processing function; therefore, a missing telephone number is more indicative of the reality of the control environment versus a data red flag.
- The telephone number field was not populated in the accounts payable database, or it is a field populated for new vendors only. These integrity issues are prevalent with data mining and need to be taken into account during any data mining planning.
- Accounts payable is a control function; therefore, the missing telephone number is a data red flag.

2. **Duplicate.** The process of locating of a second record in a database with the exact or same attributes. Unfortunately, duplicate records are often blurred by the way the data field was keystroked, either with intent or by mistake. Therefore, the ability to search for duplicate records that are not exact matches but are the same record becomes the challenge. This problem often occurs with duplicate addresses. Stripping out the alpha, spaces, and special symbols from an address field leaves a numeric string. The result is that an exact match routine will identify two vendors with the same numeric string.

PRACTICAL**GUIDANCE**

Using Databases for Data Mining Search Routines When Data Is Duplicated in a Data Field

Example: A data mining search routine is developed to search for the entities with duplicate telephone numbers within a specific database, such as vendors. Finding different vendors with the same telephone numbers may indicate:

(continued)

(*continued*)

- A duplicate telephone number between two vendors with different addresses may indicate a pass-through vendor scheme.
- A duplicate telephone number between two vendors with the same address may indicate a bypassing of controls.

3. **Matched.** The process of matching a record in the primary database to a record in a secondary one containing one or more data fields. The match could be a duplicate or be unrelated exception for the data filed match.

PRACTICAL**GUIDANCE**

Using Different Databases for Data Mining Search Routines for Duplicate Data

Example: Searches are performed to match items, such as telephone number, found in two different internal databases, such as vendors, customers, and employees.

- A match between the vendor database and the employee database would indicate that a company employee has an ownership interest in a vendor.
- A match between the customer database and the employee database would indicate that a company employee has an ownership interest in a customer.
- A match between vendor and customer may indicate a revenue recognition issued associated with the round-trip scheme.

Example: Searches are performed to match items, such as telephone number, found in two different databases, one being internally used and the other from an external source.

- Searching for matches of telephone numbers between a vendor database and the yellow pages results in finding vendors having the same telephone number, but different names or addresses. Be careful, this analysis may produce a lot of false positives. The routine will need other filtering techniques to be effective; for example, a fraud scenario involving an assumed entity scheme would need to use a filtering technique like determining if the vendor database had a change to telephone number or address in the scope period.

4. **Changed.** The process of identifying a data field that has been changed one or more times. There are two approaches to take in this situation; one is to analyze the change file, and the other is comparing the database from one date to another date. The problem with the second approach is that is does not identify the date when the initial change occurred and when it was changed back. Another consideration is when master file data is embedded within a data table versus linked to a data table.

PRACTICAL**GUIDANCE**

Using Databases for Data Mining Search Routines for Data that Has Changed

Example: A data mining search routine is developed to find entities with changes made to their telephone numbers in a database. Often, a change as simple as a telephone number will indicate unusual conditions, such as:

- Change from a land line number to a cell phone number.
- Change in telephone number and change to bank account number.
- Change in telephone number with no change in address.
- Change in telephone number that matches an existing telephone number in the database or a duplicate change has been made.

5. **Nondescriptive.** The process of identifying data fields that are intended to obscure the identity or location of an entity.

PRACTICAL**GUIDANCE**

Using Data Mining Searches to Identify Nondescriptive Data Fields

Example: The auditor needs to determine if the use of a telephone number data field was used to disguise the identity or location of an entity.

- The telephone number is a toll-free one so that there is no correlation to a physical location.
- Answering service numbers in a designated geographic area.
- Telephone numbers associated with mailbox services.
- Mobile telephone numbers may be identified by exchange number, area codes that do not correlate to the city and state.

Second-Tier Analysis The second tier of analysis is the searching for a specific data pattern or frequency within the transactional data that correlates to an entity structure. Items to be searched for include:

■ **Pattern.** The first step is to start with a data field and identify the various patterns that relate to that data field. Numbers tend to be sequential, interval, random, out of order, missing, containing alpha characters or special symbols, project numbers, or any other like pattern.

PRACTICAL**GUIDANCE**

Pattern Analysis

Example: A data mining search routine is developed to search for patterns within vendor invoice numbers.

■ A sequential pattern of invoices would correlate to favored-vendor or false entity schemes. This type of pattern is consistent with an unsophisticated perpetrator; therefore, a data mining routine should easily detect it.
■ A random pattern of invoice numbers found within the scope period needs to be interpreted before any inconsistencies can be determined. Specifically, is the range consistent with the vendor's industry, perceived size, or dollar volume of activity recorded in the books? Clearly, this analysis will require a higher degree of auditor judgment.

■ **Frequency.** The count of the occurrence of the event in correlation to the norm or the fraud scenario. If a norm does not exist, the frequency count tends to be a subjective number based on auditors' experience or an arbitrarily selected number.

PRACTICAL**GUIDANCE**

Frequency Analysis

Example: A data mining search routine of vendor invoices can be used to connect the frequency of invoices to specific fraud scenarios.

(continued)

(*continued*)

■ A scenario with a false entity and involving false billing could be detected by searching for vendors with a maximum and minimum number of invoices.

■ A scenario with a false entity and involving a pass-through scheme could also be identified in the same manner; however, the maximum number of invoices is more indicative of the scenario as compared to the minimum number of invoices.

■ **Logical order of the transaction.** Dates tend to be before an event, after an event, or the same day as the event.

PRACTICAL**GUIDANCE**

Logical Order

Example: Any disruptions of the logical order of the vendor invoices found in a data mining routine of the invoice may be indicative of a fraudulent invoice.

■ **Logical range.** Control numbers are typically sequential; therefore, a control number below the starting point or greater than the starting point stands out.

PRACTICAL**GUIDANCE**

Logical Range

■ Low vendor invoice numbers are indicative of a new company; thus, any long-standing vendors having low invoice numbers may indicate a false entity being created from a dormant vendor.

■ Use of accounting software will automatically start invoice numbers at a low figure unless set by the person using the software. If that person sets the number abnormally high, then the reason for such action should be determined.

■ An invoice number should correlate to the incorporation date. Although the vendor incorporation date is not usually included in the vendor master record, the example illustrates how correlating data can indicate a data red flag, such as if the first invoice number in the accounts payable file was 10519, and the company had incorporated two months ago, that invoice number is obviously not consistent with the age of the corporation.

- **Insufficient characters in the field.** In some cases, fields may have an expected number of characters, for example, sales orders. The number of characters in a product description field would vary by organization. In this case, the auditor would establish an arbitrary number of characters as a minimum or maximum.
- **Negative or positive.** Most data fields have a norm of either positive or negative.
- **Circumvention.** The processing of structuring a transaction to avoid a control level. In a case where a transaction would exceed a control level, thereby making it more visible, the perpetrator intentionally splits the transaction into two or more to avoid the control level.
- **Off-period transactions.** Recording a transaction during atypical business hours, either for the organization or the person processing the illicit transaction. This off-period may include holidays or weekends.

PRACTICAL**GUIDANCE**

Other Transactional Data Analyses

- Insufficient characters, negative or positive, circumvention, and off-period transactions that are not relevant to the invoice number could all indicate a fraudulent transaction.
- Remember, not all categories relate to each data element.

- **Mistakes.** Individuals make mistakes both intentionally and unintentionally.

PRACTICAL**GUIDANCE**

Common Mistakes

Example: A data mining search routine results in a finding of invoice numbers that are duplicates or not consistent with invoice dates. Auditor shouldn't jump to the conclusion that a fraud scenario is occurring. They should always consider the possibility of human data-entry error and determine if the mistake was intentional. Inputting duplicate invoice numbers is a common mistake made with data-entry, while having an invoice number entered in an order not consistent with the invoice date is a little less clear.

Third-Tier Analysis The third tier of data analysis correlates the frequency of the pattern to the fraud perpetrator. Within the selected transactions, the transactions should be correlated to the logical creator or the transactional anomaly. In the best of worlds, we can match the transaction to a specific individual, but this is often not possible, so match the transactions to the next smallest group, such as a department, via a department number or abbreviation.

Fourth-Tier Analysis The fourth tier of analysis correlates the dollar activity to the entity structure and the fraud perpetrator, with the absence of dollars indicating the exception is a data integrity issue versus a fraud issue. Remember, fraud is about dollars, not about data anomalies, which means that the existence of anomalies doesn't always mean there's fraud, too. Data is constructed by human beings, and human beings are hopelessly flawed and error prone. So, anomalies are numerous for a variety of reasons ranging from data input errors to bad software. Therefore, before performing extensive fraud audit testing, link the associated dollars to the data anomaly. In many instances, there will be no dollars associated with the event.

Entity Structures and Search Routines

Prior to implementing the search routines, a decision needs to be made as to whether all entities or just the active ones are to be examined. Active entities can be identified by a code or dollar activity. If just active entities are used, then a report should be generated to ensure all inactive entities have no financial activity or recent changes to key fields, such as address or bank account number. The reason to exclude inactive vendors is that there is no dollar exposure, and they will cause data anomalies that most likely are false positive. The types of active entities to search for fraud in are created entities and assumed identity entities.

Created Entity The created entity structure is when the perpetrator of the scheme creates an entity for fraudulent purposes. The decision for the auditor is to determine a look-back period. An annual audit may focus on one year, whereas a first-time audit may look back several years. Generally, since most frauds become evident in five years or less, the auditor may choose a five-year look-back period. Remember, transactions should be obtained from the same number of years that are in the look-back period from the creation date.

The created entity is either a truly false entity or a real entity in the business place that the perpetrator assumes. The starting point is to identify those entity structures that are new to the business system. Therefore, the key data field is the entity creation date. The second level of correlation is the individuals with the ability to create new entities. The direct access opportunity would focus on the person(s) with keystroke capacity to add a vendor. The indirect access would correlate the new vendors to the department requesting the new vendor. In addition to the creation date, the analysis may focus on the record creator correlated to off-period transactions.

Assumed Identity Entity The assumed identity entity occurs when an internal employee takes control over an existing entity within the business system. Focus is on the update field or the change file. The change file may be better to use in this case because it captures all the changes, whereas the update field is the last date that the master file was updated. The key fields are address, bank account number, telephone number, and government registration number.

Controlled Addresses for False Entities The perpetrator needs to have an address for the false entity that he controls. On the simplest level, the individual will use his home address. The next level of address control is a mailbox service company. These companies can be identified via the Internet or the yellow pages. In large cities, companies are known to rent an address at prime real estate locations. Therefore, in order to have an address at such an upscale location, a company may rent one.

In both, the created entity scheme and the assumed identity scheme, fields that control access are critical fields to search.

STRATEGIES FOR DATA MINING

There are several specific strategies for employing data mining, including off-period transactions, circumvention of dollar control levels, internal control avoidance, and speed of decision or payment.

Off-Period Transactions

The focus of the data mining is on the time and date the transaction was created or changed. Off-period is obviously relevant to the nature of the organization and the individual responsible for the transaction. First, establish a before time and an after time. Then search any transaction dates falling on a weekend or holiday. The ultimate result is finding the individual who prefers to initiate fraudulent transactions when no else is in the office.

Avoidance or Circumvention of Dollar Control Levels

Approval controls are a key aspect of the internal control system. Avoiding the internal control system is a basic tenet of committing fraud; therefore, this strategy focuses on the processing multiple transactions below a control level. The perpetrator deliberately avoids the control level by using small amounts numerous times versus a large-amount transaction just once that would be above the threshold. Therefore, aggregate analysis or average dollar analysis correlated to the number of transactions might indicate an attempt to avoid the control. Also, the determination of what constitutes "small dollar" is proportional to the management position responsible for the transaction.

The second approach to avoid dollar control levels, called structuring, typically occurs when the dollar size of the transaction is initiated by someone other than the perpetrator, for example, a purchasing contact. The individual will create two or more transactions so that no one transaction exceeds the control level. Searching for transactions that occur within "x" number of days of each other that in the aggregate exceed the control level indicates a case of control avoidance. Since business cycles tend to be 30 days, the use of a 30-day parameter is deemed reasonable.

Another type of structuring occurs when multiple transactions are processed through different entity structures. These transactions can be detected by duplicate master file tests or searching a pattern of transactions initiated on the same day and time by the same person.

Internal Control Avoidance

The concept is similar to that of the dollar control avoidance discussed previously. The search is for a pattern and frequency of avoiding a control. Since the control in question varies upon the system, a list of examples follows.

- In purchasing goods or services, search for transactions that have no purchase order or the purchase order is the same day as the invoice. The use of an open purchase order for multiple invoices may reduce the amount of checking performed by accounts payable.

■ In revenue systems, processing a sales order with an override code would avoid the internal computer checks.

■ Any manual transactions that are recorded in the automated system at a later date provide a way to avoid computer edit controls.

■ Processing a transaction in a contra manner to avoid normal controls and reduce the visibility of the transaction. Searching for positive or negative numbers is an easy way to search for contra transactions. In one company, sales adjustments were processed through the sales journal versus the sales adjustment account. The entry in the sales journal was to record a negative sale transaction or, in essence, posting a debit to the sales journal. The purpose of the entry was to effectively void the original invoice. Then another sales invoice was created with a current date. The object of the scheme is to make the receivables appear current when in fact the receivables are over 180 days. Searching for contra entries almost always has an interesting story.

Speed of Decision or Payment

It is not uncommon for passwords to be shared or compromised within an organization. In automated systems requiring electronic initiation, two approvals occurring within seconds or minutes or each other, by two different user IDs, may indicate the same person is performing the function or that segregation of duties may not be operating as described.

The disbursement of funds may occur at a faster pace with fraudulent transactions than with normal business transactions. One indicator occurs when normal payment terms are within 30 days, and a certain vendor is always paid in 10 days. The speed of payment points to a vendor preference, which may be associated with an overbilling scheme or the temporary-vendor scheme.

 LIMITATIONS OF DATA MINING

Although a powerful tool in detecting fraud, data mining has its limitations, too. Certain schemes will allow for the auditor to drill-down in order to explore the population of transactions, but even drilling down to the raw data may not be enough to identify specific fraudulent transactions, especially if the auditor's knowledge of fraud schemes is narrow or he or she gives up too soon. For example, the terminated ghost employee scheme dictates a data mining routine be used to search for all terminated employees. Then a second search is undertaken to separate the terminated employees who use direct deposit versus manual checks as methods of receiving their pay. For the direct deposit employees, if there is no change evident in the bank account information gathered, then the terminated ghost scheme is not occurring. Consequently, for terminated employees who received a paper check instead of direct deposit, further data mining with internal databases may not be possible. However, obtaining check clearing information from the bank may be able to detect a change in pattern as where the payroll checks for terminated employees were negotiated.

Also, some schemes just do not lend themselves to data mining in general, for example, the use of product substitution in a vendor overbilling scheme, whereby inferior goods and services are supplied, then billed at a higher rate. If there are quality control inspections of shipments received, those shipments are graded for quality, and those grades are placed in a database, then data mining may be useful in detecting the scheme. Also, it is possible, in extreme cases, that the level of credits or adjustments may provide a clue. Most likely, these options don't exist, so physical inspection of the goods is the most reasonable manner of detecting the scheme.

 SUMMARY

Whole books have been written about data mining, in addition to doctoral dissertations, and even college degree programs have been developed about it. So, how can we make such a large body of knowledge just one component of our fraud audit? Well, if it's any consolation, you don't have to have a degree in it to know what a useful tool it is in locating fraud in the core business systems. Besides, you can always add an IT expert to the fraud audit team if you are overwhelmed by the technological aspects of the process. Just like you shouldn't be afraid of tackling fraud, you shouldn't push data mining away because it is foreign to you. It is a powerful tool that is needed in this day and age of enormous databases. Everyone and everything has a data profile, and so it is with fraud. Data mining seems to be made for finding fraud, so embrace it like it's your new best friend.

CHAPTER EIGHT

Fraud Audit Procedures

F RAUD AUDITING IS A response to the risk of fraud in core business systems. It uses all the skills of traditional auditing, but with a different aim. The aim of fraud auditing is the application of audit procedures to a population of business transactions to increase the likelihood of locating and recognizing fraud scenarios. Fraud audit procedures by design are intended to recognize the fraud scenario. For recognition to occur, there must be a link between the concealment strategy and the gathering of evidence external to the fraud opportunity. The intent of this link is to refute the validity of the representation made through the concealment strategy.

BASIS OF FRAUD AUDIT PROCEDURES

When designing fraud audit procedures:

- Do not test the existence of internal controls, but rather the authenticity of the representation of the document or internal control. This may seem like a case of semantics; however, the difference is critical to the understanding of why a traditional audit differs from a fraud audit.

Testing for evidence of the control is not always sufficient to detect fraud, whereas fraud audit testing procedures are designed to reveal the truth.

▪ Do not rely on, or assume that, a falsity on the part of management occurs in the transactions, assertions, and representations.

▪ Fraud audit procedures are designed to target the concealment strategy. Fraud, by its very nature, involves trickery and concealment. The perpetrator uses concealment strategies to provide the illusion that the transaction is a valid one and the activity authorized. Fraud audit procedures by design are intended to collect evidence that perpetrators cannot taint by their actions.

▪ The fraud audit procedure must be designed for the fraud scenario, focusing on both the entity structure and the action component of the fraud scenario.

▪ The fraud auditor must understand the associated red flags that can be observed through a fraud audit procedure.

▪ A fraud audit procedure gathers information that is continually linked to other information obtained from all the fraud audit procedures.

The proceeding practical example is intended to illustrate the difference between the fraud audit approach and the control approach.

PRACTICAL**GUIDANCE**

A Document Shows an Entity to Be a Corporation

The Control Approach

Procedure: Find evidence of a control.

1. The vendor registration control procedures have accepted the vendor as an authorized one.
2. The invoice approval procedures indicate that the goods have been received from an approved vendor.
3. Therefore, the control approach indicates that the transaction is a valid one.

The Fraud Audit Approach

Procedure: Find evidence of a representation.

(continued)

1. Authenticate that the entity is a corporation:
   a. Verify through government records that the corporation is an authentic one registered to conduct business.
   b. If yes, then the fraud audit approach indicates the entity is a legal corporation.
2. Identify the red flags associated with the fraud audit procedure:
   a. Do the names of the officers correlate to employees or other known names?
   b. Does the incorporation date correlate to the vendor creation date on the accounts payable master file?
   c. If not, there are no overt reasons to question the authenticity of the representation.

LEVELS OF FRAUD AUDIT PROCEDURES

Decision tree logic aids in designing a fraud audit program that responds to the fraud risk in a manner consistent with the risk. No, that statement is not meant to define risk by using the term *risk*; instead think of risk in this usage in terms of degrees. To address the degree of risk, there are two levels of fraud audit procedures within a fraud audit program:

1. Red flag testing procedures associated with the fraud scenarios.
2. Fraud audit testing procedures concerning inherent fraud schemes within the core business system.

Red Flag Testing Procedures Associated with the Fraud Scenarios

Use of decision tree logic provides a process of identifying and resolving fraud red flags recognized during the audit. This process is continually evolving for the auditor given its step-by-step nature, but it leads to a necessary end point for the auditor's work in a logical, carefully planned, and structured manner.

The decision tree begins with a decision of whether a trigger red flag has been observed through the audit. If yes, fraud audit testing procedures are performed. If no, another decision is made involving whether the totality of the awareness red flags is sufficient enough for the auditor to render fraud audit testing procedures necessary. If yes, fraud audit testing procedures are performed. If no, the auditor's work is complete.

Therefore, fraud audit procedures are performed on any transaction:

- Where a trigger red flag has been observed.
- Where the totality of the awareness red flags raises the auditor's professional skepticism.

The outcome of the fraud audit procedures is either that the red flag is resolved or the transaction is identified as suspicious and an investigation is deemed warranted.

Fraud Audit Testing Procedures Concerning Inherent Fraud Schemes That Reside within the Core Business System

The fraud risk assessment identifies fraud scenarios that reside in core business systems. The decision tree logic starts with the identification of predetermined events with two possible outcomes. Think of a coin toss, but in this case instead of heads or tails, the outcome will be that the audit response will focus on either refuting a possibility of an event or establishing the likelihood of an event. The decision to go down the road to either refute or establish is a matter whatever technique is typically followed. For the purposes of this discussion, the decision is to determine whether the entity structure is false or real, and once the entity is determined false, we proceed to identify the inherent schemes that link to the entity structure. Then, once inherent schemes have been linked to the structure, we disprove or corroborate the scheme.

The following guidelines should be considered in developing the logical order of auditing the schemes within a primary risk category. A Practical Guidance box immediately follows to illustrate these guidelines.

- Keep in mind that determining that an event has not occurred is easier than determining if one has. For example, a financial statement audit establishing that a revenue transaction did not occur is clearer than trying to establish that a revenue transaction was recorded in the wrong period. Using the premature revenue scheme, detecting premature revenue is easier when the customer returns the revenue in the subsequent period versus when the customer retains the revenue and submits payment for the item. Within the asset misappropriation category, once the vendor is determined to be a shell corporation versus a real corporation, it becomes obvious that a fraud has occurred.

- The order will be impacted by the primary risk category. In corruption schemes, the starting point is looking at the opportunity to influence the decision, with the end point being bribery. In financial reporting, the order is influenced by the major account classifications of: assets, liabilities, owner's equity, revenue, and expenses. Asset misappropriation focuses on the nature of the secondary risk category to establish the appropriate audit approach.
- Documents to establish the legitimacy of the event that are created and stored external to the organization are more reliable than documents that are created and stored internally. The fraud auditor must give careful attention to the documentary evidence supporting the fraud opinion.
- The nature of the scheme can be audited using traditional records. For example, in a vendor overbilling scheme involving the provision of goods or services that are received, but are not of the stated quality, examination of receiving documents may not detect the product substitution scheme.
- The nature of the scheme requires investigatory procedures. For example, the operations manager and the vendor are operating in collusion to actually repair equipment, but the repair was unnecessary. Scenarios of this type are better suited to investigatory procedures.
- The degree of certainty principal for the scheme can be determined with direct evidence versus circumstantial evidence. Direct evidence by its nature tends to be more convincing.
- The fraud conversion cycle occurs on your company's books versus that of a third party.

PRACTICAL**GUIDANCE**

Fraud Scenario of a Favored Vendor in Collusion with the Procurement Supervisor with a Kickback

Decision tree logic when auditing for the fraud scenario is located after this Practical Guidance section. Here is an example of the auditor's walking a transaction through the decision tree.

1. Is there a trigger red flag for favored status? Auditor answers yes because the vendor's invoices are in sequential order (1000, 1001, 1002, 1003 . . . etc.)

(continued)

(continued)

2. Apply favored status fraud audit procedures. Auditor performs the fraud audit procedures to identify who sourced the vendor for use and finds the procurement supervisor requesting this vendor for use by reviewing of the vendor creation forms and through interviews with staff members.
3. Is the red flag resolved by the fraud audit procedures? Auditor answers no because the finding leads the auditor to believe there may be a favored relationship between the procurement supervisor and the vendor by review of the vendor creation forms and through interviews with staff members.
4. Is the favored status known to management? Auditor answers no because management states that the bid with the highest best value for money score should always be used and no additional information was provided by the procurement supervisor to management. The vendor with the highest best value for money score was not selected.
5. Is there a trigger red flag for kickbacks? Auditor answers yes because of the nature of the relationship between the vendor and procurement supervisor, as well as the nature of the vendor as a pass-through entity identified through interviews with staff members and by review of packing documentation.
6. At this point, it is important to note that the decision tree does not have the auditor perform any forensic audit procedures for the kickback. This vendor will be noted in the audit report for further investigation, and because there are no forensic audit procedures, the auditor would be able to perform for kickbacks, so this is a logical ending point in the decision tree.

 ## DESIGN OF FRAUD AUDIT PROCEDURES

Every fraud audit procedure has its strengths and weaknesses. The sophistication of the perpetrator can trick the auditor into a false conclusion. The experience of the auditor combined with professional skepticism will influence the success of the procedure. All of these facets must be considered in the use of the fraud audit procedures.

Each procedure will assist the auditor in gathering evidence that must be linked to other information in formulating an eventual conclusion. Instead of pursuing a course of dissecting the pros and cons of each procedure, the auditor should follow the principle of buyer beware regarding professional skepticism in the acceptance of evidence.

Another guideline to remember is that if at first you don't succeed, try, try again, and then again. The point is that it sometimes requires several testing procedures to reveal the true nature regarding an entity. Remember, it's the degrees of risk.

Linking the Procedure to the Scenario

A fraud audit procedure must be designed for a specific fraud scenario. This link is of key importance. For example, the difference between schemes with created entities versus schemes with assumed entities is like night and day. In the assumed identity scheme, the address on the documents will not match the address obtained via legal existence verification, whereas the created entity address will.

A fraud audit procedure is a vehicle to refute the representation made via the concealment strategy. It bears repeating: the concealment strategy is the weakness in a perpetrator's plan. Therefore, once the concealment is refuted, the fraud scenario becomes obvious. However, the fraud audit procedure must overcome the degree of concealment sophistication.

Totality of the evidence is an important aspect to consider in revealing a fraud scenario. The gathering of evidence and the continual linking of all the evidence may reveal the fraud scenario. For example, in a pass-through fraud scheme, the legal existence verification procedure revealed the name of a past officer of the corporation. At the time, the name had no specific reference to the transaction; however, in reviewing the packing slip, it was noted that the sales representative name on the packing slip matched with that of the past officer. Without the totality of the evidence and the continual linking of information uncovered, the scenario would not have been revealed.

Entity Verification

All inherent frau\d schemes are anchored to an entity structure. Establishing whether the entity was created by the perpetrator is the starting point for fraud audit procedures. Organizations have internal control procedures that are intended to control the process. Separation of duties is designed to ensure that one person cannot identify, approve, and record the entity.

False Entities

Fraud scenarios involving vendors, customers, and employees tend to use a false entity structure to commit the fraudulent activity. Within each category, there will be permutations that will impact the fraud audit testing procedures. The most common false entities are the following:

- The entity was created by the perpetrator, vendors, or customers. Vendors and customers are either legally created or exist in name only. When the entity exists in name only, the entity verification procedures will detect the false entity. For legally created entities, the fraud auditing testing procedure should link the incorporation date to first business date. As a guide, when the entity incorporation date is within 90 days of first business transaction date, that is a red flag of a false entity or a favored entity.
- The perpetrator assumes the identity of a real entity being a vendor, customer, or employee. In this permutation, the perpetrator is using the identity of a real vendor, customer, or employee. Therefore, the address or telephone number within the company master file for the entity should not match the address or telephone number of the entity verification procedures. A caveat exists in the pass-through fraud scheme where one of the perpetrators is employed at the real source of the goods or services, so it is possible to obtain a match of records.
- False entities in payroll. The traditional ghost employee scheme is a false entity; however, the majority of the ghost employee schemes occur by assuming the identity of a real employee.

Generally, once the fraud audit procedure obtains creditable evidence the entity is false, the need for an investigation arises.

Real Entities

When the entity is determined to be a real entity, there are generally three possible outcomes:

1. Favorite entity status indicates the entity is real, but there may be a real or perceived conflict. If there is a conflict, the fraud scenario would be dependent on the nature of the account, or no fraud scenario is occurring.
2. The fraud scenario links to a real entity, whereby a decision tree would aid in the determination of the type of scenarios occurring.
3. No fraud scenario is occurring. When the entity is established as a real entity, a decision tree can direct the auditor to the inherent scheme structure for the applicable core business system.

Entity Verification Procedures

The four entity verification procedures are physical presence, legal creation, business capacity testing, and reference checking. The first step in entity verification is to determine that the control procedures were adhered to in recording the entity into the business system. Identification of the names associated with establishing an entity structure should be performed for comparison purposes in future fraud audit procedures. The intent is not control testing, but the gathering of information to establish a basis for entity verification.

The order of verification is verify legal existence, verify physical existence, test business capacity, and check references. The first three procedures can generally be performed in a covert manner, however, reference checking tends to be overt, so the procedure is generally performed last.

Verify Legal Existence

- Government registration. All entities have a legal registration. Employees have birth records, and corporations have registration requirements with an applicable government office. The first step is to establish whether the entity is legally created, then gather identifying information that can eventually be linked to other pertinent information. Names of registrars; officers' addresses; and dates related to entity creation, dissolutions, or changes tend to be the critical information gathered.
- Customers and vendors that are not incorporated may have filed a doing business as (DBA) certificate. The lack of a DBA certificate is typically a red flag. Such a certificate can provide the name of a small business owner, although it is not uncommon for small business owners not to file a certificate.
- Small businesses may not be registered in the state matching the address. While small businesses are required to file as a foreign corporation doing business in the state matching the address, not all small business owners are savvy enough about these requirements, especially in regard to their tax descriptive information. Therefore, a national-level search for legal registrations maybe required.
- Trade associations. When an entity is a member of a trade association, a business's membership provides evidence that the entity is a real one. This verification may also be a useful test for incorporated businesses. One reason small business owners join a trade association is the opportunity to purchase insurance in a group plan. It should be noted that the absence of membership should not be considered as evidence of a false entity.
- Use Internet search companies, such as Lexus Nexus, which gathers public record information that is made accessible to clients. A search of a

company on Lexus Nexus can find if any public records exist on the company and what type of records they are.

Verify Physical Existence

▪ Telephone verification. By contacting the entity, you verify physical existence by the mere fact of the call's being answered. Then it becomes a question of how the call is answered. How the call is answered is part of the evidence associated with the audit judgment of whether the entity is real or false. By calling, the possible outcomes are the telephone is disconnected, someone answers in the name of a different entity, or someone answers in the name of the entity in question. Interview skills are the critical skill to ensure the success of the procedure. Here a few practical tips:
  ▪ Use a telephone in the area code of the company you are auditing. Area codes from out of the area may create a suspicion about why you are calling.
  ▪ Be prepared to provide an explanation about why you are calling. Possible explanations are updating records, resolving internal problems, or original documents have been misplaced. Try not to raise suspicion at this stage of the audit.
  ▪ Have the documents readily available to ask questions or provide answers.
  ▪ Avoid calling multiple times; a second telephone call raises suspicions.
  ▪ Remember the entity you are calling may have Caller ID. Therefore, do not indicate that you are someone other than the person associated with the number identified.
  ▪ The manner in which a call is answered must be consistent with the anticipated business size. Does the business volume correlate with the audited company usage?
▪ Internet search engines like Google can determine what physical structure is located at the known address, and whether the address is consistent with the entity structure. Often, the created entity scheme will use a personal residence address. Remember that many small businesses operate from the owner's personal residence, so in this case, reference checking may be preferred in order to reveal that the entity does not conduct business.
▪ Site visit. By visiting the site, it can be determined what physical structure is located at the known address and whether the address is consistent with the entity structure. Private detectives often will perform the procedure for

a nominal charge, so the use of one may be useful for verifying entities that are not located in your geographic area.

- Public records can determine whether a government or business recognizes the entity as a real entity, and that the address is recognized by other entities. A legal instrument filed by banks securing a loan indicates that the bank believes the entity is real.

- The IRS web site can provide federal identification verification, which will determine whether the federal identification number or Social Security number matches the name associated with the ID number. In many parts of the world, corporations will have a Value Added Tax (VAT) number, which can be confirmed with a government ministry.

- The Internet has extensive databases and search engines to gather information. At the simplest level, Google is an excellent starting point. At the advanced level, there are research companies that have made an art of how to navigate the Internet.

Test Business Capacity

- Proof of insurance. Real companies tend to have insurance. For example, companies with employees have workers' compensation insurance. The fraud testing procedure would consist of a request of the certificate of insurance. Fortunately, such a request is a normal control procedure in many companies, but for fraud audit purposes, the need is to examine the certificate to take note the date of coverage and types of coverage.

- Employees. A company telephone directory provides evidence that the company has employees. By calling the company, you are often referred to the company telephone directory when you do not know an employee's extension.

- Uniform Commercial Code (UCC) filings. A public record filed by a bank or a financing company can indicate a lien has been filed against the described asset. It also indicates that the bank recognizes the entity as a real one.

- Shipping documents, such as a bill of lading indicates the source of the shipment, therefore providing verification.

- Web sites. If a company has a website, does such a site provide matching information about the businesses and services offered?

Check References

- Professional associations. Is the entity recognized by a trade association? Such organizations can also provide useful information on trade practice and trends, which in turn can be used to corroborate representations made by individuals.

▪ Competitors. Contact competitors to establish that the entity conducts business consistent with the goods and services described on the invoice. Competitors may also provide other information regarding ownership and business conflicts.

▪ Media searches. Information published regarding the entity may provide names, services, and legal actions regarding the entity. Advertisements by the entity would suggest the existence of the entity and describe the type of services provided by the entity.

Nontangible Entity Items

Entity verification can extend beyond the existence factors listed above and can pertain to smaller internal factors, such as inventory number, product number, and so on. Data mining should focus on new, deleted, or changed entity numbers. The testing procedure would focus on the authenticity of the transactional data associated with the entity number. Financial statement audits sometimes focus on these nontangible entity items. For example, inventory schemes are often associated with false entity, whereby in order to inflate the inventory, management will create false inventory numbers and record nonexistent inventory. So, identifying new inventory numbers with inventory increases at the end of the year is a good place to look for false inventory schemes.

Fraud Audit Procedures Verifying the Inherent Scheme Action

An aspect of an inherent fraud scheme is the action of the fraud scheme. A fraud audit procedure would need to be customized to the applicable inherent scheme. Procedures to verify the action element of the inherent scheme follow.

▪ **Document confirmation procedures.** This procedure involves contacting the entity to verify the document submitted is authentic. It is used for documents purported to be externally created by a vendor or customer. These procedures are associated with vendor bids, customer orders, and shipping documents.

▪ **Event confirm procedures.** This procedure involves the process of confirming directly with the customer or vendor that the event occurred as describe on the internal document. Often, documents are available from vendor or customer web sites. For example, in an actual construction audit, trip tickets were obtained to support a delivery of materials.

▪ **Reasonability tests.** The ability to determine that an event has occurred is not always easy. Therefore, a secondary approach is to establish, with a reasonable degree of certainty, that the event has occurred.

▪ **Use of industry experts.** Experts may be available from a variety of sources, both internal and external. Employees not involved in the business unit or core business system may be a valuable source of information. Librarians can assist in the research of an assertion; for example, in a purchase audit of paper, a paper conversion formula was confirmed through a librarian's assistance. Sometimes you may need to pay a fee to an expert in order to corroborate an assertion. For example, in an audit involving printing expenditures, a print expert was able to show how a client was being overbilled.

Recognizing that it is not expected of you to know everything about every business or industry and that enlisting the aid of those recognized as experts in a field is not a sign of being incompetent bolsters the possibility of a successful fraud audit outcome. The moral of the story is that no one works in a vacuum.

▪ **Pretext visits.** Meet with actual established vendors on the basis of future business. Such a procedure was used on an actual audit, which allowed the gathering of necessary industry pricing information to establish an overbilling scheme.

▪ **Evidence of work performance.** The concept differs from establishing business capacity by the gathering of evidence that the event did occur versus its having the capacity to occur. By establishing a database that captures date and time information, which can then be compared to an actual event, the reasonability of the event consistent with the time and date reported can be made.

 ## SUMMARY

In this chapter we introduced you to the use of decision trees in fraud auditing. Decision trees, in general, are nothing new, but they have proven to be very useful in fraud auditing for a number of reasons. Most important, they aid in designing a fraud audit program that responds to the fraud risk in a manner consistent with the risk, meaning they are an adaptable tool. It is this ability to adapt that enables its use to keep the fraud auditor on the correct path of finding the fraud scenario that applies, like a GPS system, or not. Unfortunately, since fraud hides, we probably need a road map that shows all those back roads that only the locals know.

CHAPTER NINE

Document Analysis

M ANY OF THE HIGH-PROFILE cases of fraud over the last 25 years were concealed from the auditors by the falsification of documents. In hindsight, the auditors failed to detect the fraud for several reasons, one of which is the lack of professional skepticism. These results indicate the need for increased professional skepticism, or as referred to in Chapter 4, awareness. However, awareness in this context alone is not sufficient. Hence, the ATM approach to building a fraud audit program provides a methodology that incorporates fraud red flags into the fraud audit process.

The brainstorming sessions discussed in Chapter 4 are directed at the "A" in ATM, representing the awareness needed by the auditors. An increased awareness of fraud is necessary for a fraud audit program to work successfully. We don't want to lose our way and fall back on the traditional audit methods and apply *those* to fraud. This awareness encompasses the components of a fraud audit program that are singular to it. Specifically, the components are data mining, which allows the auditor to *locate* the fraud, and fraud audit procedures, which allow the auditor to *recognize* the fraud. It is the latter component that is separated into two distinct areas of testing procedures: the red flag testing procedures and the fraud audit testing procedures.

Fraud audit testing procedures and red flag testing procedures are designed to validate the authenticity of documents and the performance of internal controls. As we have seen in the previous chapters, detailed audit steps and specific red flags must be included in the planning of the fraud audit program, typically done via the brainstorming sessions. So you may be asking, where does the document analysis come into all this? We've gone three paragraphs into the chapter introduction and no mention of documents. Well, we aren't really introducing anything new in this chapter with regard to the actual building of a fraud audit program. We are just trying to establish for you how document analysis fits in, and to do so, we are just trying to tie together everything about a fraud audit program we've discussed so far in the chapters leading up to this point.

 ## DOCUMENT ANALYSIS AND THE FRAUD AUDIT

The red flag testing procedures are based on *observing* indicators in the internal documents and internal controls. In contrast, the fraud audit testing procedures *verify* the authenticity of the representations in the documents and internal controls. While internal controls are an element of each, they are not the same as the testing procedures performed in a traditional audit. Considering that fraud audit testing procedures are the basis of the fraud audit program, the analysis of documents will differ between the fraud audit and the traditional audit.

Why, exactly, would the analysis of documents be different? Well, business systems are driven by paper documents, both imaged paper documents and electronic documents. Approvals are handwritten, created mechanically, or created electronically through a computerized business application. Therefore, the ability to examine a document for the red flags of a fraud scenario is a critical skill in the detection of fraud.

 ## LEVELS OF DOCUMENT EXAMINATION

It should be noted that within fraud auditing, there are levels of document examination: the forensic document examination performed by a certified document examiner and the document examination performed by an auditor conducting a fraud audit. Clearly, the auditor is not required to have the skills of a certified fraud auditor; however, the auditor should understand the difference between the questioned document examination and the examination of documents for red flags.

Questioned Document Examination

Forensic document examination is the application of sciences to the law. The forensic document examiner, using specialized techniques, examines the documents and any handwriting on the documents to establish the authenticity of them and to detect alterations. The American Academy of Forensic Sciences (AAFS) Questioned Document Section and the American Society of Questioned Document Examiners (ASQDE) provide guidance and standards in the field of document examination.

For example, the American Society for Testing and Materials, International (ASTM) Standard E444–09 (Standard Guide for Scope of Work of Forensic Document Examiners) indicates there are four components to the work of a forensic document examiner. These components are the following:

1. Establish genuineness or no genuineness, expose forgery, or reveal alterations, additions, or deletions.
2. Identify or eliminate persons as the source of handwriting.
3. Identify or eliminate the source of typewriting or other impression, marks, or relative evidence.
4. Write reports or give testimony, when needed, to aid the users of the examiner's services in understanding the examiner's findings.

Some forensic document examiners (FDEs) limit their work to the examination and comparison of handwriting, however, most inspect and examine the whole document in accordance with this ASTM standard.

Fraud Audit Document Examination

The fraud auditor also focuses on the authenticity of the document, with two fundamental differences:

1. **The degree of certainty.** With forensic document examination, the forensic certainty is based on scientific principles. Fraud audit document examination is based on visual observations and audit experience.
2. **Central focus.** Fraud audit document examination focuses on the red flags associated with the fraud scenario. Forensic document examination focuses on the genuineness of the document or handwriting.

Being *aware* of the principles of forensic document examination will assist the auditor in knowing when and how to use the services of a fraud document examiner in a fraud audit.

DOCUMENT RED FLAGS

As discussed in Chapter 4, one of the categories of red flags is the document red flag. Remember, the auditor needs to be aware of how a fraud scenario occurs, but also employ a methodology in detecting fraud. These abilities are certainly needed in order to be successful in the identification of document red flags. Specifically, a document must link to the fraud scenario and the key controls of the core business system.

The document must be examined for the following categories: document condition, document format, document information, and industry standards. Within these categories the concept of missing, altered, and created should be applied to the document or the document information. The second aspect of the document examination is linking the document to the internal controls.

A document that links to a key control should generally correlate to a *trigger red flag*, whereas documents for nonkey controls generally correlate to *awareness red flag*. Why separate the red flags any further? This distinction is made once again to use the familiar to learn the new. A trigger red flag is similar to the traditional-audit use of red flags, whereby an internal control not working triggers a red flag, which correspondingly triggers a fraud audit procedure.

Linking the document examination to the internal controls is a critical aspect of developing the decision tree aspect of the fraud audit program. Using a document examination methodology aids the fraud auditor in building the fraud audit program.

Document Condition and Existence

The acronym "MAC" is a useful aid to assist the auditor in identifying the red flags and the corresponding audit response. The "M" stands for missing, either missing the entire document or missing information on a document; the "A" for altered information on a document; and the "C" for created documents or information on a document. Specifically:

"M" for Missing

A missing document is a red flag. Missing documents occur because the document was never created, was destroyed, or has been misfiled. Documents are either the basis of initiating the transaction or support the transaction. Frequency of missing documents must be linked to the fraud scenario. In some instances, missing one document may be a red flag, although typically repetition is necessary to warrant fraud audit testing procedures. The audit response should focus on the following attributes assuming the document links to a key control:

- Is the document externally or internally created? The existence of externally created documents can be confirmed with the source, assuming the source is not involved in the fraud scenario.
- Is the document necessary to initiate the transaction or is the document a supporting one? Documents used to initiate a transaction had to have existed at some point; therefore, logic dictates that the document was destroyed or misfiled.
- One, two, or all three of the following questions could apply to internal documents:
  - Is there a pattern of missing documents associated with the same entity?
  - Is there a pattern of missing documents associated with an internal employee?
- Does the document support a key control, therefore being a trigger red flag, or is the missing document attached to a nonkey control?

With regard to missing information on a document, several questions arise, one of which is: are there tears, torn pieces, soiled areas, or charred areas that cause information to be missing? To address any of these situations, finding a similar document type is needed to determine if the intent of the document has changed because of the missing information.

Another question is: is information obliterated (e.g., covered, blotted, or wiped out)? Overwriting is commonly used to obscure existing writing. Correction fluid is also a common method, but the underlying writing can be read and photographed using transmitted light from underneath the document. Scratching out writing with a pen will obliterate writing successfully if it results in the page being torn. Spilled liquids can also obliterate writing. How many staff meetings have been interrupted by spilled coffee on the meeting notes?

Has any information been erased? Chemical erasing fluid leaves evidence in the form of stains. Chemical washed areas are difficult to detect even with infrared lighting. Erasures of pencil markings can be detected through the impressions left. For computer-generated text, some inkjet inks are water soluble, making them easy to erase; however, there will be a stain. Toner ink can be erased by scraping, but this method will leave damage. Overall, deciphering erased information generally depends on the material being erased, the time between the writing and erasing, and any restoration.

For computer-generated and printed documents, it is very difficult to determine if there is missing information because of the difficulty in determining an original from a copy. Comparison documents may help to determine exactly what information was removed.

"A" for Altered

Altered pertains to changing or adding information to the original document. The information may be altered manually or through the use of desktop publishing capabilities. For example, manual changes tend to be visible through a difference in handwriting, and electronic documents would generally be altered via the software used to create the document. Any altering of information would be detected through the same red flags as adding information.

In the context of fraud, forgery is the first thing that comes to mind in any discussion of the altering of documents. *Forgery* is a legal term applied to fraudulent imitation. It is an alteration of writing as to convey a false impression that a document itself, not its contents, is authentic, thereby imposing a legal liability. It is an alteration of a document with the intent to defraud. It should be noted that it is possible for a document examiner to identify a document or signature as a forgery, but it is much less common for the examiner to identify the forger. This is due to the nature of handwriting, whereby a forger is attempting to imitate the writing habit of another person, thereby suppressing his own writing characteristics and style, and in essence, disguising his writing.

Electronic alterations tend to focus on the alignment of the information with original information, type font or type size, and electronic header information reflecting a date change after original recording of date and time. One thing to be noted with computer-generated and machine-printed documents is that they are a relatively new development in document examination and, as such, are now considered a subspecialty. The complexity of the analysis of the computer-generated documents requires an expert in such analysis for the examination of the questioned documents.

"C" for Created

A created document pertains to any document prepared by the perpetrator of the fraud scenario. This type of changed document can include added or created documents or added and created text on a document. The document can be prepared by an external source (e.g., a vendor in an overbilling scheme) or an internal source (e.g., purchasing agent that created false bids). By the way, the fraudulent invoice included in Chapter 6 is one that was created, but for educational purposes only, of course! Some signs of document creation can include the age of the document being inconsistent with the purported creation date, or the document lacks the sophistication typically associated with normal business standards.

Added or created text can occur with the use of ink or whatever type of writing instrument was used on the original. It can also be performed through cutting and pasting sections of text, then photocopying the document to eliminate any outline. When pages are suspected of being added in this manner, a comparison of the type of paper used for the original and the photocopy should be made. In terms of computer-generated and machine-produced documents differences in the software used may result in text differences.

Created approval signatures are forgeries of the approver's signature. Some signs are:

- No attempt to resemble the original signature.
- Freehand or tracing of the original signature.
- Original signature obtained through trickery.
- Approver signs the document to provide the illusion of forgery.

With documents created by the perpetrator, there is a direct link between the sophistication of the creator and audit detection. The auditor should be aware of the following similarities that can exist between created documents and the originals:

- The created document compares to known standard template documents.
- The created document has a form number that coincides with those purchased from a document supply house.

- The created document template coincides with known templates in small business software or templates found in standard word processing software or spreadsheet software.
- The created document format is consistent with the sophistication of the business.
- Substitution. The creation of documents through means of substituting the original document happens when an original document was used to initiate a transaction, and then the original is substituted by creating a new similar document or altering the original document.

Document Information

As MAC shows us, fraudulent document information can be considered missing information, incorrect information, or information inconsistent with normal business standards. Therefore, the auditor needs to have the requisite business and industry knowledge to presume the appropriate red flags pertaining to document information.

Incorrect Information

As highlighted in the MAC discussion, the information on a document is obviously wrong or in error. This information is incorrect because of typos, document condition, use of a document format differing from known sources, or use of information that simply does not exist. The level of sophistication in concealment is very low in such cases; therefore, the auditor should consider them a first-level red flag target.

Identifying Information

When discussing document information, the focus typically is on those pieces of information on a document that serve as identification. This information may include information that identifies the entity, the transaction being documented, and the source of the information. Some items of entity information would be address, telephone number, web sites, and e-mail addresses. Refer back to our phony invoice (Figure 6.5 in Chapter 6). The items pertaining to the transaction itself may include when it took place. Therefore, a red flag may be if the transaction was created at off-period times or dates. Any control numbers pertaining to the transaction are also to be noted; a red flag may be if control numbers are illogical in reference to a sequential pattern or out of sequence by number or date. Another red flag would be if the source of the information is unknown or is not recognized as a known source.

Internal Procedure Information

Internal procedures are also associated with red flags, especially when information that is required by company procedures is missing or incorrect. Therefore, for an auditor to identify a red flag associated with internal procedures, she must have an understanding of the organization's procedures and what type of information is created in the implementation of those procedures. Some red flags regarding types of information created by internal procedures are the following:

- Arithmetic errors caused by use of improper rates.
- Control numbers do not have the proper number of integers or alpha characters.
- Control numbers that are duplicate or not contained in the expected range.
- Alpha descriptions are inconsistent with company standards.
- Required data fields are blank.
- Identifying information correlates to dormant sources, expired sources, or aged sources.

Industry-Specific Information

Industry-specific information concerns information that external entities would provid as part of the document. Therefore, associated red flags would pertain to information that is inconsistent with industry standards. The red flags would require the auditor to have knowledge of the industry or to conduct research on industry standards. By having this knowledge or performing this research, the fraud auditor is able to consider the source of the information, the integrity of the information, and the information as it reflects current standards.

BRAINSTORMING SESSIONS AND DOCUMENT RED FLAGS

One aspect of a brainstorming session is to discuss the red flags associated with a fraud scenario. Discussions should contain the following:

- Identify the key control document supporting the business application.
- Discuss the document condition and document information expectations.

For the discussions to be general versus specific in nature, use actual company documents or documents created by external sources (e.g., a vendor invoice). Such documents can be provided to each participant in either old-fashioned paper form or through the use of some kind of audio-visual equipment. The point of this discussion is to identify critical information on the documents that would trigger red flags and the associated audit response. This is a good opportunity to also find out the level of industry and organizational knowledge the group has, so discussion should be encouraged on any previously known problems associated with the document.

 ## THE FRAUD AUDIT PROGRAM AND DOCUMENT RED FLAGS

As part of the fraud audit program, actual document red flags become the basis of the audit opinion. Therefore, some practical tips include:

- Take your time. Read the document from left to right. Use a pointer to help you focus on the specific data element you are looking for.
- Remember that information missing from the document is more difficult to find than altered or incorrect information.
- Develop a consistent approach to document examination. For example, first start with examining the document condition, followed with the document information, and last, evidence of the internal controls.
- Focus on entity aspects of the document before moving on to the transactional ones. Within the red flags, focus on the trigger red flags and then the awareness red flags.
- Do not trust your memory. Write down information regarding names, addresses, numbers, and so on. As the fraud audit process evolves, a name observed two weeks ago may now link to a fraud audit finding.

 ## SUMMARY

We entered the world of the document in this chapter. Perhaps we took a scenic route to get here, but it was a necessary direction to take. After all, before we can even discuss what constitutes a fraud red flag as far as documents are concerned, we really needed to know what a fraud red flag is, when they are discussed in the planning of a fraud audit, and how they are different from those used in a traditional audit. We previously learned how important is for the auditor to have and maintain an awareness of fraud throughout the fraud audit process. Now, we learned how this awareness is applied through the fraud audit testing procedures. Simply, an auditor must be aware of how a document is linked to the fraud scenario. If the link is through a key control, then the auditor is aware of trigger red flags. If the link is through a nonkey control, then the auditor is aware of, well, awareness red flags. Can we state it enough? Be aware. Be very aware.

CHAPTER TEN

Disbursement Fraud

S TUFF HAPPENS. FOR OUR discussion, we prefer the variation disbursement fraud happens. It's not a question of "will" it happen; it's a question of "when" it will happen. And in case you were wondering about the "how" of the proverbial when, where, and how troika, that will depend on the opportunities created within the organization. Disbursement fraud is typically thought of as occurring in the check-writing process because of the cash nature of disbursements in general. However, there are many more methods of implementing disbursement fraud than just through the check-writing process. It can be found in an accounts payable function where there is internal or external collusion with a vendor or when management initiates a transaction through the authorization of the organization's treasurer. So, checks, while an important document, are not the exclusive document to talk about when discussing disbursement fraud. Purchase orders, invoices, wire transfers, even packing slips can be essential documents in detecting this type of fraud.

 FRAUD RISK STRUCTURE

A fraud audit addresses disbursement fraud in the same manner as discussed in general in the preceding chapters with the first step being a determination of whether the entity is a false one or a real one. Then, depending on which it is, the fraud risk assessment would focus on the action element of the inherent scheme. For disbursement fraud, the action element is how the theft of monetary funds takes place. The decision then becomes which inherent fraud scheme is most likely occurring.

Establishing a fraud risk structure is the starting point for identifying the fraud scenarios that can occur through an organization's core business systems. In the case of disbursements, that system would entail the organization's bank accounts. Fraud risk structure refers to the auditor's ability to fit or structure the schemes within the organization, the relevant business systems, and the general nature of the general ledger account. To illustrate this process, we give you three actual case-based examples involving fraudulent disbursements. The first case concerned accounts receivable, where dormant credit balances were falsely issued, first by the changing of the customer's address, then a false request was made on behalf of that customer. In the second case, a bookkeeper issued checks in the name of an actual company, and then diverted the payment when it falsely endorsed the checks. In the third case, an insurance claims adjuster issued a check in the name of a house-insurance policy holder who did not file a claim.

These three situations appear different at first glance, but are in fact the same inherent scheme, whereby the perpetrator takes over the identity of an actual entity. In each, the action element involves an event that did not occur, for example, a customer did not initiate a transaction, payment was not received, and no damage occurred. However, the concealment strategy differs slightly for each, considering the nature of the transaction or the nature of the industry. So, how does the auditor decide upon a fraud risk structure given all these nuances? Remember our opening statement: Disbursement fraud happens and, therefore, the question of "when" needs to be answered. So, the audit procedure is to determine whether it was a real or false entity that caused the event or in these cases nonevent. Then, in the proceeding situations, a comparison of the fraudulent disbursement bank account location to known previous bank account locations is performed to reveal the discrepancy.

More specifically, for the first case, the data red flag is the proximity of the change of address in relation to the request for a refund. Confirmation of the transaction with the real customer is performed involving examination of the canceled check to verify either the endorsement on the check, the bank that negotiated the check, or with an electronic payment, the account number. With a little luck, the employee committing the scheme used the same account as her payroll direct deposit. However, if she did not use her personal account, comparisons to previous customer remittances would also detect the scheme.

In the second case, the bookkeeper did not create false invoices to support the disbursements. The missing invoices would be a red flag. Examination of the canceled checks would reveal endorsement discrepancies. Otherwise, comparing the bank account number on the checks associated with the missing invoices to the bank account number on the checks for any invoice on file would reveal the discrepancy.

For the third case, confirmation with the homeowner would reveal that no claim had been filed. Since companies are sometimes hesitant to contact the customer, the auditor would need to examine the documentation and reasons for the claim. For example, if the claim is for wind damage, then checking with the local weather bureau or newspapers will reveal whether any high-wind storms, tornados, and so on occurred in that vicinity on the date of the alleged damage. Examination of the bank account number on the claim check to the customer's policy payment check would reveal any discrepancy.

Terminology

As can be seen even in our simply stated cases above, one of the common problems in building fraud audit programs is the tendency to use terms interchangeably, especially when it comes to false entities and billing schemes, as is being discussed in this chapter. Therefore, it is recommended that the fraud audit program include not only the fraud risk structure, but also the definitions for the terms used so everyone can be on the same proverbial page. For the purposes of our discussion of disbursement fraud, the following definitions will hopefully provide some clarification of the concepts being discussed. Besides, to interchangeably call an overbilling scheme a pass-through scheme or simply a billing scheme is just plain wrong.

Front companies: A vendor that has no active business purpose and is typically created for the sole purpose of illegal activity. Variations include:

- *Fictitious:* A vendor that does not legally exist.
- *Shell:* The vendor is created legally, but does not function like a true company. It exists solely on paper, has no physical address or employees, and does not produce goods or provide services.
- *Pseudo-real:* The vendor is a real vendor, but has no prior business conducted with the organization or is dormant relative to doing business with the organization. In terms of schemes where the vendor has no prior

business with the organization, an internal employee at the organization in essence steals the vendor's identity by providing false address and/or bank information, resulting in the vendor's being newly created within the master file. With the latter definition, where the vendor is dormant, the existing address and/or bank information in the vendor master file is changed by the perpetrator.

▪ *Temporary or limited use:* The perpetrator takes advantage of the fact that vendor verification procedures ordinarily do not exist for vendors that are expected to receive only one payment. Can also apply to fictitious or pseudo-real companies as defined above.

▪ *Look-alike or similarly named:* The vendor uses a look-alike or name similar to a known, real company to deceive and hide its fictitious nature. Can also apply to fictitious or pseudo-real companies as defined above.

Billing schemes:

▪ *False billing:* The organization pays for goods or services that are not delivered. The vendor is usually fictitious, although the scheme can also be committed by a real company in collusion with an employee of the organization.

▪ *Pass-through billing:* A real vendor provides goods or services to a front company, which in turn provides the goods or services to the organization with a markup on price. The only function of the front company is that it provides a pass-through of the goods or services. These schemes are a combination of false billing, overbilling, and conflict-of-interest schemes, a circumstance that just lends itself to the overall confusion when the phrase "billing scheme" is just tossed around.

▪ *Overbilling:* A real vendor overcharges the organization for the actual goods or services that are provided. The scheme is typically committed in collusion with an employee of the organization, but may also be used without collusion, whereby the vendor takes advantage of known internal control weaknesses.

▪ *Temporary-holding:* Payment is made to a false vendor, which has a similar name as the actual vendor. The payment is then held in a bank account controlled by the perpetrator. While payment is eventually forwarded to the real vendor, the perpetrator temporarily invests the diverted funds, thereby personally benefitting from any earnings gained in the interim.

▪ *Speed of payment:* The vendor invoice is paid more quickly than normal payment terms.

Fraud Risk Structure and Embezzlement

The legal definition of embezzlement according to *Black's Law Dictionary* is "the fraudulent taking of personal property with which one has been entrusted . . . the criminal intent for embezzlement . . . arises after taking possession." For the purposes of our discussion of disbursement fraud, embezzlement is simply the theft of monetary funds. It is a type of fraud risk, one that is typically associated with disbursements because they are the actual payment of monetary funds by someone entrusted to make those payments. The terms *embezzlement* and *disbursement fraud* aren't interchangeable. The distinction between embezzlement and disbursement fraud must be made to understand the concept of a fraud risk structure.

The fraud auditor's job doesn't involve the criminal intent aspect of the definition of embezzlement, but rather how the personal property (monetary funds) is taken. So, the auditor's first step, as always, is to determine if the entity is false or real. If it is false, and a front company has been established, then the assessment would focus on the action element of the inherent scheme. Therefore, embezzlement schemes that are inherent to false entities would include various false billing schemes, pass-through billing schemes, and illegal activities committed by or within the organization.

If it is a real company, then several inherent schemes are possible, and the auditor needs to narrow down the possibilities by fitting the schemes to the organization, the relevant business system, and the nature of the general ledger account. For example, the billing schemes most often found in real entities concern overbilling and have many variations. Overbilling may be carried out by a vendor's taking advantage of poor internal controls, or it can occur when a vendor is in collusion with an internal employee prior to or after procurement. It also can occur with a vendor in collusion with an internal employee after procurement in many ways, including:

- Fictitious invoice submitted by vendor.
- Fictitious charges on a real invoice.
- Overcharging on price.
- Charging for a higher quantity of goods or a greater amount of services than delivered or provided.
- Charging for a higher quality of goods than delivered (product substitution).
- Charging for goods or services that are not needed by the organization.
- No recovery or chargeback for credits or returns.
- Intentional duplicate payments.

In addition to billing schemes, another inherent fraud scheme found in real entities involves theft of checks. Again variations abound. For example, the theft of outstanding checks can occur when a perpetrator voids the original check and reissues the check, typically a manually created check, for the same amount and in a name controlled by the perpetrator. Another variation is when a check is issued in the name of the perpetrator, but the cash disbursement journal lists a valid name. A third example is the situation where there is counterendorsing of a check made originally to a real company, and the theft occurs through the second endorsement.

Also to be included in the discussions to follow are inherent schemes, such as temporary-holding schemes and speed of disbursement schemes. Although not billing schemes, per se, they both involve the theft of funds.

Data Analysis

Two consecutive data searches must be performed in our fraud audit data mining: The first is designed to search for false entities through the master file data, and the second, the transactional data. Use of two fiscal years' data is recommended, with the current partial data being optional. The overall objective is to obtain specific file data for the following time periods:

- Expenditure files for scope period: two complete years.
- Purchase order file for scope period: four complete years.
- Disbursement files for scope period: two complete years for all checks, wires, or electronic transfers.
- Vendor master file consistent with the expenditure file.
- Vendor master change file: two complete years.
- Optional files:
  - Vendor master file for beginning of scope period.
  - Employee master file.

Master File Information

1. Search for duplication in key information, specifically, vendor name, address, telephone number, bank account number, e-mail addresses, and government identification numbers.
2. Search the vendor master change file for changes to vendor name, address, telephone number, bank account number, e-mail addresses, and government identification numbers.

3. Note any missing key information because it may indicate a control to access strategy.
4. Match key information to employee databases.
5. Match address information to known mailbox service companies within a geographic radius of the accounts payable function.

Off-Period Transactions

1. Expenditure or disbursement transactions recorded at nonbusiness hours, by vendor and record creator.
2. Expenditure or disbursement transactions recorded on Saturdays, Sundays, or holidays, by vendor and record creator.
3. Vendor master file records created at nonbusiness hours, by vendor and record creator.
4. Vendor master files records created on Saturdays, Sundays, or holidays, by vendor and record creator.
5. Vendor master file changes to address or bank account number that occur at nonstandard business hours.
6. Vendor master file changes to address or bank account number that occur on Saturdays, Sundays, or holidays.

Detecting Internal Control Avoidance

1. Experience has shown that the circumventing of dollar control levels seems to be a prerequisite to internal control avoidance. This analysis is performed to search for invoices, which in the aggregate exceed a dollar control level within a prescribed date range, but where each individual invoice is below the dollar control level.
2. Match purchase orders and invoices to identify invoices with no purchase order or purchase date equals or exceeds invoice dates.

Vendor Invoice Analysis

1. Compare the first vendor invoice number in the scope period to the last invoice number in the scope period, then calculate an invoice number range, which is correlated to the number of invoices in the scope period. Note any sequence changes. Also calculate a date range, which is then correlated to invoice number range. Note any inconsistencies.
2. Note a pattern of invoices with a Saturday, Sunday, or holiday date.

Purchase Order Analysis

1. Note use of aged purchase orders. In this scheme, accounts payable is applying a false invoice to an old purchase order.
2. Identify open purchase orders. In this scheme, accounts payable is applying a false invoice among the many invoices applied to the purchase order.

False-Entity Data Analysis

We have made the determination of whether an entity is real or false a general tenet throughout this book. Now, when talking of disbursements we can get specific as to how to make such a determination in the context of a core business system. Two examples of linking the type of entity and disbursement fraud through data analysis are provided below, one if the vendor was created and the other if the vendor was assumed.

Example 1: Created Identity

1. Identify all vendors with a creation date within the scope period.
2. Link the associated expenditure records to the vendor master file.
3. Create a report with the following information: vendor name, vendor number, creation date, total records, aggregate dollars, the maximum invoice amount, the minimum invoice amount, and the average invoice amount.
4. Identify all invoices with a creation date within the scope period.
5. Identify the first expenditure record and compare the invoice date to creation date and the incorporation date.

Example 2: Assumed Identity

1. Identify all vendors with changes in the scope period with changes to the address, bank account number, or telephone.
2. Search for inconsistencies between address fields and area codes and government registration numbers.
3. Search for duplicate key information.

 ## AUDIT APPROACHES

In the following discussion, we have chosen to distinguish fraud schemes by whether an entity is determined to be real or false. Hopefully, by separating them, the audit approaches, although seemingly similar, will reflect the importance of the first step of entity determination.

Schemes Involving False Entities

Once it has been determined that an entity is false, there are several scenarios that may be detected, with false billing and pass-through billing the most obvious. Outside of billing, there is an area of illegal activities that includes disbursement fraud particularly as it relates to money laundering. Remember, the audit procedures for the entity structure were discussed in Chapter 9.

False Billing

The scheme is simply that the perpetrator has billed the company for goods or services that were not provided or an event that did not occur, and the company is a false-entity scheme. The concealment strategies are false invoices, false approvals, and the use of false companies to receive the payment. Therefore, the audit approach is to confirm the event did or did not occur by using an independent database not under the direct control of the perpetrator. The challenge for the auditor here is locating an independent database. In terms of predictability, the auditor would factor in that this scheme typically occurs for services, although small dollar purchases for tangible goods would be likely. Also, false billing can occur through a real vendor.

Aged or dormant purchase orders can be used internally to commit a false billing scheme. In such a situation, someone in accounts payable applies false invoices against purchases orders where a project has been completed. The vendor typically has also become dormant; therefore, the address or bank account is changed to allow for the diversion of the payment.

Pass-Through Billing

This scheme requires a minimum of three entities: an actual supplier, a shell company, and the organization purchasing goods or services. The scheme operates in the following manner: The purchasing organization places an order with the shell company. The shell company places the order with an actual supplier, who then ships the goods to the purchasing organization. This action results in an invoice being sent to the shell company, who subsequently sends another invoice to the organization. Fraud occurs because the shell company makes a profit by charging a higher price to the organization actually receiving the goods. As a guideline assume the mark up ranges from 5 to 15%.

Once again there are many variations, for example, when a sales representative at the supplier establishes a shell company. The sales representative sells goods to the shell company. Then the shell company sells the goods to the purchasing organization. The shell company provides a kickback to the organization's purchasing agent for purchasing the items from the shell company versus the actual supplier. Just like the proverbial shell game (pun intended), replete with sleight of hand, except in this case it's an invoice that gets shuffled around. But wait. There's more. In another variation, the purchase agent sets up the shell corporation and commits the scheme without the direct knowledge of the actual supplier. Still following the shell around? Then here's one more variation, where an organization is managing a cost reimbursable contract for a customer. The customer directs the organization to purchase goods and services from a specific vendor, which is functioning as a pass-through for the customer's employee. In essence, all these variations operate the same way, with the differences occurring at the point of opportunity.

The scheme, regardless of variation, presents many fraud detection problems, the first one being that it will most likely comply with all of the internal controls. Second, the goods and services were received by the organization purchasing them. Last, the pass-through scheme mirrors a legitimate business broker model.

When trying to predict the likelihood of such a scheme's taking place, the auditor should realize that the scheme typically occurs in supply items that aren't subject to inventory controls. Recently, we have seen the scheme operate where the internal purchasing agent sets up a company that allegedly has an expertise in procuring a particular item. In this case, the pass-through scheme operates as a buying specialist in a particular market. The singularity of the item allows for a predictability factor of the pass-through scheme's actually occurring.

The audit approach would use the false entity audit procedures, alerting the auditor that a problem exists. Second examination of the packing slip for the goods would indicate that the goods were shipped by the actual supplier, then billed to the shell company, and delivered to the audit-subjected organization. Examination of the packing slip and the corporation registration documents for individual names may provide a match, whereby the same person's name appears on documents for two different entities.

Illegal Activities

Shell companies are used by organized crime groups and by individuals committing tax evasion or hiding assets; they may be used by corporations to conceal bribery, gain access to markets, or obtain contracts. The corporation may also pass funds through multiple, actual companies as a way to conceal the original source of the funds. These actions are very similar to the layering process involved in money laundering.

Schemes Involving Real Entities

It may seem that all disbursement fraud detected in real entities involves some variation of an inherent overbilling scheme. That assumption is probably caused by the fact that overbilling schemes relate to the opportunities presented. A vendor having knowledge of an organization's internal controls can find fraud opportunities by discovering the weaknesses with those controls. Then there are disbursement fraud opportunities involving collusion between the vendor and an organization's employees. Outside of overbilling, there are more inherent fraud schemes, such as those involving the speed of reimbursement, theft of checks, treasury transactions, and employee reimbursement. Some of these schemes may appear to overlap with overbilling, so they are included herein.

Overbilling

Overbilling schemes occur when a vendor intentionally inflates its margins through false representations on its invoice. These schemes become evident when focusing on vendor's margins versus the dollar amount on the invoice. For example, a false change in price from a $1.00 to a $1.05 is just a nickel, but also a 5% increase to the vendor's margin. Obviously, the pattern and frequency of the event is an important consideration in evaluating the difference between error and fraud.

From the perspective of opportunity, such a scheme typically operates through collusion of an internal employee with a vendor or through a vendor's taking advantage of poor internal controls. How the overbilling occurs will differ by what circumstance creates the opportunity for the vendor to intentionally overbill.

Opportunities Created by Internal Controls   As stated previously, vendors can overbill an organization without the involvement of an internal employee by taking advantage of internal controls or exploiting the lack of an internal control. Specifically, vendors learn that companies have exception tolerances built into their payment system for operational efficiency. The opportunity is based on knowledge of the materiality of the difference and the fact the vendor is a real entity conducting business with the organization.

An example of a vendor utilizing this knowledge is when a vendor is aware that the company policy is to automatically pay an invoice that is within a certain percentage of the purchase order. The vendor intentionally inflates the unit price, but stays within the tolerances. Focusing on the percentage increase versus the numeric increase of the unit price provides a predictability factor for the auditor.

In certain industries, there are accepted practices recognizing that minor differences between the purchase order amount and the invoice amount is not deemed a breach of the implied contract. In these cases, the consistency of the overcharges as to quantity amount or price variance would indicate that the overcharges were intentional rather than caused by any randomness associated with the nature of the industry practice.

Companies also have different control procedures for small dollar expenses that are subject to schemes. For example, a vendor submits a small dollar invoice that is automatically paid without a purchase order because the dollar amount is below a predetermined amount. You may be thinking, so what, it's only a small amount. However, there was a reported scheme where a shell company vendor billed millions of dollars for toner cartridges that were not ordered or received using this same method of billing.

The vendor may also be aware that small dollar invoices are applied against an open purchase order without further checking. In this variation, the vendor submits false invoices among the real invoices knowing that the invoice will be applied against the open purchase order. The red flag here is the pattern of frequency of small dollar invoices within the pattern of large dollar invoices.

Vendors learn that internal control procedures may not operate with sufficient due diligence to detect the intentional overbilling. Short shipments and product substitution schemes are classic examples of using such knowledge to commit fraud. For example, a vendor knows that a company's verification procedure calls for a comparison of the description on the box to a shipping invoice versus a physical inspection of what is in the box; therefore, no one is validating the quantity or quality. These schemes are more prone to occur with noninventory items or where detecting the product substitution is beyond the skill of the receivers.

The predictability factor with overbilling schemes operates on the concept that the vendor will learn about the control weaknesses within the company's procedures. The auditor should perform a fraud penetration assessment of known internal control weaknesses. A penetration assessment by design is intended to determine how to process a fraudulent transaction through the business system. Once the penetration assessment is designed, the auditor would develop a data mining plan to search for the transactions consistent with the known control weaknesses.

A second predictability factor of these types of schemes occurring involves the vendor's taking advantage of tolerances. The auditor should develop data mining routines to search for frequency and pattern of abuse. An example is when the vendor intentionally submits invoices above the purchase order, but within the accepted tolerance. The data mining routine starts by summarizing total purchase orders and total invoices. The routine is designed to identify vendors that overcharge at a high frequency with a pattern that is within an allotted percentage. Since management is not involved, the audit procedure would necessitate the obtaining of management confirmation of the acceptability of the frequency and pattern of overbilling.

The data mining routine for small dollar schemes focuses on frequency and percentage of small dollar invoices in relation to large dollar ones. The audit should focus on the reason for the small dollar invoice amount. Vague invoice descriptions, special add-on charges or "per manager" instructions would be document red flags of the inherent schemes. Audit software can also be used to search for these phrases within the invoice line in the database.

A third predictability factor of overbilling schemes involves the opportunity to commit this type of scheme. The vendor takes advantage of the known due diligence in performing a control procedure. For example, temp hiring agencies are supposed to ensure that individuals are properly screened and qualified to be hired on a temporary basis. Since the agency knows that the company relies on it for these checks, it feels confident that it can provide individuals that do not meet the stated qualification requirements. So, when the accounting department requests a temporary employee with CPA qualifications, the agency intentionally submits an individual with accounting experience, but not one with certification.

It should be noted that in the preceeding examples there could exist collusion with operating management. The small difference in these cases versus the ones discussed previously involves the concealment strategy when management is involved.

Collusion with the Vendor Employees Prior to Purchase Orders   Overbilling schemes can occur prior to issuance of the purchase order. The fraud opportunity is associated with an employee's purchasing authorization, specifically, the level of authority the person has to enter into a purchase agreement and the level of authority to authorize payment. If purchasing procedures identify a vendor as a sole source in the bidding process, that transaction is readily identifiable. However, when an operations person buys directly from a vendor, the purchase is still a sole source. Overbilling schemes prior to issuance of the purchase order occur as follows:

1. The employee negotiates directly with the vendor. This happens in parts of an organization where the purchasing authority has been formally delegated to the employee. In this instance, interviews with relevant management would denote such questionable delegation.
2. The employee exceeds his or her purchasing authority or circumvents purchasing procedures and purchases directly from the vendor. In this instance, invoices without purchase orders or purchase orders issued after the invoice are a red flag.

When the scheme occurs prior to the purchase order, typically there are no overt signs of the overbilling within the documents supporting the disbursement. However, excessive socialization between the vendor and the employee is a behavioral red flag of the fraud opportunity.

In reality, the red flags show up in the procurement process. However, when the procurement occurs at an operations level versus the purchasing department, sufficient documentation may not be available for the purchase decision process taking place. The audit procedures will require independent verification of management representations.

Collusion with the Vendor Employees after Contract/Purchase Order Issuance When the overbilling occurs after the issuance of the contract, the red flag is a change between the purchase order/contract and the vendor's invoice. These schemes involve collusion with the vendor and occur by some aspect of management override. The vendor typically provides a kickback to the internal employee.

The first scheme is the false charge scheme where the real vendor submits invoices for false charges. It is also possible that accounts payable employees are processing false invoices through a real vendor and diverting the payment. Regardless of the fraud opportunity point, the false charges are concealed among the real charges. The type of false charge and the party committing the false charge scheme will determine whether data mining or document examination is the appropriate technique to search for the false invoice.

In a scheme where the vendor is in collusion with an employee regarding false invoices, data mining is a critical step because the document is created by the real vendor. The data mining would focus on invoice numbers, invoice dates, product description, and purchase order information. For example, text searches are an effective technique to locate vague descriptions or terms like *special charge*.

In a scheme where accounts payable is processing false invoices through a real vendor, the key is to search for differences among the invoices (document category of a red flag). The first step is to establish the norm for information on the invoice. The second step is to search for invoices that are not consistent with the normal invoicing procedures. The data mining could be as simple as visually scanning the invoice file. Data mining could also search for invoices applied to aged purchase orders that have an open dollar balance. Similarly, data mining can be performed by searching for invoice anomalies with open purchase orders.

Sometimes an element of a real invoice is a false charge. Typically, it will be a charge that would appear to be legitimate, such as taxes or handling charges. In the case of reimbursable expenses, the expenses may be false in total or some aspect of the expenses is false. The data or document red flag would be the existence of a charge that typically doesn't exist for the organization.

Overbilling also occurs when the invoice price or rate on the vendor invoice is higher than the rate on the original contract. The higher rate is usually supported by a phony reason, and a manager uses his position of authority to approve the higher rate. Performing a data mining search routine that compares unit prices on the purchase order to the unit prices on the vendor invoice is needed to uncover this scheme.

Similarly, the scheme operates when the invoice quantity is for more than the amount provided. How it is carried out depends on the nature of the goods and whether the goods are obtained by a receiving function or an end user. Besides collusion with a vendor, the difference could also be caused by internal theft, theft by the transporter, and theft by the receiving function.

Product substitution schemes are another variation of schemes involving collusion because the vendor is typically shipping an inferior good or providing an inferior service. Product substitution schemes are not typically detectable through data mining procedures unless the nature of the substitution causes a frequency of credits or adjustments that are recorded in the accounts payable system. Interviewing end users of the product or service is a good way to locate product substitution schemes. Examination of a packing slip from the vendor's inventory control system versus the vendor's invoicing system would detect the differences also. Otherwise, physical inspection of the items provided is the typical audit procedure.

Within the product substitution category, the following schemes may occur: vendor indicates the item is comparable; knock-off principle where the item is falsely labeled; country of origin is falsely labeled or the item is contaminated and will produce health hazards or other fitness issues. Product substitution is probably more common than the audit profession recognizes or understands. At some level, the need for industry experts who are affiliated with the auditor will be required.

With regard to service product substitution, the scheme occurs when the service is provided by an individual at a lower qualification level and billed at a higher rate. These schemes tend to occur in services where qualifications are critical to the rate structure. Since the schemes are difficult to detect through examination of vendor invoices, it is often necessary to access vendor's internal records.

No discussion of vendor billing schemes is complete without mentioning intentional duplicate payments. Intentional duplicate payment schemes can occur in many different ways with many different combinations of opportunity. The illusion of a duplicate payment is the concealment strategy, some examples include when:

- A vendor submits multiple invoices to take advantage of poor internal controls.
- A vendor is intentionally paid twice, and then provides a kickback to the employee responsible for approving or processing the duplicate payment.
- A vendor is intentionally paid twice and, when requested to reimburse the company, the vendor's reimbursement for the duplicate payment is diverted.
- A vendor is intentionally paid twice by accounting, and the second payment is diverted by accounting personnel. The duplicate payment is part of the concealment strategy by the accounting staff.

Data mining for duplicate payments is easy when it involves direct matches on invoice numbers, invoice dates, or invoice amounts. The search can occur on invoice numbers that match numerically, but an alpha or special symbol that has been added to avoid the internal control will complicate that search. So, while performing a search purely on duplicate numbers would detect the scheme, there is extensive manual review of the invoices to eliminate false positives. If the accounts payable department processes a false invoice through an actual vendor account and diverts the payment, data mining can be performed that would focus on any anomaly with an invoice number, such as invoices not within the anticipated range and discrepancies with dates and invoice numbers. This is an effective method when the false invoices have alpha characters and the actual invoices are numerical only.

As with duplicate payment–based schemes, collusion with a vendor involving accounts payable is typically found when there is no recovery of credits for returns and adjustments from the vendor. These schemes typically occur between the end user and the vendor. If the item is an inventory item, matching inventory adjustments to the accounts payable file would detect the scheme. If the scheme is committed by someone in accounts payable, then aged-unapplied credits would be a data red flag. Otherwise, the scheme is an unrecorded item and does not lend itself to data mining procedures.

Speed-of-Disbursement Schemes

The cliché "timing is everything" applies here. Data mining searches involving dates are very useful with schemes relying on timing—for example, a search is done for vendors that routinely receive payment in a shorter period of time than normal payment terms. The aim of the search is to compare invoice dates with the check payment dates. If an invoice date is falsified in the system, comparing the record date to payment date would reveal the scheme.

This type of scheme may directly involve collusion with a vendor or it may not. For example, the temporary-holding scheme does not involve collusion with a vendor. In this scheme, the perpetrator wires the money to a temporary account that the perpetrator controls. The perpetrator holds the funds for a designated time period. During that time period, the perpetrator invests the funds, thereby earning income from the invested funds. After the holding period, the funds are wired to the actual intended vendor. While the scheme doesn't require collusion with a vendor, it does involve collusion, typically with a high-ranking employee in the finance department. The collusion could also occur within the organization or with a banker. The scheme is usually associated with one legitimate vendor that has a material amount of payments. Again, a data mining routine can be employed that focuses on timing, in this case, the comparison of the actual date to the vendor invoice data or the date the record was created. Specifically, the search is for a pattern and frequency of a disbursement within 15 days or less of the invoice date. The audit procedure for this scheme consists of a direct confirmation of the actual vendor's bank account number. This bank account number will not match the bank account number used by accounts payable. Also, a request should be made for the vendor to confirm the dates that the payment was received by them. Note any discrepancy where the vendor's receipt date is later than the accounts payable payment date.

Another type of timing scheme, this one involving collusion with a vendor, relates to early payment between a vendor and an internal employee. The early payment scheme operates on the assumption that the vendor pays a kickback for early payment of its invoice. Data mining searches aimed at comparing invoice dates and check dates as performed above with the temporary-holding scheme are effective with this variation as well.

Theft-of-Check Schemes

The primary type of theft-of-check schemes is predictable when there are checks clearing after being 60 days outstanding. Simply, a check that clears after 60 days outstanding is more likely to be stolen, indicating a check substitution scheme. The data mining search could be performed manually or automated. The manual version calls for reviewing bank reconciliations for outstanding checks that appear one month, but are not listed the second month. From a data mining perspective, obtain from the bank the detail of checks cleared during the month and compare the date on these checks to the date in the cash disbursement journal. Once the checks are identified, compare them. Either the face of the check will not match the cash disbursement journal or the endorsement will reveal a discrepancy.

Treasury Department Schemes

Temporary-holding schemes that do not involve collusion with a vendor, but collusion with a high-ranking financial officer, typically in an organization's treasury department, were discussed previously in the section on timing schemes because they are based on the time value of money notion we all learned in Econ 101. Similarly, foreign exchange schemes operate the same way in that they take advantage of swings in currency valuations when monies are wired internationally. Typically, all wire transfers of money are the responsibility of an organization's treasury department or treasury officer, which is why they are mentioned in this section. The data mining searches and audit procedures are similar to those discussed in the timing section.

Employee Reimbursement

False reimbursement schemes occur when an employee submits a request for reimbursement that the employee is entitled to receive based on company policy. Since the employee is entitled to the disbursement, data mining is not effective in the detection of the scheme.

The following two scenarios were meant to be illustrative of the type of scenarios the fraud auditor may detect:

Example 1: Specifically, the scheme occurs when the employee submits false documentation supporting the reimbursement request. In this scheme, either the event did not occur or the costs have been inflated by the false documents. Also, since the documentation is often comprised of photocopies of the original documents, for example, receipts, document examination is not usually effective in detecting the scheme unless the employee makes an overt alteration to the document.

Example 2: Another type of employee reimbursement scheme concerns employee status changes when said employee does not notify the organization of the change. For example, employees working outside of the country for a period of time, often referred to as expatriates, tend to receive various allowances associated with family. Typically, in order to receive the benefit, the employee's family joins the employee on the overseas assignment. Once the benefit starts, the family returns to their home, but the employee continues to receive the allowance. In this case, the nature of the allowance or reimbursement would determine the appropriate audit procedure. However, confirmation procedures with the service provider noted on the submitted documents is an apt audit procedure to follow in this case.

In reality, employee reimbursement schemes are driven by how the program operates. In my 30-plus years of auditing, I have enough stories to fill a book.

Extortion of Vendors

What discussion of fraud would be complete without including some extortion? Disbursement schemes involving extortion typically involve an internal employee withholding payment to a real vendor that has legitimately provided the goods or services. The scheme can occur in either of two ways, through operations personnel who hold the invoice on a false pretense or through accounting personnel who do not enter the invoice into the accounts payable file. The data mining search is the reverse of that discussed with timing schemes in that we are looking for invoices that are paid beyond normal terms. Detecting the scheme through data mining searches depends on whether the scheme occurred within the scope period because a vendor may have been paying a bribe for years to ensure the prompt payment of its invoices. Under this circumstance, these schemes are typically discovered through a vendor complaint.

 SUMMARY

Disbursement fraud is one of the most prevalent kinds of fraud, as is evidenced by the variation of schemes discussed in this chapter. The opportunity to embezzle cash seems the most tempting of all the frauds that can be committed, since it can occur with the theft very small amounts, where an employee views it as a benefit rather than theft. The analogy would be to view an organization as the human body. Disbursements are the circulatory system with cash being at the heart of the matter. Although the heart is not the largest muscle in the body, it is the most vital and, therefore, typically the first thing looked at when a health problem arises. So, the fraud auditor is the cardiologist who finds the leak or clog, whether big or small. The auditor's tools to fix the problem aren't a scalpel or sutures, but the determining of a fraud risk structure and implementing of the correct fraud audit procedures.

CHAPTER ELEVEN

Procurement Fraud

F RAUD IN THE PROCUREMENT process is always a worry for management and auditors alike because it involves the fraud risk category of corruption, and corruption may be just as nebulous as it sounds. One reason for this difficulty is that collusion is found in most corruption-related fraud schemes, and we know from our discussion in previous chapters that collusion typically involves internal and external parties. It is the external part of this exchange that is the most problematic because outside party records are not accessible to the auditor.

Procurement fraud, for the purposes of our discussion, refers to the corrupting of the purchase decision-making process to ensure a specific vendor is awarded the contract. With numerous differences in these decision-making processes existing, it is critical for the auditor to know the industry and the types of procurement activity that is distinctive to an industry. Throughout this book, we have discussed how fraud auditing operates best by digging down to a class of transactions level, so the auditor needs to go beyond the required bid documents in order to understand how the documents can be falsified (i.e., they are corrupted). Specifically, auditors need to understand the business, how to be overt in their audit procedures, how the business process can be corrupted, and how to locate and recognize a corrupted decision. The immediate discussion consists of examples of each of these points. They may seem like an oversimplification, but we don't want you to get bogged down in a lot of extraneous facts and miss the point.

Understanding a business sounds relatively simple, but an auditor needs more than just surface understanding. Now, we don't mean you go undercover and perform actual jobs to get that understanding. Here's an example of what we mean: Say a company entered into a contract with a printing company to publish an employee handbook for $100,000. The auditor's assessment of the internal controls indicated they were sound, so the auditor examined the bid file, noting three bids from three different companies. Even though all three bids were technically sound, and the company selected the lowest-price bid, the auditor knew the importance of economic substance was critical with these bids. With this factor in mind, it was found that two of three printers selected specialized in direct mail printing. Therefore, while the two printing companies had the capacity to print the employee manual, their printing equipment was not designed to print large quantities in a cost-effective manner. As a consequence, the auditor would have reported that the competitive bidding process was flawed because two vendors were not qualified for the printing project. In order to come to this conclusion, the auditor had to have enough understanding of the printing industry to know the capacity constraints.

In addition to understanding the industry, auditors need to be overt in their audit procedures. Now, you're thinking, fraud is covert, so why are auditors required to be overt in detecting it? What we mean is that auditors need to directly address the risk of fraud. Here's an example: Internal auditors identified that all of a company's advertising expenses associated with printing occurred through one print broker. The print broker used one printer for large runs and one printer for short runs. Based on further analysis, the auditors had determined that their company was the only client that the print broker serviced (i.e., a sole source). The auditors did a great job in identifying a potential fraud opportunity, yes? The answer may be no, since while the facts sounded suspicious, the sole source situation may just indicate a bad management decision. The auditors had to determine if collusion exists, whereby the print broker earned an inflated profit in order to pay a kickback to a company employee. Therefore, the auditors needed to request both the printer's invoice and the print broker's invoice for the job in order to compute a gross margin and associated profit percentage. If the gross profit is determined to be reasonable by printing industry standards, then the risk of procurement fraud is diminished in favor of the poor management decision outcome.

Auditors need to understand how the business process can be corrupted. Now you may ask if understanding the industry includes understanding how the business processes can be corrupted. What we are really talking about is not the corruption in the sense of diminishing the internal controls involving the procurement process, but rather recognizing problems with the process. For example, in a construction project, management opted to use a best and final offer competitive bid environment. The internal controls surrounding the process were excellent, with a high degree of redundancy and monitoring surrounding the process. At first glance, the control environment seemed impervious; however, one of the ways of circumventing the process was to issue a change order to the primary trade contractor providing plumbing services. Then an electrician was hired under the plumber's change order. This circumvention of the competitive bidding resulted in the electrician's receiving additional work at full rate versus at the competitive bid rate.

Along the same lines of business process corruption, auditors need to understand how to locate and recognize corrupt decision making. This recognition will depend on whether the business relationship is one-time or ongoing. In an ongoing business relationship, behavioral red flags become more evident. Also, there is a trend evident on pricing, whereby vendors' requests to bid and winning bid patterns become more obvious. For example, a company put its annual reporting printing out to bid. The auditor examined the bid file and all procedures were complied with and the lowest-price vendor was selected. Also, it was noted that the printer chosen had a good reputation for quality. However, upon examination of the three previous years' bidding process, the auditors learned that even though the same three vendors were requested to submit bids, the same vendor received the contract in each year. With one-time contracts, the auditor should search for a deviation from the process that could have provided the winning vendor a competitive advantage. If a competitive advantage is indiscernible, then a determination needs to be made if the other bidders were technically competent for the engagement.

FRAUD RISK STRUCTURE

If you haven't figured it out by now, corruption is the key element in procurement fraud. Corruption is defined as the destruction of the integrity in the decision process by an individual conducting business under their official capacity. From a legal perspective, laws around the world will have their own definition of a corrupt act. Corruption also has been categorized as either major or petty. Major corruption occurs when a required service would not be obtained without paying a sum of money to an individual, so major corruption has an element of extortion. Petty corruption, referred to as facilitation or grease payments, is designed to speed up a process that the individual is legally entitled to receive.

How corruption presents the opportunity for fraud is the question that needs to be answered. To find such an answer, we can focus on typical corruption–opportunity combinations found with procurement fraud, such as:

- Employee in collusion with a vendor.
- Vendors in collusion amongst themselves.
- Vendor alone.
- Employee alone.
- Directed by the customer of a cost-reimbursable contract.
- Foreign corrupt practice issues.

The Collusion–Corruption–Opportunity Connection

In building a fraud risk structure, the opportunity for corruption has to be recognized in determining the inherent fraud scheme. As seen in the preceding list, many of these situations involve collusion. For example, if it has been determined that the inherent fraud scheme entails false statements, then focus is on the employee in collusion with a vendor, whereby a concealment strategy could be the creation of bids in the name of two real vendors at amounts higher than the collusion-related vendor. Sometimes the fraud terms of *collusion, corruption, bribery, conflicts of interest,* and so on get used interchangeably or incorrectly because they are defined within varying context (e.g., legal). Hopefully, the examples given in this chapter's introduction and throughout the chapter will provide an effective working terminology of these concepts. We also have to mention other areas involving collusion that tend to get blurred in detecting corruption opportunities, these being favored vendors, nepotism, and discrimination.

Favored Vendor

With favored-vendor schemes, the selection process favors a vendor without proper disclosure and approval. Such a favored status may have occurred by the virtue of a personal relationship with company employees, prior employment with the company, or an extended business relationship with the company. The scheme occurs with the general knowledge of management, although usually there is no specific documentation showing management approval. There is no bribe or kickback, so the action element is a form of policy manipulation rather than an illegal act. Obviously, favored vendors may be viewed as a conflict of interest based on how company policies are written in regard to ethics. Often employees are required to recuse themselves from working with a vendor because of a preexisting relationship. For example, there's the situation where a government employee stated a conflict of interest and recused himself from a project because his daughter is employed by the consulting firm bidding on the job.

Nepotism and Discrimination

Nepotism is the process of hiring a vendor based on a family relationship. The benefit of such a hiring is not usually one of financial incentive, but rather the relationship presents an ease to collusion. On the surface, the relationship may provide an appearance of favoritism as described in the previous section. However, if in fact a financial incentive is the benefit, then a bribery scheme is highlighted. In the cases where employees act alone, many times companies will ask on an employment application if the person applying is related to anyone already employed there for the purposes of denoting the potential for nepotism.

Discrimination is the process of not considering a vendor or disqualifying a vendor based on a discriminating factor. At minimum, this practice will create adverse publicity for the organization. Clearly, discriminatory practices such as these are not performed with an economic benefit in mind.

Bribery, Kickbacks, and Extortion

So far our discussion has focused on the element of collusion and its role in the corruption–opportunity connection concerning procurement fraud; however, we don't wish to confuse fraud schemes that employ collusion with those that involve abject bribery. Bribery schemes occur when the perpetrators intend to corrupt the competitive bid process for economic gain. The challenge for the auditor is to gather sufficient evidence of the intent to deceive. "Intent" bears attention because direct evidence of the bribe cannot be established within the audit process. Auditors do not typically have access to the personal or business records necessary to establish that a bribe has been paid. However, in many bribe schemes there is an element of overbilling built into the process, and therefore, the existence of overbilling could provide circumstantial evidence that a bribe did occur.

Many times the concepts of bribery, kickbacks, and extortion become blurred especially in any discussion involving fraudulent behavior. For the purposes of our discussion of procurement fraud, all three include the element of corrupt decision making, but they differ as discussed in the following sections.

Bribery

Bribery is a price, reward, gift, or favor bestowed on or promised to an individual in order to pervert the judgment of, or influence the action of, a person in the position of trust. The types of bribery cases that immediately come to mind are those involving politicians who receive gifts or sizable campaign donations in exchange for awarding a governmental contract to a corporation. Even though our focus is on procurement, the elements of an exchange of favors and corrupt decision making are evident.

Kickbacks

A kickback is a return of a portion of a monetary sum received for the false administration of a contracted service or delivery of a good. Kickbacks are typically associated with vendor overbilling schemes, but they enter into our procurement discussion because of the element of contracts being corrupted.

Extortion

Extortion occurs when an employee obtains something of value from a vendor through coercion. It may also occur when a vendor coerces an employee to issue a contract to the vendor. Extortion differs from bribery and kickbacks because a mutual accord is missing due to outside agents such as intimidation, threats, and so on.

Data Analysis

Data analysis with regard to procurement fraud may appear simple; after all, the transactions for purchasing are rather centralized in any organization, aren't they? We have already discussed examples where economic substance of a transaction is a key analysis. A complexity factor is added with the determining of bad decision making from corrupt decision making in the procurement process. Knowing how the process operates per industry helps, but it's not a panacea, because if there is collusion, the auditor is barred from the outside party portion of the necessary data. So, the focus of our audit becomes the action element of procurement fraud schemes occurring with the corruption of processes or documents, especially contracts, or sometimes both. If we just concentrate on the transactional processes, then analysis of economic substance or data mining searches of purchase invoices will encompass the total of our data analysis. However, given the relationship of procurement and contracts, document examination becomes a part of our analysis as well. Performing data analysis like we did with overbilling schemes may lead auditors to end their search for fraud at that point, which in the case of procurement fraud would mean the effort will probably fall short. It is with this reasoning that our discussion of data analysis with regard to procurement fraud is directed at the auditor having knowledge of the inherent fraud schemes pertinent to procurement fraud as our starting point.

Bidding Corruption

Bidding is the point at which the procurement process is at its weakest. Vendors, employees, even customers can corrupt the bidding in a variety of ways.

Bid Avoidance   Bid avoidance is the structuring of the procurement process to circumvent or avoid standard bidding requirements. This isn't control avoidance as found with other areas of fraud, whereby a vendor has knowledge of an organization's controls and, therefore, knows how to avoid them. Instead, this is a situation of the tail wagging the dog, whereby those making the procurement decisions corrupt the structuring process to the point where only a particular vendor can be used. Types include:

- **Structured purchasing.** The process of issuing multiple purchase orders to the same vendor, where each order is individually below the bid threshold level, but the purchase orders exceed the control threshold in the aggregate. A data mining search routine similar to those used in cases of disbursement fraud can be employed. For example, search for purchase orders from a vendor, which in the aggregate exceed a dollar control level within a prescribed date range, but where each individual invoice is below the dollar control level.
- **Split bids.** The process of awarding two vendors a purchase order for the same product to avoid the control threshold, whereby the two vendors are controlled by a common parent. A data mining search routine can be developed for any purchase orders that have been split.

- **Contract amendment.** The process of awarding the vendor additional projects without following the competitive bid process. Typically, change orders occur for a variety of reasons, such as when an owner changes requirements, unforeseen circumstances, contractor recommends changes, and errors in the original requirements. Review of contracts for amendments is needed.
- **Sole source.** The process of procuring goods or services without using the normal, competitive bidding process. This implies that there is only one vendor that can provide the goods or services needed and that, in the end, competitive bidding would yield the same result. This type of situation is very difficult to detect and requires overview of the bidding process looking for any loopholes.
- **Exigency purchase.** Purchasing that is deemed urgent to bypass control thresholds and competitive bidding procedures. You need to answer the question of just what constitutes an emergency in the type of project taking place.

False Statements   False statements encompass creating false bid documents and using false or real company names on the bid documents, thereby corrupting them. Data mining routines as described in the data analysis section in Chapter 10 on disbursement fraud can be used in this situation as well, whereby real or false vendors are determined as are the associated false documents.

Favoring of Key Control Points   This is defined as establishment of a need by submitting a purchase order at peak demand times or under exigency conditions in order to increase the probability of paying a higher price for goods or services, thereby increasing vendor margins. The frequency of these events needs to be determined, such as just how many orders are processed during peak demand time or as urgently needed.

This also refers to specification settings, whereby the product/service specifications are designed to favor a certain vendor over others. Types include:

- Vagueness or lack of clarity in specifications allows for the vendor to bid in a manner that appears to be cost effective when in fact the pricing is higher than the other vendors. Assume the specifications call for a price per case. The industry standard is 48 units per case, when in fact the selected vendor is providing 24 units per case. The lack of clarity on the quantity per case allows the false awarding of the purchase order. The auditor should determine the industry standards for communicating specifications on quantity, quality, or product description or confirm the exact number being provided.

▪ Given that restrictive specifications favor the preselected vendor, the auditor should compare the selected vendor's sales literature to the request for proposal (RFP). If the RFP has a high degree of similarity to the vendor's sales catalog, it is likely that the bid was structured to favor the vendor.

Bidding Exclusion This scheme involves the identification of vendors that have the capacity to bid, then structuring the bidding process to exclude qualified vendors that would otherwise be ready, willing, and able to offer competitive pricing or include unqualified vendors to provide the illusion of competitive bidding. Examples include:

▪ Excluding qualified vendors by not including the vendor in the bidder's list. The auditor should search for other qualified vendors through trade associations, yellow pages, Web searches, or discussions with other subsidiaries or audit departments in similar industries. The use of Web postings for RFPs is an effective control to minimize the risk.

▪ Failure to mail or distribute RFPs as stated in the bid file. The auditor should confirm that all vendors on the list received the RFP. The use of Web-based postings of RFPs minimizes the risk of the scheme.

▪ Providing vendors with false or misleading RFPs to discourage the vendor from bidding on the purchase. The auditor should confirm with all the vendors on the list that they received the same RFP.

▪ Limiting the search for qualifying vendors. The process places arbitrary limits on the geographic boundaries on the vendor search. The auditor should corroborate the business need for the limits established.

▪ Dissimilar vendors to provide illusion of search. The vendor name, SIC code, or company description indicates that the vendor is a comparable source when in fact the vendor business structure is not consistent with the true needs of the company.

Vendor Selection

These schemes involve the changing of procurement processing criteria, either the evaluation of vendors for selection or the actual selection process.

Vendor-Evaluation Criteria Manipulation   There are numerous ways the criteria for evaluating vendors can be manipulated to favor certain vendors over others. Some of these ways include:

- A vendor criterion is established to favor the selected vendor. With advanced communication, the vendor can respond in a manner to maximize the existing criteria. The auditor should determine if the criterion is valid or created to favor the vendor.
- The vendor criteria are established after the bid opening. The auditor should establish when the vendor criteria were established.
- Request for proposals have intentional defects that are known to the favored vendor.
- Vendor prepares specifications. It was known that the vendor establishes the RFP, and then bids on the contract.
- After the fact, financial adjustments due to specifications. The key here is that the select vendor has prior knowledge of the financial adjustments, which allows the vendor to bid arbitrarily low.

Vendor-Selection Process Manipulation   These schemes involve the actual selection process and the ways such processes can be manipulated to select particular vendors over others. Examples include:

- Vendor bypasses normal review process.
- Communicating other vendors' pricing information to the favored vendor. Pricing information should never be disclosed unless the terms of the RFP indicated that a price negotiation phase will follow the submission phase. If price disclosure occurs, the auditor should determine that all vendors had an equal opportunity to reconsider their pricing based on the competition's pricing. In reality, the practice encourages vendors to submit higher prices on the original quote.
- Lost bids or information: The purchasing agent destroys a vendor's submission of a bid. The auditor should contact vendors on the RFP that did not submit a bid and confirm the fact. It is also a good idea to inquire about the reasons the vendor did not submit a bid.
- False calculations of vendors' cost. In reality, cost calculations are not as simple as one unit price multiplied by a quantity. In those instances where multiple price considerations exist, the auditor should recompute the anticipated costs.
- Vendor selection criteria favor a specific vendor via the selection process.

- Creating criteria after bid opening.
- Changed criteria after bid opening.
- Scoring system favors a specific vendor.
- False statements regarding vendor assessment.

Management Override These schemes influence vendor selection when management intentionally authorizes the selection of a vendor. This scheme occurs when management bypasses control procedures or authorizes the selection of a vendor not having the best overall price.

Advance Communication of Information An employee with knowledge of the selection requirements or future requirements or changes provides information to one vendor to the detriment of other vendors. The changes typically relate to either actual needs versus projected needs or future changes.

Vendor Corruption

Vendor bid rigging is the process of vendors colluding among themselves to determine which one will be awarded the contract and what price. These schemes do not usually involve internal employees and are perpetrated without knowledge of management. The schemes include:

- Unresponsive bids to provide the impression of competitive bidding where, in reality, suppliers agree to submit token bids that are usually too high.
- Bid suppression is agreed upon among suppliers either to abstain from bidding or to withdraw bids. The vendors know the company has to get its supplies from someone, thus, by suppressing the bids, they inflate the bidding in the long-run.
- Bid rotation is employed, whereby the preselected supplier submits the lowest bid on a systematic or rotating basis. This fraud happens when there are like projects up for bid on a continual basis. Instead of harming profits by bidding low, vendors collude to ensure high bids are received. The scheme depends on the bids being high enough to offset the awarding of projects at low bid in the aggregate.
- Market division is an arrangement among suppliers not to compete in designated geographic regions or for specific customers. You tend to see this type of fraud happening where corporations split up the country because of distribution routes. Less shipping time and distance means higher profits.

Vendors-in-Collusion Characteristics   There are certain characteristics associated with both vendors in collusion and vendors corrupting purchasing agent decision making. Specifically:

- The same company always is awarded a particular bid. Suspicion arises if one or more companies continually submit unsuccessful bids.
- The same suppliers submit bids, and each company seems to take a turn being the successful bidder.
- Some bids are much higher than published price lists, previous bids by the same firms, or engineering cost estimates.
- Fewer than normal bids are submitted.
- A company appears to be bidding substantially higher on some bids than on other bids, with no apparent cost differences to account for the disparity.
- Bid prices drop whenever a new or infrequent bidder submits a bid.
- A successful bidder subcontracts work to competitors that submitted unsuccessful bids on the same project.
- A company withdraws its successful bid only to be subcontracted work by the bid-awarded contractor.

Collusion and Vendor Bid Rigging   There are several noticeable economic aspects where vendor bid rigging becomes more probable. For example, collusion is more likely to occur if there are few sellers. The fewer the number of sellers, the easier it is for them to get together and agree on prices, bids, customers, or territories. Collusion may also occur when the number of firms is fairly large, but there is a small group of major sellers and the rest are "fringe" sellers who control only a small fraction of the market. Also, the probability of collusion's occurring increases if other products cannot easily be substituted for the product in question or if there are restrictive specifications for the product being procured. The more standardized a product is, the easier it is for competing firms to reach agreement on a common price structure. Design, features, quality, or service are all items that increase competitiveness.

Repetitive purchases may increase the chance of collusion, because the vendors may become familiar with other bidders, and future contracts provide the opportunity for competitors to share the work. Additionally, collusion is more likely if the competitors know each other well through social connections, trade associations, legitimate business contacts, or shifting employment from one company to another. Also, bidders who congregate in the same building or town to submit their bids have an easy opportunity for last-minute communications.

Vendor Collusion and Pricing Fixing   We would be remiss in our discussion of vendors in collusion without mentioning price fixing directly. Price fixing is the main ingredient in many of the vendors-in-collusion-driven schemes described because it is an agreement among vendors to control the prices at which they sell their goods or services. There are many forms of price fixing that can take place in these schemes, such as establishing, eliminating, or reducing pricing discounts; adopting a standard formula for computing prices; maintaining certain price differentials between different types, sizes, or quantities of products, and pretty much any manner of dissolving a competitive difference between vendors.

Vendor-Alone   Two schemes are predominantly found with vendor-alone bid rigging: the defective pricing schemes and conflict-of-interest schemes. Defective pricing is the intentional falsification of or an inaccurate submission of information regarding costs or prices in reference to a contract. Simply stated, it is the intentional understatement of costs, by the vendor, for the sole purpose of winning the contract, generally with the intent of later increasing the costs through change orders. Conflict of interest is, as discussed previously, where an employee has a covert interest in a vendor conducting business with their company. Again, focus is on overbilling.

Employee-Alone Procurement Corruption

Three schemes are often operated by employees acting alone. One involves disguised purchases, whereby an employee procures an item for his or her personal use. Now, we obviously aren't talking about petty office supplies here; however, the item may have the appearance that it will be used for business purposes. The conversion is hidden through purchase documentation that was created or altered to present a false description. These tactics are usually implemented through employee credit cards.

Another scheme involves an employee's procuring an item that is consistent with his or her job, only to sell it for personal gain. The scheme may seem similar to a theft scheme; however, the difference lies with the person diverting the item for resale being the same person authorized to procure the item. The item may be physically received by the company or the item may be shipped directly to the resale point. The red flag is that total purchases exceed the needs of the company.

A conflict of interest occurs when an employee has an undisclosed legal or beneficial interest in the vendor. The employee either directly or indirectly causes purchase orders or contracts to be issued to the vendor. The scheme also may involve overbilling; however, it is suggested not to mix the two schemes. Interestingly, it is more likely that a conflict of interest will be uncovered through overbilling audit procedures than through conflict-of-interest audit procedures.

Customer Directed

In cost-reimbursable contracts there are two parties: the customer and the company awarded the contract for goods or services, referred to as the supplier. In this fraud scheme, an employee directs the supplier to use a specific vendor, referred to as the subcontractor to the supplier. The supplier procures goods or services from the subcontractor at the price dictated by the employee. A kickback occurs between the customer and the subcontractor. The supplier may or may not be involved in the scheme, but does at a minimum serve as a conduit to the fraud scheme.

Foreign Corruption Practices Act (FCPA)

For the most part, our discussion of procurement fraud has concerned corruption against an organization. The FCPA focuses on corrupt acts committed by an organization to further its interests. The law addresses issues of who is covered by the law, what is prohibited, what is allowed, exceptions, and defenses to the law. The internal auditor should be alert to the red flags of FCPA violations in order to bring such issues to management's attention in the appropriate manner. Some of these red flags are:

- Commission payments that exceed company or industry standard.
- The subsequent structuring of the payment into multiple foreign bank accounts.
- Payments to shell corporations or entities that have no apparent qualifications or sufficient business history.
- Contracts that do not contain standard anticorruption provisions.
- Lack of transparency in expenses and accounting records.
- Payments to consultants that were recommended by a government official.

Contracts and Procurement Fraud

One cannot discuss procurement fraud without mentioning contracts, because when one typically thinks of procurement, he thinks of those procurement departments in large multi-international corporations that manufacture items like airplanes, wind turbines, supercomputers, and so on. Even though we have discussed construction projects, we have pretty much ignored contracts to this point because our focus was not on fraud occurring in procurement departments per se, but rather bidding-intense schemes and the schemes involving any employee authorized to purchase goods and/or services. Also, it may seem to auditors that they might need an attorney on the audit team because of the amount of documentation examination involved with detecting procurement fraud through the abuse of contracts. However, the attitude must prevail that, where there are contracts, there is the likelihood of fraud. Knowing the types of schemes inherent to large projects or purchases requiring contracts provides the auditor with the necessary skills to tackle this fraud. There are schemes specific to procurement on a large scale, as discussed in the following sections.

Progress Payment Fraud

Progress payment fraud occurs when a contractor applies for payment during the course of a contract. The contractor fraudulently certifies that costs were incurred that are eligible for reimbursement or fraudulently certifies that no encumbrances exist when, in fact, they do; or the contractor falsifies the percentage or stage of completion. Two potential negative outcomes occur, one involving the time value of the money, and the other is when the contractor files bankruptcy, thereby failing to complete the work consistent with the stage of payment. It should be noted that in construction projects, when a contractor fails to pay a subcontractor, a legal liability is created. It is for this reason that the obtaining of a partial lien waiver at the time of the progress payment becomes an important control to have in place.

Nonconforming Materials

These schemes involve a contractor's substituting goods or services that do not conform to those specified in the contract. These goods may be knockoffs, defective, or may even contain hazardous materials. Even the "made in country" labels may be false. Think of the recent toy recalls where paint containing lead was used. Now, clearly, these cases would be the responsibility of regulatory agencies, but the auditor can inquire as to management's quality assurance controls to ensure the schemes are not occurring.

Cost Mischarging

Cost mischarging occurs when costs not allowable under the contract occur. The following is a list of schemes indicative of mischarging:

- Fictitious charges and overbilling schemes with the difference being that these schemes are located in the procurement process, which requires additional digging by the auditor.
- Charge not allowed under the contract. This scheme requires document examination by the auditor, who has to know how contracts are structured for the organization. If charges are automatically processed, then a data mining search routine can be implemented looking for charges that perhaps are coded differently or are atypical for the vendor.
- Contract specific. A contract typically has terms and conditions that bind both parties to it. In this situation, the expenditure was either specifically excluded or not specifically identified in the contract.
- Contract interpretation. A situation where the contract language may have different interpretations. One case that comes to mind involves the building of a dementia unit in a religious-affiliated nursing home. The CEO, who happened to be a nun also, asked if an altar could be purchased for the meditation room, considering that the loan agreement allowed for the purchase of tables. In her mind, an altar constituted a table, but to the bankers, the contract stipulated tables. Thus, the altar had to be purchased with funding from donations to the project and nothing fraudulent occurred. Thank heaven.
- Contract references to governing rules and regulations and cost principles that determine the allowability of a charge. Many times, large construction projects rely on government bond issuances, and with public funding, no matter how partial the funding is, there are specific rules, regulations, and cost principles that have to be followed. Of course, with the large monetary amounts needed to fund these types of projects, the temptation to commit fraudulent acts also exists. Just pick up a newspaper on any day and there is probably a story involving these types of schemes.

- "Whereas" clauses also provide a gray area because with every rule there is an exception. For our purposes, we have to ask if those exceptions are allowed.
- Charges not related to the contract. The expenditure did in fact occur, but the goods or services did not relate to the contract. Given the size of projects requiring extensive contracts, there is also the opportunity to hide things, sometimes expensive personal-use things.
- Charge improperly allocated to the contract. The expenditure did in fact occur, but a percentage of the charge allocated to the contract exceeded the effort associated with the charge. Payroll costs are often associated with this scheme, and therefore, a data mining search routine may be helpful.
- Charge is part of indirect cost. Often, contracts will allow for the cost of administering the contract. The contract charges may be a percentage calculation, actual costs, or an indirect cost rate. Indirect costs can be a real headache because each cost may be calculated in a different manner. Therefore, the auditor needs to know how each indirect cost is calculated before searching for anomalies.

AUDIT PROCEDURES

We have belabored the point that procurement fraud is associated with the corruption of the purchasing decision-making process. Whether it is a matter of vendors manipulating purchase documents or abuse of contracts, something is being corrupted for a benefit that is not warranted. So, what audit procedures need to be followed to detect corruption? First, the auditor has to obtain knowledge of the procurement processes found in the organization, then employ all the tools she has to detect it. When discussing all the types of schemes associated with procurement as we have in this chapter, we find with such an assortment that one single approach isn't going to cut it. We have to dig, and dig deep. It's time to drop the shovels, folks, and bring out the heavy equipment.

Audit Approach Steps

We have discussed that collusion, as it is found with the procurement process, focuses on vendors. Bribery, kickbacks, and extortion are secondary concepts to collusion. The same logic that we employed in determining whether an entity was real or false applies. However, in this situation, the determination is whether the procurement process was corrupted. To answer this question, here are five simplified audit approach steps:

1. To show how the purchase decision-making process was corrupted, the auditor needs to establish that the representation made by the purchaser was false.
2. Determine that the purchaser knew that the representation was false. Does the purchaser acknowledge that the representation is false or that he should have known it was false?
3. Can a connection be found between vendor and employee-purchaser? We have already discussed just how difficult it is to make this connection, primarily because of a lack of access to outside vendor records. However, instead of being deterred by this roadblock, the auditor needs to dig as much as possible into the employee's actions, as they are documented, to uncover the opportunity for collusion.
4. Determine whether the employee did receive a financial incentive to award the contract from the vendor. This step appears to be the simplest, given that in all probability, we clearly know who has contract authority.
5. Last, establish that the financial incentive did in fact corrupt the purchasing decision. The quid pro quo.

Fraud Red Flags and Audit Procedures

We stated that procurement fraud necessitates that the auditor use all the available fraud-detecting skills available. This means that data mining searches are needed to locate where corruption can be taking place within the procurement system, then the use of fraud audit procedures, which includes recognition of the fraud red flags associated with the inherent procurement fraud scheme. When it comes to red flags, now may be the time to have "the talk." The red flags of fraud talk. We have seemingly bandied about various categories and types of fraud red flags throughout this book, and the very term *red flag* has become a part of the general lexicon. It is this categorizing of a generality that causes us to pause, and perhaps regroup. Remember, instead of sampling and testing as with traditional audit programs, a fraud audit program requires steps to locate and recognize fraud. We do these things by being aware of the red flags particular to the fraud scenario we have located and recognized.

Also, remember, that the noun *corruption* is a primary classification of fraud, and the act of corrupting is described as a secondary classification of fraud, while our given in procurement fraud schemes is the corruption of purchase decision making. Now that we have established that linking, we can approach procurement fraud schemes by breaking corruption into three areas for discussion: bidding corruption, vendor corruption, and employee corruption.

Bidding Corruption Schemes

We have already discussed bidding corruption schemes as involving bid avoidance, false statements, favoring at key control points, and management overrides. Now here are some definitive audit approach steps to take with each.

Bid Avoidance   Data mining is used in a fraud audit program to locate fraud because it tends to be highly effective in detecting the patterns and frequencies. With that rational in mind, the key data mining fields for bid avoidance are the following:

■ Commodity code: An alphanumeric system designed to identify products and services. We want to identify purchases in the aggregate that require a bidding process.
■ NAICS codes: Codes developed by the Office of Management and Budget, which replaced the SIC code, to classify businesses. We perform this data mining search routine to identify when multiple vendors are used to circumvent a bid level.
■ Bid codes: These codes help identify the types of bids used by an organization, for example, sole source vendor bidding or system-wide contract bidding. This code is critical, but seldom found in procurement systems. If the code does exist, it should be the first recommendation in the auditor's report.
■ Buyer name: Data mining search routines of buyer names can reveal a pattern of purchasing by an individual. We are trying to locate the points of opportunity by doing such a search.
■ Line item detail: The vendor invoice obviously contains a history of purchases. If the information is accurately entered into the system, such as unit pricing, number of units, product code, and product description, then reports can be created to identify bid avoidance on a vendor

level. Once a vendor has been identified and if accessible, the vendor's sales reporting system can typically provide the same detail.

- Linking the purchase order detail to the invoice detail is a relatively easy report to generate through data mining searches because the information is readily available, and it should highlight any anomalies, patterns, or frequencies between the two types of source documents.
- If all else fails, then performing a data mining search routine using general ledger codes may work. Unfortunately, this process may require an extensive manual review of the activity involving common purchases.

False Statements   Given that these schemes involve written bids that were corrupted, data mining routines are somewhat ineffective because the fraud is in the documents themselves. The exception would be in searching for a pattern of favoritism in the bidding process over an extended period of time. Data mining search routines could also help in identifying all purchases that exceed the bid level.

The fraud red flags involve document examination, specifically, the commonality of the bids as to paper type, font size and style of the print, layout of the documents, and errors in the documents. In addition to examining document-to-document, a visit to the vendor's web site may reveal inconsistencies in information, whereby you have to question whether the vendor actually provides the product or service. One last testing procedure would entail matching the information submitted by the bid-winning vendor with that provided on the losing bidders' documentation.

Favoring at Key Points   The fraud audit approach requires the auditor to have an understanding of the products regularly purchased by an organization in order to recognize any peculiarities (e.g., a vague product description is a red flag indicating bid rigging). Clearly, the auditor will not recognize a vague description without knowing the industry standards of the purchased item.

Management Override   Data mining tends to be less effective in cases involving management overrides because the fraud is hidden in the decision-making process. Also, depending on the sophistication, the documents may not contain one red flag. Now, what do we do, you ask? Well, there's always the interviewing of individuals involved in the procurement process. Often, in a management override situation, employees are uncomfortable being interviewed because they don't want to be implicated when it is their supervisor who participated in the bid rigging. Therefore, the auditor needs to display those finely honed interviewing skills to ask the right questions in the right manner. Yes, it makes one tend to long for the days of the three-martini business lunch, but regardless of the setting, the following types of questions are a good start:

- Has a senior member of management been overly involved in the purchasing process?
- Has a senior member of management encouraged the use of a specific vendor?

Vendor Corruption Schemes

Just to clarify a point, when distinguishing between real and false vendors in the area of procurement fraud, we don't imply that it is the same as determining real and false entities as a first step in the audit approach as was done in other areas of fraud schemes, like disbursements. We don't want to go down the wrong road here and spend all of our efforts in determining whether a vendor is real or false because our focus is on whether the vendor is corrupting the purchasing process.

Predetermined Pricing   This inherent scheme is the most difficult to detect because all parties to the purchasing transaction are participating in the scheme. The inherent scheme is similar to bid rigging because of the element of collusion. The concealment strategy is having the documentation on file supporting the awarding of the contract. The following red flags may be evident:

- Pricing on losing bids is extremely close to the winning bid, or the losing bids are round amounts, whereas the winning bid is an odd amount.
- Over a period of time, there will be a pattern for similar purchases, where the same vendor receives the contract and the same vendors do not.
- Is there an overall pattern found with the bidding for a variety of contracts where the same vendor is awarded the job and the same vendor or vendors lose it?

Advance Communication of Information   These schemes involve providing a vendor with a competitive advantage. This advantage may be providing additional time to prepare the bids. As with any fraud involving timing, a good place to look is with vendor-sent e-mails. Searching subjects lines that may contain the project name or provide some reference to a bid proposal deadline are a good starting point. If the information concerns future changes, a data mining routine would be performed to identify all expenditures associated with the contract in order to detect differences between expenditure date and change date.

Another area of detecting advanced communication of information involves any discrepancies in purchase-projection amounts and actual purchase amounts. In this situation, a postexpenditure analysis that compares the actual quantity purchased to the projected quantity should be performed. If there is a significant difference, the next step is to identify intent, whereby the auditor needs to establish whether the manager knew or should have known that the bid projections were understated.

Favored Vendors   The data mining routines performed to determine false entities also can be applied in detecting favored vendors. The favored vendors we are referring to in this instance are vendors with one customer. This type of scheme is usually an overbilling one occurring in the procurement process.

Vendors in Collusion   This inherent scheme is extremely difficult to detect, so it generally becomes known through whistleblowers. The previous red flags may indicate a fact pattern that is suggestive of vendor bid rigging. If the auditor believes there is creditable evidence of vendors operating in collusion, the audit process should convert to an investigation within the legal sense of the word.

Vendor Alone   There are several areas of schemes that involve vendors working alone as opposed to being in collusion. However, that does not mean there is no collusion going on, as you can determine with the brief descriptions of the audit approaches employed in the schemes that follow:

- **Defective pricing.** The scheme operates through the submission of either false documents supporting the cost assertions or pricing information that is not correct for the current marketplace. It's all about the price in either case, but in the latter, the acceptance of pricing information may indicate collusion between vendor and employee(s). The auditor will need to validate the pricing information with the specific vendor or through marketplace pricing information.

- **Conflict of interest.** The fraud audit procedures associated with determining false entities may disclose a conflict if an internal employee lists his own name or address on the incorporating papers. The auditor's success in detecting this scheme will depend upon their understanding of how to use public records. Typically, corporation records filed with a secretary of state list the registrar name and the officers of the corporation. Therefore, the information, being self-reported by the registrar, is not verified by the governmental agency.
- **Price fixing.** The nature of a price-fixing scheme dictates the appropriate audit procedures. Vendor web sites are an excellent source in determining if the vendor's pricing is consistent for the project being bid on. Vendor sales catalogs may also provide such pricing information. The auditor needs to research the pricing over an extended period of time to account for economic factors that influence pricing. Therefore, the audit procedure is to look for any pricing anomalies that are inconsistent with market trends.

Employee Corruption

Procurement fraud schemes involving the employee alone typically focus on the concealment strategy. The employee disguises the purchasing documentation, thereby corrupting it. The audit procedures needed to detect such schemes are discussed in the following sections.

Disguised Purchasing These schemes refer to when an employee purchases items in the course of business for personal use. The data mining search routines should focus on key words in the document text, vendor names (no, we won't name names, but you could probably think of a few off the top of your head) that would indicate a nonbusiness purpose, and a frequency that exceeds the normal buying pattern for the employee. Often, the vendor name is sufficient enough to flag a potential problem area.

Disguised Purchasing and Resale This scheme is similar to the disguised purchasing one; however, instead of personal use, the objective is personal gain through resale. Greed plays a major role in this scheme, so data mining search routines are performed that will identify purchases by specific commodity code, including the dollar amounts and volume purchased. Another area to consider is finding out exactly what the company purchases on a regular basis that would have value for resale.

When the goods purchased are controlled through inventory records, then the auditor should focus on usage. However, the scheme typically operates with supply items where the usage records most likely do not exist. Therefore, the auditor will need to start with the purchased item and determine where and how it was used. We want to find out if the quantity purchased is consistent with the quantity needed and utilized.

Other Agents of Corruption

Corruption of the procurement process does not just involve vendors and employees; that would be too easy now. Think of the procurement process. Who is involved? The vendor supplies the product to the company, and then the company uses the product in the development of another product, which is eventually sold to a customer. So, vendors can corrupt the process, and employees of the company who are authorized to make purchases can corrupt the process, and finally, the customer can corrupt the process. The main scheme that involves the customer typically occurs with cost reimbursable contracts. Therefore, the auditor should focus on both expenditures as they apply to cost reimbursable contracts and any vendors added to the master file during the contract period. If there are any matches, an interview with the purchasing employees may reveal the most significant red flag, that being when an employee informs the auditor that a customer recommended the vendor in question.

 SUMMARY

If you remember one thing from our discussion of procurement fraud, please remember that it involves the corruption of the purchasing decision making and, subsequently, the manipulation of the procurement process. The intricacies of the inherent fraud schemes depend on whether the focus is on the procurement department or simply those authorized to make purchases. Typically, there are contracts involved, and their complexity is directly proportional to the size of the project. Someone quipped that you need to just look for where the lawyers are circling.

The fraud auditors will need use of all their detection tools in finding procurement fraud, such as knowledge of the industry, knowledge of the procurement process, data mining searches, document examination, and even, dare we state it, contract law. Two difficulties are evident. One is the inability to access outside agent records, specifically, those of the vendors. Another is the auditor's not digging deeply enough and perhaps even stopping with the first fraud scheme that appears evident, even though it may not be inherent to procurement. Don't think of corruption as a gelatin-like concept that's too slippery to get hold of and therefore undetectable. Remember, it's out there, hiding like all the others.

CHAPTER TWELVE

Payroll Fraud

I N TERMS OF THREAT likelihood, the chance of fraud's occurring in the payroll process is very high, with one or more instances per year. Any employee filling out a time card has the opportunity to falsify the hours worked. What compounds the problem is that supervisors tend to develop close personal relationships with the employees they supervise, so they may look the other way when hours are falsified to help an employee going through difficult times or just to keep good employees. Perhaps they just do not believe it can happen based on the mutual respect that has been reached in their supervisor–subordinate relationship. Conversely, if the relationship is a bad one, a supervisor may spend a considerable amount of time supervising employees versus work flow. Even though it's a common occurrence, most payroll fraud will not have a material impact on the organization. The exception, of course, is with smaller companies where payroll tends to be the largest expense.

When it comes to business systems, no other system is bypassed as much as payroll, because there are typically numerous proliferations of "unofficial" systems that seem to spring from the "official" one. Everyone on the payroll knows the system and, therefore, knows the controls in place. This knowledge lends itself to the bypassing of the controls. The opportunity to circumvent the controls is too easy, and once one person does it, of course, everyone follows and the unofficial becomes the official to everyone's way of thinking.

The conflict between practice and intent makes the fraud difficult to identify. For example, a professor needs someone to work on a research project he is conducting. He identifies a student in class who would be perfect for the job, and asks her if she is interested in working on it. Once she is told how much the job will pay, the student agrees and starts work immediately. The professor/supervisor completes all the paperwork and submits it to human resources. Two weeks later, the student/employee receives her first paycheck. All the controls appeared to be in compliance from a documentation standpoint. However, the fact of the matter is that most of the controls were circumvented. For one thing, having the professor responsible for directly hiring people opens the door to establish ghost employees on the payroll. What if the professor, having a multimillion-dollar research grant and under outside pressures from a gambling addiction, is tempted to use his knowledge of payroll controls to obtain nonexisting employees' salaries in order to get a larger portion of the grant pie, as it were?

With these "unofficial" systems, it can be difficult to distinguish whether payroll circumvention is indeed fraudulent. For example, a company with many subsidiaries initiated a salary freeze due to the bad economy. However, within the company, certain departments or units had a profitable year and so to circumvent the salary freeze, those employees were awarded bonuses in lieu of salary increases for the year. Obviously, the salary freeze said nothing about bonuses, but what was the intent of the freeze?

 FRAUD RISK STRUCTURE

A fraud audit focuses on payroll fraud differently than with disbursement fraud where we start with searching for real/false entities. Oh, sure, you're thinking, this after 11 chapters of pounding into our heads: determine if it's a real or false entity. Before you get your ledgers in a bunch, let's explain why entity type is not first priority. The entity structure is not as critical as with the vendors because most payroll fraud schemes involve real employees. With payroll, we are working with a classification of inherent schemes: ghost employees and compensation-falsifying schemes. Therefore, analyzing opportunity becomes the starting point of predicting how inherent schemes could occur in the payroll system. Overall, the predictability factor for ghost employees is strong as compared to compensation fraud. Compensation fraud, like overtime schemes, is more people related versus having knowledge of control circumvention. Regardless of whether the schemes involve fictitious employees or falsifying compensation, data mining routines are needed, but on a more complex basis than those used with disbursement fraud.

Speaking of disbursement fraud, the operative question there concerned the "when" of the fraud's occurring, while in the case of payroll fraud, the operative question is "who" is committing the fraud. Is it an individual or an organizational unit? Although fraud committed by one person is just as common as fraud committed by a group of people, there are cases, as with the disguised compensation scheme, where the entire organizational unit may be benefiting from the fraud scenario.

Data mining searches by simply examining the payroll database may not be effective in identifying fraudulent transactions. Overtime fraud cannot be detected by examining the payroll database unless the employee is claiming a noticeably excessive amount of hours. It might be more effective to match the payroll database to a security access one, whereby you can identify any employees whose reported hours differ between those listed in each of the databases. It is recommended that you select one inherent scheme and then develop the data mining search accordingly. The volume of data contained in payroll systems is always a challenge as you find that necessary details become buried within a variety of places. Also, the document phase of the examination may not be effective because of how the fraud scenario occurs and the level of collusion present. For example, in many overtime schemes, the time card will be consistent with the hours paid. Therefore, detecting overtime fraud through time card examination will not be successful unless the time card has been visibility altered.

Terminology

In the hopes that the definitions section in Chapter 10 helped you weave your way through the discussion on disbursement fraud, the following is a similar list, but these definitions pertain to payroll fraud, of course.

Ghost employees are individuals listed in the payroll register who are not providing services, but who are receiving a paycheck. Some types include:

- **Fictitious ghost employee.** A nonexistent employee placed on a payroll, allowing the supervisor to falsify time reporting and divert the employee pay.
- **Terminated ghost employee.** An employee who exists at the time of hire, but is terminated without notifying human resources. At the time of the audit, the employee may be:

- ▪ Terminated in the system by the supervisor or at the supervisor's request after the supervisor has decided to stop perpetrating the scheme.
- ▪ Not terminated in the system and still being used to perpetrate the scheme.
- ▪ **No-show ghost employee.** An employee who is a real person, but not one who provides actual services to the company. The employee may or may not be in collusion with the supervisor carrying out the scheme.
- ▪ **Preemployment ghost employee.** An employee whom the supervisor places on payroll prior to the commencement of work.
- ▪ **Temporary ghost employee.** A type of employee who bypasses the normal hiring procedures due to the nature of being a temporary hire.
- ▪ **Family ghost employee.** A family member placed on payroll who provides no actual services to the company.
- ▪ **Rehired ghost employee.** A staff member who has been terminated and, at a later date, is placed back on payroll as a current employee.

Payroll adjustments and allowances are any changes to the database fields or subsystems in the payroll function that allow for changes to compensation. Some types include:

- ▪ **Salary adjustment.** A database field allowing manually calculated lump-sum adjustments to payroll calculations.
- ▪ **Other salary adjustment.** A database field allowing payments to an employee for various reimbursements.
- ▪ **Other compensation.** Various data fields influencing retirement, health benefits, and personal leave calculations.

Data Analysis

Many of the same tests used on the vendor master file in previously discussed data mining routines will provide similar results for payroll (e.g., duplicate address searches will work in searching for employees). However, expanding the analysis to include payroll-related databases is needed, of course (e.g., data mining routines on employee master file data elements may detect several different ghost employee schemes, while searching payroll databases is necessary for salary adjustment or overtime schemes). Again, it is up to the auditor to interpret the data in determining which inherent scheme is most likely occurring.

Challenges in Data Mining for Payroll Fraud

Data mining searches in payroll-related databases are necessary to detect fraud within that system; however, because of the high volume of data that exists in these databases, there are challenges in performing such searches. The following list highlights some of these challenges:

- A high volume of false positives may occur. A search for duplicate bank account numbers is a good routine to use for ghost employee detection; however, the search routine may produce many duplicate account numbers if there are members of the same family employed by the company and they use the same bank account for their direct deposit.
- Privacy concerns associated with downloading data into a nonsecure environment. There have been enough high-profile cases involving identity theft on a mass level that should convince anyone using information as sensitive as that found in payroll and personnel systems to use the highest of security protocols with the data.
- Matching payroll data to other databases to verify work performance is a critical step in any payroll data mining routine. Problems do tend to occur whenever you try to link two or more databases. The most prevalent of these problems is when different class codes and line numbers are used for the same information.

Overall, you have to be aware that certain schemes are just not detectable through the use of data mining. Some routines will not produce a positive hit on a fraud scheme, but rather a group of employees that fit the fraud profile. So, the auditor will still need to make a judgmental sample.

For every data mining routine we develop, a certain class of nonfraudulent transactions will be linked to the analysis. For example, in comparing the hours paid to the hours worked via a computer security access log is not going to work if the employees do not use a computer workstation as a part of their job duties. Therefore, any work performance testing may require stratification (i.e., multiple routines are needed to be performed sequentially so that one set of results is used in a subsequent search to arrive at groupings or classes).

To complicate things even more, payroll data typically has two levels, the first comprised of summary data fields, such as gross payroll or total hours worked for the calendar year, and the second, the payroll register level, contains all the detail regarding the actual payment of wages. So, once again multiple search routines may be required matching data to subdata.

Data Mining Planning

With those stipulations in mind, data mining must be performed to detect fraud schemes in the core payroll business systems; thus, careful planning is required. The first step in creating a data mining plan is to understand how the payroll system calculates a paycheck and how the data comprising the calculations are stored:

- Gross pay entails two sets of calculations. The first is the calculation of gross pay based on hours, piece work, or annual salary. The second calculation is the salary adjustments, which increase gross pay within a specific payroll period.
- Net pay also entails two sets of calculations. The first is the net pay calculation resulting from wages. The second is the identification of all adjustments to the net pay. Payroll systems may have fields or transaction types that are added to the net payroll calculation (e.g., reimbursement for expenses).
- Employees have numerous deductions from their paychecks for items, such as taxes, health, retirement benefits, and various other voluntary deductions. The payroll system either calculates the deduction or the deduction is manually entered into the system. The adjustments are either recurring or one-time, and they provide opportunities to increase net pay.
- The calculation of employee hours worked for the payroll period involves systems that are typically automated and feed into the payroll system. The systems often have the ability to adjust, change, or add hours. Understanding how this system operates is critical to linking overtime fraud schemes to a perpetrator.
- Work performance databases exist throughout a company. The challenge when working with these systems is their reliability. It is hoped that these systems can be linked to the other payroll systems via an employee number that is common to all the systems.

Data Mining Reports

The following describe the data mining reports we use in our practice to identify fraud within the payroll systems:

- The comparison of calendar year gross payroll to calendar year net payroll. The report should contain the following information:
  - Employee number, name, job code, department code, and start date.

- Total gross payroll; should reconcile to the annual wage statement.
- Total deductions.
- Total net payroll. This should be calculated from the check table versus the net payroll field.
- The report is searching for an employee whose net payroll is a high percentage of their gross payroll.
- This report is effective in searching for false adjustment schemes to net payroll.
- Statistical reports on payroll data. These reports will need to be able to summarize by employee, job title, and organizational unit. The report should also provide aggregate dollars and a frequency count as well as:
  - Salary and hourly providing aggregate dollars and employee count.
  - Counts by active, terminated, or temporary.
  - Standard hours and overtime hours.
  - Bonus payments that are included in gross payroll.
  - Number of employees paid via direct deposit or check. The report should be summarized by department and job title.
- Number of payroll payments by employee. If the employee either started or terminated in the current year, that should be produced. The count should be produced from the disbursement table. The report is designed to search for employees receiving additional payroll checks.
- Employees receiving payroll checks after their termination date. There may be a number of valid reasons for this to occur; however, it is also indicative of a terminated ghost scheme.
- Number of manual payments. This will be identified by a transaction code, check sequence number, or date that does not correspond to regular payroll dates.
- Gross payroll report of all employees in payroll or human resources who have the direct ability to commit a payroll fraud.
- A contra report. In theory, all deduction fields should be a subtraction from net payroll. However, a negative number in a deduction field would increase net payroll versus reduce net payroll.
- Listing of all journal entries that are designed to transfer payroll amounts either gross or net payroll to a nonpayroll general ledger account.

Example of Data Mining for Payroll Fraud

The fraud strategy for a perpetrator is to keep gross pay low and net pay for the ghost employee high. The simplest test is to compare annual gross pay to annual net pay, then compute a percentage of net to gross and sort on the percentage field high to low. We want the report to result in a list of employees with a high net-to-gross pay.

The premise is that ghost employees will minimize all voluntary deductions, since they tend not to participate in retirement programs and health insurance programs for obvious reasons. Tax withholdings will be at minimal amounts, too. A ghost employee probably won't have much if any sick time, personal time or vacation, or holiday time.

Matching the payroll file to other files may be one of the more effective ways of detecting a fictitious employee. However, the problem is that no one database may be effective for all classes of employees and the data in the secondary database may not be reliable. Also, finding a key data file to link the two databases together is one of the real-world difficulties in performing these type of matches. One of the more useful nonpayroll databases is a security access database used for building, parking lot, and computer system information. A data mining search on such a database would provide a report that contains a summary of the number of access attempts in a one-month period. The aim is to find employees having no access attempts or a limited number of attempts compared to other employees.

AUDIT PROCEDURES

Given that payroll fraud exists on an employee level of an organization, and that any false entities are people, the audit approach can bypass the usual initial step of determining whether an entity is real or false, although the skills needed in the entity determination can be thought of as the same when determining whether the employee is a variation of ghost employee. The following is a list of effective audit procedures that can be used if the fraud risk structure identifies payroll fraud.

- Perform a payoff procedure in which the auditor meets each individual selected and requests a government-issued identification. Compare the employee's identification to actual forms of the identification for signs of alteration or creation. Remember that when a perpetrator presents a false identification, it may be useful to ask a few questions that only an employee working in that department would know.
- Search for evidence of work performance through available databases: computer access, telephone records, security systems, and parking lot

access. In a retail environment, check through the cash register sign-on procedures. The key is to locate a database that the perpetrators did not consider.

■ Examine documents in the department that would require a manual notation. Any such documents provide a standard of comparison for handwriting.

■ Interview employees regarding other names associated with the department. Does the ghost employee's name come up?

Terminated Ghost Employees

There are two types of terminated ghost schemes. First, the manager keeps the terminated ghost on the payroll for a limited period of time. Second, the manager keeps the terminated ghost employee on the payroll indefinitely.

In the first scheme, the data mining should group the employees by the method of payment, either direct deposit or a payroll check. For the scheme to operate with an employee who was paid via direct deposit, the manager will need to change the bank account number. Therefore, the data mining routine is to search for terminated employees, paid through direct deposit information that indicates any changes to bank account numbers. The employees paid via manual check will not have an overt change, so they will require document examination.

In the second scheme, the key is to search for changes in the employees' personnel data, such as addresses, and/or in their payroll information, such as a change in bank account for direct deposit. The indefinite terminated ghost may eventually take on the identity of the fictitious ghost or a no-show ghost.

Audit procedures for terminated ghost employees include:

1. The key aspect is where and how the checks are negotiated at the end of the payroll period to the beginning of the payroll period. Also, compare the endorsement on the check at the beginning and end of the process.
2. Examine work schedules for evidence of the employee name.

Preemployment Ghost Employee

The scheme involves a supervisor's placing an employee on the payroll prior, typically one pay period, to the commencement of work, whereby the supervisor diverts in some manner of duplicity that employee's pay to him- or herself. Data mining searches would key on any new employees and match them to the date of their first paycheck and/or time card.

Audit procedures for preemployment ghost employees include:

1. Compare first payment period to other relevant databases to establish a work performance commencement date.
2. Interview employees to determine their recollection of when their start date was.

Rehired Ghost Employee

When an employee is terminated, another employee, typically a supervisor of the terminated employee, will place that person back in the payroll system by falsifying a time card and diverting the pay. This scheme may sound like the variations discussed previously for the terminated employee; however, the difference is that the terminated employee is not maintained in the records, resulting in a gap.

The audit procedures are similar to those used for terminated ghost employees except the focus is on searching for the gaps. After searching for a list of terminated employees, a search is performed for a later time period for any of those employees, either in the time card records or payroll records, or both.

No-Show Ghost Employee

The no-show ghost employees mimic real employees, making it difficult to ascertain any information that we usually look at in identifying ghost employees in general (e.g., they will have regular tax deductions and contributions to benefit programs). We said difficult, not impossible, because the no-show ghost is a real person who typically has a relationship with the hiring manager, or there may be a family or personal tie. Therefore, the key is to find the relationship between a supervisor and a no-show. Cases abound where people hire their relatives, possibly making a no-show job one of the oldest professions in recorded history. Sometimes the employee does the job, maybe not too well, but he or she does show up to shuffle some papers around, perhaps, therefore, although wasting the company's money, they are not considered no-show ghost employees. Remembering my first due diligence audit concerning the acquisition of a company, we identified that the CEO's son was listed in the payroll. Further investigation determined that he did in fact perform necessary job duties and a reasonable salary rate. The relatives we are interested in when considering payroll fraud are the ones who are hired, never set foot in the company, and never attempt to do a day's work for the company. There's a fine line sometimes, like in the case of college athletes who are given campus jobs for considerable pay for things like turning on the lawn-sprinkler system once a week.

So, data mining searches need to be performed that highlight the fact that a no-show does not perform the job duties for which he or she is being paid. The first step is to search for possible no-show employees, then perform secondary searches to uncover a lack of job activity. Just a bit of advice: When looking at job duties being performed or not, it is helpful to know what duties and responsibilities the no-show job title has listed in its corresponding job description. The following is a list of effective primary and secondary searches when dealing with no-show ghost employees:

▪ Duplicate last name search. The search will produce many false positives on common last names. Therefore, there will need to be a secondary search on the name data, such as zip code or bank routing number.

▪ Duplicate name in the payroll file and the health insurance benefit file or the life insurance beneficiary file.

▪ When searching for names in the security access files results in no activity for an employee, a secondary search is needed matching the names showing no activity in the security access database to those in the payroll databases.

▪ Specific name searches on senior executives who could have a family-member employee within some other part of the company.

▪ A duplicate address search match requires a secondary search for bank account numbers to determine if there is a match there as well.

▪ A search on direct deposit information, for example, bank routing number and bank account number, results in a match requiring a secondary search through personnel and payroll databases looking for matches on zip code and cost center.

Audit procedures for no-show ghost employees include:

1. Interview employees in the department to establish if the name is known by fellow employees.
2. Identify evidence of work performance.

Temporary Ghosts

Hopefully, your databases will have a code distinguishing temporary employees from nontemporary employees. If not, the difference between the start date and the termination date may be an indicator. Obviously, the second approach will create false positives on the data mining search. The temporary employee is a real person, but because of the temporary nature, hiring controls may have been bypassed. Control over temporary employees is usually vested with a local manager, making such bypassing uncomplicated. Data mining for temporary employees focuses on those coded in the payroll system as temporary.

Audit procedures for temporary employees include:

1. Confirm the existence of the employee through a telephone interview.
2. Search for evidence of work performance.
3. Interview coworkers.

Overtime Reporting Fraud

With overtime reporting fraud, we need to identify all employees who are paid in excess of the number of hours for their position. In most payroll databases, there will be a field that accumulates employee hours throughout a fiscal year. The field is populated from each payroll register, and since actual hours paid for each payroll period are located in each payroll register, that particular database is crucial in detecting overtime fraud. The aim of a search of this register is looking for the pattern and frequency of hours. The exercise is not difficult, but can be time consuming to access all registers and then develop a search routine for a particular pattern. Focus is on both individuals and clusters of employees within the same department or work shift. You are looking at clusters of employees to detect collusion in overtime abuse, a form of disguised compensation, or any kickbacks to supervisors that are approving all the overtime.

One caveat concerns those employees receiving a salary and being eligible for overtime pay as well. This situation often occurs in the healthcare industry where nurses, who are typically salaried professionals, receive overtime pay any time they work beyond normal hours for a pay period (e.g., working nights, weekends, and holidays). Things can get confusing when a nurse's normal shift is during these times, so the pay scale may differ from the nurses working a typical Monday through Friday daytime schedule. In general, you have to know the criteria of an organization's pay scales, what job titles are eligible for overtime pay, and how that overtime pay is reimbursed.

Since opportunity is a key element with this type of payroll fraud, there are several known points of opportunity to look for:

- Employees falsify their time keeping because their supervisor unknowingly approves overtime. This opportunity can occur in a staggered workday or by the supervisor's not carefully checking time cards or not being present during the overtime hours or just a general neglect of their duties.
- Employees operate in collusion to falsify their payroll hours. Once again, this will occur without the knowledge of the supervisor.
- Employee and supervisor operate in collusion. The supervisor may be receiving a kickback, or it may be a form of disguised compensation.
- Employee forges the approval of the supervisor. In an automated time card system, this would occur through a weak password control procedure.
- An employee working in payroll overstates another employee's hours or his own when entering them into the payroll system using information from a properly approved time card. The original time card is then either destroyed or altered, or a new version is created.

Understand that the point of opportunity is relevant to the document examination rather than the data mining (e.g., a missing time card is a red flag of the overtime scheme). Such red flags aid in the determination of whether the scenario is being committed by a single employee or if it is a disguised compensation scheme. If committed by one employee, you can assume the scheme in an ongoing one, whereby a time card would be missing in several payroll periods for an employee. If the scenario is a form of disguised compensation, time cards would be missing for a group of employees, typically, from the same department.

Disguised Compensation Payroll Schemes

Disguised compensation schemes occur as part of a management's effort to increase an employee or group of employee's salaries. Once again, examination of the payroll registers is critical in detecting this fraud. The first step is to identify all the database fields that comprise the gross pay calculation and the net pay calculation. Then generate a data mining report that summarizes the dollar amounts and frequency of the adjustments by the field.

The salary adjustment field in a payroll register exists to provide lump-sum adjustments. Retroactive merit adjustments and performance bonuses are two typical examples. The databases often include a field referred to as "other," which exists for nonsalary adjustments, such as travel reimbursement and allowances. Both types of fields provide an opportunity to fraudulently adjust an employee's compensation.

One example of utilizing these fields occurred when a manager provided his employee with weekly salary adjustments for local travel. By doing so, he was increasing the employee's gross compensation beyond the salary maximum for that job title. Searching these fields in the database would show high frequency of use atypical of the job and an aggregate amount of salary beyond the maximum allowed for the job title.

Unfortunately, such a data mining routine isn't always effective. For example, a construction company requires employees to travel to job sites in a large region. The company pays a travel per diem that is included in employees' paychecks. The adjustments field in the database logically shows a high frequency of use for salary adjustments and high aggregate salary amount. Therefore, our ability to differentiate between legitimate and fraudulent adjustments was not possible since there could be fraudulent adjustments buried within the travel ones.

Disguised Compensation Nonpayroll Schemes

There have been many reported examples of executives who have enhanced their total compensation through nonpayroll items such as interest-free loans, company apartments, company vehicles used by family members, corporate planes and boats, lavish personal parties, entertainment falsely described as business related, and so on. The key to detecting such schemes is to be aware of the opportunities. The audit procedure should focus on whether the item was known and approved by the board compensation committee. A personally favored second test is determining how the company would react if the perk was publicly disclosed. Think of the public outrage when financial firms continued to give large bonuses after they received government bailout money and proceed along those lines.

Payroll Department Schemes

We have been discussing employees and supervisors committing payroll fraud and pretty much ignoring the gazillion-pound gorilla in the room known as the payroll department. Obviously, a payroll department is the gatekeeper for most payroll fraud, considering that the department's employees have the greatest opportunity to enrich their own compensation through their own fraudulent behavior or from getting kickbacks from other employees doing likewise.

The audit program should always require the examination of the annual compensation of all employees that have direct access to the payroll system or indirect access via a supervisory role. This consideration applies to large and small organizations. For example, the corporate controller in a small company typically has broad authorization, and can adjust their salaries, then journal transfer the excess wages to accounts that would not draw immediate attention.

Payroll-Related Schemes

There are numerous schemes that are related to payroll either directly or because they involve the hiring and use of employees within personnel functions. Descriptions of these schemes and examples are discussed in the following sections.

Temporary Hiring Agencies

Typically, schemes involving temp agencies operate though collusion with an organization's operations, whereby the temp agency overbills for the number of employees provided and the operations manager certifies the overbilled amount. The focus of such schemes is on the relationship between employees of a department that would regularly use temps and those outside of the organization.

Another variation is when the temp agency actually hires and pays an employee who works temporarily for a company, so the company doesn't have to deal with paying benefits or required withholdings. The company may interview the employee to approve his or her hiring while agreeing to pay the agency a fixed hourly amount. The agency, in turn, agrees to pay the employee a lesser amount than that being reimbursed from the company, or hires a less-qualified individual at a lower wage. A gray area is reached as to whether the company knows that the agency is inflating its profits. Even if it does know, it may be satisfied with the work of the hire and think of this as a nonissue. Still, you have to ask if there is a form of collusion going on with a kickback provided to someone at the company from the temp agency, and why would the temp employee accept such an arrangement? She may feel that by accepting the position at the lower wage, she leaves the door open to being hired on a full-time basis directly by the company, or she feels that the goodwill established with the temp agency will lead to other jobs in the future. While the jury is still out on these types of hiring practices, the circumvention of payroll and personnel systems does present the opportunity for fraud.

Health Insurance

Health insurance is such a needed benefit that it is often the subject of payroll fraud schemes, whereby the benefits administrator is receiving a kickback from nonemployees or terminated employees for admission into the company health insurance plan. The scheme would require the benefits administrator to be in collusion with the nonemployee. Detection can often occur when active payroll data is reconciled to employee's paychecks, whereby the portion paid by the employee is listed as a withholding on thepay stubs.

Allowance Programs

One fondly remembers allowances as the amount he or she got as a kid for doing weekly chores around the house. Although getting the money without having done the chores wasn't officially an act of fraud, when we talk about allowances in regard to payroll, the opportunity for it cannot be overlooked. Allowance programs, such as tuition reimbursement, moving expense reimbursement, relocation fees, and the like, are prone to fraud because the receipts may be copies or created ones through desktop publishing software. Typically, like the kid who thinks he deserves an allowance without doing chores, the employee rationalizes that the program is unfair or he is entitled to more because the program does not cover all normal, reasonable expenses. Such schemes operate in the following manner:

- The employee falsifies his or her eligibility for the program.
- The employee falsifies the occurrence of the event that creates the eligibility.
- The employee provides false or altered documents to support the reimbursement.

How the fraud occurs will depend on the nature of the of allowance program such as:

- Tuition reimbursement would occur through a falsified grade report.
- Moving expenses would be inflated thorough falsified receipts or the vendor's overbilling the company and the employee's receiving a kickback.
- Expatriates (as discussed in Chapter 10) often receive higher allowances for their families being with them, but still receive the same amount after the family returns home and the company is not notified of it.
- Rental allowances would occur through false leases and false rental receipts or through the landlord's inflating the rental payment and provide the employee with a kickback.

The audit process should focus on the authenticity of the documents and independent verification that the event did, in fact, occur.

Discriminatory Hiring Practices

As we have discussed with other variations of payroll schemes, hiring practices offer an opportunity for fraud. With regard to discriminatory practices, a supervisor may have a tendency to hire or not hire employees of a certain race, gender, religion, physical condition, and so on. Detecting such practices involves a global perspective on company hiring, whereby personnel databases will show the tendency to hire or not hire persons on such factors. Remember your nineteenth century history and the stories about the waves of Irish immigrants escaping the potato famine in their homeland by looking for jobs in the New World, and being met with signs in local shop windows that stated "no Irish need apply"? We cannot think of that type of blatant hiring discrimination happening today. However, if you learned anything in reading this book, it's that fraud is anything but blatant.

Conflict-of-Interest Hiring

A scheme of this type typically occurs when a senior-level employee hires an employee where some sort of relationship exists. The relationship can be of a romantic nature, repayment of a political favor, a college buddy, and of course, a family member. We discussed no-show employees where there typically is a relationship between the supervisor and a person hired who does not really perform work, but receives pay. With conflict-of-interest hiring schemes, we are concerned about hiring controls being circumvented and not payroll systems as in the no-show case. Interviewing coworkers may reveal if the hire is a conflict of interest.

Misuse of Employee

The scheme occurs when a supervisor requires a company employee to perform noncompany duties during work hours or after work hours. The Speaker of the New York State Assembly had his wife transported by state employees in a state automobile. Regardless of the legal analysis of the situation, the general public opinion was that was a misuse of state resources. The point of this war story is to show what is meant by noncompany duties and what constitutes misuse of an employee.

To some, having an administrative assistant make coffee for a meeting could be thought of as misuse. To others, it would not be a misuse unless the person asked had an integral participatory role in the meeting. It appears that misuse depends on the view of the person being misused. Larger companies have specific duties and responsibilities clearly on record with their personnel departments, which aid in determining if an employee is working outside of these duties and responsibilities, thereby being misused. However, we cannot ignore the fact that sometimes we do things on the job outside of our required duties because we have the ability to do these things. Then it becomes a matter of frequency to the point where doing so becomes an actual job duty.

Trying to detect misuse is difficult. Knowing an employee's job duties and responsibilities can be effective in showing the performance of duties outside the scope of the job title. Interviewing the employee who is being misused may not be effective because she may be concerned that telling someone of the misuse will cause her to be fired or maybe she does not even think of it as misuse. Interviewing coworkers may be a better method if such an interview can take place in an environment where fear of any retribution can be minimized.

 ## SUMMARY

The number of payroll fraud schemes seems endless, made more so by the knowledge that payroll is more than likely the largest expense to an organization. Then compound that expense by numerous separate acts of fraud, and it all seems too much. How can we detect all those fraud scenarios? You have to be thinking with all the linking that needs to be done in a fraud audit, the size of the resulting chain in the case of payroll fraud would span the globe. It is like looking for the proverbial needle in a haystack, but it helps to think of payroll as just one big haystack and not a bunch of big ones spread over acres. No, the payroll systems are rather antisocial; therefore, they typically do not commingle or interact with the other core business systems or outsiders. They may share characteristics with other core business systems, however, like automated functions, and it is these common characteristics that make the detection of fraud just that much more a focused effort on part of the auditor.

CHAPTER THIRTEEN

Revenue Misstatement

I T SEEMS THAT REVENUE is all any company outsider, like investors, market analysts, and bankers, care about. They question things like how do revenues equate from quarter to quarter and what does that revenue increase mean for my dividends? And, of course, the standard: what's the bottom line? So, company executives like CEOs and CFOs are pressured to focus on revenue. For the CEO, it is a matter of the books looking "healthy" to those company outsiders. For the CFO, it is a matter of properly recognizing revenue. Remember, the CEO is operating as the face of the company to the outside world, while the CFO is the head bookkeeper and, being so, must know all the gray areas of financial reporting regulation. Although concerned with varying aspects of revenue recognition, the actions of both of these highest-of-level executives are needed in order for revenue recognition fraud to occur.

For the auditor, revenue recognition requires an understanding of the industry and the organization. The auditor needs to have the ability to apply and interpret the principles of revenue recognition to the audit program. It sounds simple; however, there are many widely accepted revenue recognition procedures and many situation-specific ways to interpret and apply each of these procedures. Just as organizations are different, the kinds of revenues they generate are different. Consequently, these different types of revenues need different recognition and reporting methods. Therefore, they also need an audit program tailored to their uniqueness.

FRAUD RISK STRUCTURE

Instead of providing some key terminology like we did in the previous chapters, we start our discussion on an equally basic level, just so we are all on the same page again. So, we begin by asking: When is revenue recognized as such? To the layman who uses the terms *income, revenue,* and *profit* interchangeably, it is simply when you sell a product and receive payment for it. If only life were so simple. Fortunately, fraud auditors have GAAP. Look in any principles of accounting text and you'll find something like: "Revenue is recognized when amounts are realized and are earned," followed by these assertions (i.e., "general rules" for revenue recognition):

- A transaction has to occur, entailing an exchange.
- The conversion of income to revenue is essentially complete.
- The price is fixed and determinable.
- Collection is reasonably assured.

Our discussion involves transactions that are for goods and services in exchange for a monetary amount, and not barter transactions. So, when we state selling goods or products the revenue is recognized at the date of the sale, and when discussing services, the revenue is recognized when the services have been performed and are billable. Again, it all seems so simple. The reason we drudge up all this seeming minutiae is that to the perpetrator of fraud it is just this simplicity that presents the opportunity to commit and conceal fraudulent behavior. When we talk of fraud, how to conceal the true nature of the transaction is critical, and therefore, the objective is to have the business transaction look like a real one.

Fraud Risk Structure and Revenue Misstatement

The fraud risk structure is the starting point for identifying the fraud scenarios that can occur through manipulation of revenue recognition. Specifically, the search for revenue fraud begins with understanding how management has historically misstated revenue. Revenue fraud can be categorized into four major groups, with each group having several general schemes and several industry-specific fraud schemes. Although it seems like revenue fraud would predominantly occur at large corporations because of the pressure for positive results that rests on high-level executives, revenue recognition fraud can occur at smaller companies also for varying reasons.

Every fraud scheme involves a method of concealment singular to that scheme. In the case of revenue recognition fraud, how the individual implements the concealment strategy varies on the perpetrator's position in the organization and the company's internal procedures. Therefore, the auditor should give primary consideration to opportunity in relation to the system under audit. Other items to consider include use of computerized systems versus manual systems, required documents, internal controls, and corporate governance issues.

How the true nature of the transaction is concealed becomes the weak point of the fraud scheme, because if the auditor can identify the concealment and then the questionable transaction, the fraud should become apparent. In some instances, more than one layer of concealment techniques is employed to hide the true nature of the business transaction. By layers, we mean that you have to look beyond the actual accounting for a transaction (e.g., journal entries to general ledger to financial statements) because the transactions will appear as real. Knowing how the false transactions can be made to "look" real gives the auditor the knowledge to dig deeper and investigate transactions that are susceptible to fraud. The following is a list of the most commonly used concealment strategies involving revenue:

- Creating false documents or altering real documents with fictitious information.
- Fictitious delivery of the product or service. This will occur through the creation of false documentation.
- Real delivery to false or hidden locations. Here, the company ships product to noncustomers for the illusion of sale through the use of freight forwarders, other company warehouses, and concealed or false locations, or consignment locations. Or the company ships to distributors without title transfer.
- Shipment of nonexistent or incomplete product. Occurs through the actual shipment of a container that is either empty, filled for weight purposes, or an incomplete product.
- Shipment to a real customer who did not order the product. Management ships an actual product to a customer who never ordered the item.

- Concealment of returns. Requires the delaying of the return until after the audit period, recording the return as something other than a return or a combination of efforts to conceal the return and the adjustment.
- Subsequent credits or adjustments. Since the fictitious revenue cannot be realized, the receivable must be cleared through credit memos or actual adjusting entries.
- Disguised customer remittances. The documentation supporting the source of the remittance is altered or created to provide the illusion of realization.
- Use of company funds to provide illusion of customer remittances. Here, the company uses multiple bank accounts, subsidiary bank accounts, or foreign bank accounts.
- Lapping scheme to provide illusion of customer remittances. Other customers' remittances or credit balances are applied to the fictitious revenue.
- Undisclosed terms and conditions. The customer is offered verbal terms or side agreements that are not disclosed to the auditor. Or the auditor can also be given draft documents, altered copies, or false documents.
- Right of return not disclosed. The customer is provided the opportunity to return the product through a trial period, approval period, or some other program.
- Created, altered, or fictitious documentation.
- No documentation supporting verbal representations.
- Falsifying company reports to provide an illusion of an event or representation.
- Control over confirmations. With fictitious customers, the customer addresses are under the control of management. With real customers, the management team must exert some control over the response. In certain industries, obtaining responses can be difficult, so management offers assistance in obtaining the response. Last, there are cases in which the customer conspired against the auditor to falsely respond to the confirmation.
- Intentional misrepresentation by management.
- Improper criteria used in estimates.
- Collusion with outside experts to provide false representations.

Data Analysis

The primary assumptions in our discussion of data analysis with regard to revenue recognition are that we are operating on a 12-month calendar basis, that the analysis will focus on overstatement of revenue versus the understatement of it, and focus is on one product line versus multiple and varying ones. Data mining for revenue misstatement operates on the principle that the misstatement occurs either in a source journal or a general journal entry. The misstatement is recorded in a general ledger account and is either an under- or overstatement of revenue. Therefore, the first stage or layer of data mining is intended to identify the most likely place for revenue misstatement. The process is a combination of merging the data analysis with the fraud risk factors identified in the planning stage, for example:

- Determine the percentage of revenue from source journals and general journals.
- Determine the extent of revenue in each general ledger account as to the dollar, frequency, and percentage of the account from a source journal and a general journal entry.
- Determine the source of revenue from new customers and existing customers. There are two types of new customers, those customers that were created in the current year and dormant customers that have become active in the current year.
- Determine the extent of revenue recorded to noncustomer accounts.
- Determine the extent of revenue recorded in the source journal within the final month of the accounting year. The actual time period is dependent on the nature and size of the organization.
- For general journal entries with a credit to revenue, determine the extent of debits by general ledger account as to dollar, frequency, and percentages.
- Determine the aggregate dollar value and the frequency of journal entries by control levels and by user ID.
- Determine the extent of revenue that was recorded at the end of the accounting year and after the end of the accounting year.
- Determine the percentage of the account balance created after the close of the year end or month end for interim analysis.

Using Data Mining for Detecting False Revenue

The data mining needs to focus on the source journal or general journal entries to uncover the false transactions related to the inherent fraud scheme. Therefore, a key determinant is the significance of the misstatement. Consider the situation where revenue, as reported on the financial statements, is comprised of 95 percent source journal entries and the remaining 5 percent from general journal entries, which suggests the most likely area for misstatement is the source journal. Therefore, if misstatement has occurred, it is either false revenue or improper recognition.

Now let's say that revenue in the source journal is comprised of 5 percent from new customer sales (new, dormant-to-active, and house accounts) and 95 percent from existing customers. Of the new customer revenue, 1 percent was earned in the final quarter of the year and the remaining 4 percent has been realized. Therefore, material misstatement from a false revenue scheme using created customers does not meet the significance test, and the possibility of false revenue from a real customer scheme and improper recognition schemes need to be considered.

Additional analysis of transactions involving real customers shows that four customers accounted for 10 percent of sales in the fourth quarter. We then need to verify that the four real customers have in fact paid for the products. If so, the realization of the receivable eliminates false revenue through a real customer. If not, then premature recognition needs to be considered focusing on product delivery.

Disaggregated data analysis at the journal or account level may be needed to be performed based on the risk profile. For example, if the inherent scheme involves false revenue and real customers, data analysis would focus on a few large transactions to a few customers, whereby we are no longer looking at the revenue-transactional data in aggregate for anomalies. Consequently, the analysis would also focus on subsequent reversals of sales transactions in the next accounting period.

From this example, it appears that disaggregate data analysis is more likely to identify an anomaly, but we still have to start with a transactional significance analysis of the transactions on aggregate. Specifically, we need to analyze source journals to detect if entries were recorded in the improper accounting period. The general journal analysis would focus on any large entries and multiple entries of large amounts.

Another example involves a construction company that is recognizing revenue on a percentage of completion; therefore, the completed cost account is a key general ledger account in the recognition of revenue. The completed cost is comprised of postings from source journal and journal entries. Our first step is to identify, by project, completed expenditures originating from source journal including payroll, accounts payable, and other source journals and from general journal entries. The data mining search routine is performed to produce a report showing those projects with a high percentage of the completed cost originating from journal entries. The report would need to be modified to detect material misstatement that is spread over many accounts. The first step is to understand the dollar significance of general journal entries on the completed cost account. If the significance test is material, the data mining routine would focus on a frequency of general journal entries to the overall account and by their subsequent posting to a project.

If the source journal reveals inflated revenue amounts, then the accounts payable entries are either fictitious or an actual payable recorded prematurely. A data mining search routine can be performed for reversal of entries, credit or debit memos, or contra entries in the source journal. Since fictitious payables are typically reversed in the next accounting period, the data mining should focus on debits to accounts payable from a noncash account, reversals, or debit memos. The actual payable recorded prematurely is the most difficult to isolate with data mining. One test would be comparing the recording date to the eventual payment date, whereby we are looking for payment dates that will exceed the standard number of days.

Schemes with False Customers and False Revenue

Is the customer real or false? The process for data mining for false customers and fictitious revenue is similar to the process of searching for false vendors. Management may create one or more false customers to inflate revenue; however, since a material misstatement may require significant revenue distortion, the likelihood is that several false customers would be used. Items to search for include:

- New customers. The analysis should identify material sales transactions or a materiality factor in the aggregate to new customers.
- Dormant customers that become active in the final accounting period.
- Duplicate customer addresses for billing or shipping.
- High credit terms for a new customer.
- High percentage of revenue in the final accounting period.
- Revenue transactions that have no sales commission codes attached to the revenue transaction or a sales representative territory code.
- Revenue transactions that are posted to noncustomer accounts.
- Match customer database to personnel or vendor databases for matching of names, addresses, telephone numbers, or government registration numbers.
- Sales transactions with no sales order number.
- Search shipping addresses for either the same address for more than one customer or no recorded shipping to an address.

The characteristic of false revenue is, going back to our accounting principles stated previously, that there is no realization of an amount. The false revenue transaction must be reversed or the aging process must be disguised. The following characteristics of false revenues apply to both real and false customers:

- Customer accounts with significant sales, but no postings from cash receipts.
- Customer accounts with sales reversals in the next accounting period.
- Subsequent returns or sales adjustments for sales recorded in the final accounting period.
- Contra entries in the sales journals, particularly when the return or adjustment is posted as a debit in the sales journal and not posted to the sales adjustment account.
- Changing the date on the sales invoice to provide the illusion that the receivable is current. Data mining would consist of a search routine for a sales invoice numbers not consistent with the dates of the invoices.
- Subsequent transfer of a cash receipt posting would be indicative of manipulating the aging process. This is a form of lapping; however, the intent is not to hide the theft of funds, but rather show the sales transactions as realized at the accounts receivable aging date. When lapping is used, consider the following data analysis:
  - Search for customer remittance check numbers that do not follow a logical date sequence.
  - Search for accounts with frequent credit memos and other credit adjustments to the account.
  - Search for transfers from other customer accounts.
- Realization through loans from the company or an affiliated company.

Schemes with Real Customers and False Revenue

These schemes need the involvement of management to operate and pertain to the shipping of products. They include:

- Shipping products to customers who did not order them, so the goods are subsequently returned. Revenue is recognized on a non-sale.
- Shipping products to customers who did not order the product, whereby the customers are advised that the shipment was in error and they should be returned to a location other than the designated warehouse. In this scheme, management is concealing the return. The product is usually added back to inventory as an adjustment.
- Shipping products to customers who agree to hold the product for a period of time.

In each of these cases, the data mining routines should be performed to match customer returns to the dates of the sales transactions. For example, search for returns within 30 days of the sales transactions. Also, perform a data mining routine that searches for large inventory adjustments within the first quarter of the preceding fiscal year.

AUDIT APPROACH

Determining false or real entities is not our first step; instead, the approach starts with determining the significance of the risk that may exist. Is the significance of the risk at a magnitude that could result in a possible misstatement of the financial statements? In order to determine significance, an understanding of the composition of the revenue as to source journal or journal entries is needed. What are the inherent fraud schemes within this construct? Once determined, then what data red flags are evident for the specific fraud scenarios?

The following principles provide the basis for building an audit program for responding to the risk of material misstatement of revenue due to the intentional acts of management:

1. All revenue is either recorded through a source journal or through a general journal entry; therefore, analysis through appropriate data mining routines should determine the overall significance of revenue recorded in the financial statements through both sources. For example, if only 4 percent of the revenue was created through journal entries, then any occurring misstatement must be located in the source journal.

2. Revenue is either over- or understated. An understanding of management's motivation to misstate revenue is needed. If there is pressure to overstate revenue, then the current year's general journal is the source data, whereas if the intent is to understate revenue, then the preceding year's general journal is the source data.

3. The other side of the misstated revenue general journal entry will provide clues regarding the type of fraud schemes occurring. Debits to non-traditional accounts should be a red flag.

4. Revenue is either misstated by one or a few transactions or by multiple transactions that in the aggregate are material. The data mining searches should focus on large transactions, but also the frequency and aggregate dollar value of transactions.

5. Organizations are evaluated by external parties. The key operating statistics used by external organizations link to general ledger accounts. These accounts have a higher propensity for misstatement.

Documentation

Examination of documents for evidence of misstated revenue is needed to be performed involving items, such as sales contracts, shipping documents, delivery of service documents, or cash receipts. We still have to determine real or false entities, but this time it is in the form of customers. In the case of false revenue's being created through real customers, the fraudulent act revolves around whether the products are returned.

For example, if the false revenue for a real customer is not realized, then the fraudulent action revolves around the returns and adjustment accounts. If the real customer retains the goods or services, the documentation examination regarding the sales contract, shipping documents, or the delivery of service documents becomes the point of fraudulent action.

With regard to sales orders, the documentation should show a clear intent to order the product. The audit process should focus on created sales orders, non-original documents, nontraditional documents, and back-dated sales orders.

Any sales terms and conditions should support the recognition of the sales transaction. The audit process should search for:

- The unconditional right to return the product or ease of return of the product.
- Open payment terms or extension of payment terms beyond normal company policy.
- Future performance conditions.
- Undisclosed terms and conditions. Many high-profile frauds have misstated revenue by providing customers with oral terms and conditions. The audit process should focus on reasons for customer return that seem inconsistent with normal company practices or through a customer confirmation.

Statement of Auditing Standards 99

Due to the past abuses in revenue recognition, SAS 99 makes it perfectly clear that improper revenue recognition has to be a top priority on audits. Therefore, careful consideration of revenue recognition begins during the audit planning stage. Specifically:

1. Structure the brainstorming session to include a discussion of the revenue fraud schemes in relation to the specific client industry and client accounting practices. This discussion should include:
   - Identify any client practices that may create problems.
   - Review industry-specific fraud schemes.
   - Include any past problems with the client.
2. Use the fraud theory of pressures, rationalization, and opportunity to understand management's motivation for under- or overstatement of revenue. This review facilitates where and how to search for the fraud.
3. Understand how the key revenue assertions—such as a transaction has to occur entailing an exchange, the conversion of income to revenue is essentially complete, the price is fixed and determinable, and collection is reasonably assured—occur within the company by revenue source.
4. Discuss how those revenue assertions could be falsified and subsequently concealed.
5. Develop data analysis around the relevant fraud schemes.
6. Develop questions for the interviewing of management in the context of:
   - Understanding how the key revenue assertions occur in the company.
   - Identifying which revenue schemes relate to the individual being interviewed.
   - Understanding what affect the individual has on the documentation supporting the revenue assertion.
   - Inquiring about negotiation strategies with customers.
   - Identifying customers controlled by non–sales force personnel.
7. Discuss improper revenue recognition for the company. Remember that the identification of a risk of material misstatement due to fraud involves the application of professional judgment and includes consideration of:
   - The *type* of risk that may exist. As mentioned, the auditor should consider how management would misstate revenue, first at a topside level and then at the specific scheme level.
   - The *significance* of the risk: Whether it is of a magnitude that could result in a possible material misstatement of the financial statements.
   - The *likelihood* of the risk or scheme's occurring within the industry and organization.
   - The *pervasiveness* of the risk: Whether the potential risk is pervasive to the financial statements as a whole or specifically related to a particular assertion, account, or class of transaction.

Examples of Fraud Schemes Involving Revenue Recognition

Although the following examples relate to well-known frauds of larger companies, the same schemes can occur in small, privately held companies:

1. Management records fictitious revenue through a false billing scheme. *Illusion* is the key word in this fraud scheme. Management must provide representations, supported by documentation, that a customer exists, that delivery has occurred or that services have been rendered, and that the revenue transaction has been realized. Documentation will be obtained, created, or altered to support the false transactions. The overall audit approach should search for and critically examine each of the four revenue assertions described previously. Specifically:
   - The revenue transaction is recorded in the sales journal.
   - The revenue transaction is recorded through the use of either a real or fictitious customer.
   - Management obtains, creates, or alters documents to provide the illusion that the customer ordered the product or services.
   - The delivery of the product is disguised in one of many methods.
   - The realization of the receivable is concealed.

2. Improper recognition of revenue because it was either recorded prematurely or intentionally delayed to a later period. Specific characteristics of these schemes are:
   - The recognition is premature, so the revenue is not realized, and the transaction is eventually reversed after producing a temporary inflation of the revenue.
   - The revenue is eventually recognized. This fraud scheme is the most difficult to detect because the revenue recognition occurs—eventually. This delay to a later period results from a need to reflect an increase in an earlier period. The audit focus is on the sale-product delivery point matching through the appropriate documentation.

3. Creation of revenue through journal entries. Revenue is misstated simply through one or more journal entries. No customer accounts are affected. Examples include:
   - Creating revenue through the manipulation of journal entries, such as manual journal entries, top-sided entries, a series of nonmaterial journal entries that in aggregate are material, and large-amount journal entries.
   - Creating revenue through manipulation of reserves, such as bad debts.
   - Creating revenue through accrued revenue.
   - Creating revenue through manipulation of estimates.

4. Misapplications of generally accepted accounting principles (GAAP) include:

   - Misapplication of the four general rules of revenue recognition. Management intentionally misapplies one of the four assertions. The auditor needs to identify the assertions as they apply in the organization's core business systems and then determine how management could manipulate them and conceal such manipulation.
   - Misapplication of GAAP industry pronouncements. There are a number of specific GAAP pronouncements covering revenue. So when management intentionally misapplies the criteria established under specific revenue pronouncements, the auditor needs to identify the specific criteria and determine how management could manipulate it and conceal the manipulation. For example:
     - The intentional recognition of nonoperating revenue as operating revenue.
     - The intentional recognition of the full amount of revenue on fees collected up front.
     - The intentional failure to write off bad debt customers or loans.
     - The intentional recognition of revenue on bartering, consignment income, or related party activity.

Use of Real Customers

The following schemes involve a real customer that can either be a potential or an existing one:

- Recognition of revenue from customers who have not agreed to purchase the item, although all indications are that the customer intends to purchase the item.
- Recognition of revenue due to an improper cutoff procedure. This scheme is a simple matter of recording revenue that has not been delivered by the end of the accounting period.
- Recognition of full revenue based on partial shipments.
- Recognition of revenue on products or services with questionable workmanship.
- Recognition of revenue involving multiple deliverables that have not all been satisfied.
- Recognition of revenue when a right of return exists. Typically, the seller does not disclose the right of return within the sales documents.

- Bill-and-hold procedures having specific accounting principles governing revenue recognition. In this transaction, a real sales order is received from the customer; however, the terms require the seller to hold the goods until the purchaser is ready to take acceptance. The seller will need to either provide a false representation as to the terms or ship the goods to a false location.
- Consignment of income involves the transfer of the product to the buyer; however, the seller is not obligated to pay for the product until the item is sold. The terms should be disclosed in the sales contract.
- Channel stuffing is the practice of offering extremely favorable terms to move a sales transaction into the current period. The inducement must be so favorable that the customer purchases the item beyond its needs. The red flags would be large discounts or payment terms that extend beyond normal sales terms.
- Round tripping refers to sales activity where there is no measurable economic benefit to the two parties. Typically, no cash transfer occurs between the two parties and a red flag is identified when a customer is also a vendor.
- Related party transactions that are not disclosed. The business relationship is typically disguised by using a third party intermediately to disguise the business connection.

SUMMARY

By devoting an entire chapter to revenue recognition fraud, it may appear we are neglecting our topic of fraud in the core business systems. In other words, why aren't we devoting an entire chapter to the financial reporting process as a whole? Well, we will do that in our next chapter, but it really is a simple matter of the dictates of SAS 99, which makes it clear that improper revenue recognition needs to be a top priority on audits. Think carefully for a minute. What is the purpose of standardization in just general terms? Basically, we want things to mean the same. We almost all use the same word processing software so that when we send a document to someone it will be in a recognizable format. Similarly, when we pick up an income statement, we know where to look for the revenue number and because of standards; we know what those numbers mean. So, when someone who is in a leadership position within an organization fraudulently presents a revenue number, in essence, all meaning has been lost.

CHAPTER FOURTEEN

Inventory Fraud

Y OU ARE PROBABLY ASKING at this point: why have we chosen to devote an entire chapter to fraud as it occurs with inventory? The answer is simply because there isn't just one distinct core business system that presents the opportunity for fraud involving inventory. Inventory fraud can occur in just one core system or several concurrently. We have found fraud scenarios that pertain to the theft and misuse of the assets comprising inventory and fraud scenarios that involve the valuation of the inventory where it is misrepresented in the financial reporting. Of course, there are the scenarios where any combinations of systems are affected. Yes, this is a case of a multiheaded monster. But don't worry thinking it will take a Herculean effort to detect the fraud scenarios. Remember, we have the tools and knowledge, so for inventory fraud we are not interested primarily in the "why," "when," or "who" of the fraudulent act, but rather the "how." Are the assets being used in the intended manner? If not, then how are they being misused? Are the assets there? If not, then how are they being stolen? Does the inventory value as reflected on the financial statements have meaning? If not, then how was that value misrepresented?

You may think that this type of fraudulent activity would occur most frequently at businesses with large and diverse inventories, thereby allowing the perpetrator to easily conceal any theft. However, how many times in your auditing life have you heard from a small business owner who didn't realize the enormity of the inventory theft until the perpetrator/employee took some time off? You have to think that where there is inventory, there is theft, misuse, and misstatement of that inventory. The level of concealment sophistication probably will increase proportionally with the size of the inventory, and that is why knowing the fraud scenarios associated with inventories is all the more important.

 FRAUD RISK STRUCTURE

Theft is a somewhat broad term; we have petty theft, cyber theft, theft by deception, theft by extortion, theft by false pretenses, theft of services, and so on. When we talk of the act itself, we use the terms larceny, embezzlement, burglary, and stealing. The definition we are going with here is that theft pertains to the taking of business assets in the form of inventories, thereby depriving a business of them, and resulting in a failure to conduct business on the scale intended. When we speak of inventory in this context, we mean the noun and not the verb. By using the noun *inventory*, we defer to the accounting definition that denotes a business's raw materials, works-in-progress, and finished goods, the total value of which is represented in the assets on the business's financial statements. So, now that we have a basis for our discussion, here are some key references for our discussion of fraud and inventories:

- Theft: The physical movement of the asset (inventory) from the business's control to the entity's control, with entity being an employee, vendor, or customer. If it's an employee, the inventory may be removed within the normal course of his or her job duties or off-hours. Typically, if a vendor or customer is involved, then collusion is also evident.
- Theft point: Inventory may be diverted before or after a business takes possession. If it occurs before, then weaknesses in the receiving business processes are indicated. If it occurs after, then weaknesses in physical security controls are indicated.
- Normal course of business: When inventories, by their very nature, are consumed in the normal course of doing business, they cannot be examined as inventory.

Identifying Inventory Theft and Misuse

As in previous chapters when we discuss building a fraud risk structure, we consider this process the starting point for identifying the fraud scenarios. Once again our first step is to identify real or false entities, such as determining if the vendors are real or fictitious. Since collusion is often present in fraud schemes involving inventories, the more you know about the entities interacting with the core business systems involving inventory, the more effective you are going to be in locating and detecting the appropriate fraud scenarios.

Next, we focus on the action element of the inherent fraud schemes pertaining to inventories. This is the point where the opportunity for the fraud occurs. A decision needs to be made as to which inherent fraud schemes are most likely given the core business systems present in the organization. However, there is a twist with inventories concerning the core business systems. When we speak of theft or misuse, we could be referring to any number of systems such as purchasing, but if we are speaking solely of the misstatement of inventory value on the financial statements, then it is clearly the accounting and financial reporting systems that are in play.

As always, upon identification of the probable fraud scenario occurring, a fraud audit program is developed. There are two components of the audit program, one of which is data mining. The data mining component relies on the development of a fraud data profile that consists of a compilation of fraud data red flags and awareness of the concealment strategy, which acts as a guide to sample selection. By concealment strategy, we refer to how a perpetrator hides the theft or the misuse of the inventories or misstates the inventory value on the financial statements. Obviously, the concealment strategies can encompass a wide range of methods, such as the creation of internal documents reflecting a sale, transfer, or obsolescence of inventory to the writing-off of assets as obsolete.

Concealment Strategies

How the fraudulent act is concealed will depend on the composition of the inventories and what core business system(s) are being targeted to carry out the fraudulent act. The following is a list of the strategies most commonly employed with inventory fraud:

- Writing off the asset as scrap, obsolescence, missing, donated, or destroyed.
- Writing off the asset through shrinkage.

- Labeling the movement of the asset as a customer adjustment, no charge, promotional, transfer, or internal consumption transaction.
- Moving assets with no documentation supporting the transfer.
- Accepting goods without documentation or the creation of false documentation to support receipt of the goods.
- Creating false work orders.
- Creating false receiving reports as to quantity, quality, or specifications. Assets that are consumed in the course of normal business are especially susceptible to this concealment strategy.
- Creating fictitious credits to hide the shortage.
- Nonbilling of the asset sale.
- Creating false inventory counts or altering records after the physical count.

Management-Derived Inventory Fraud

When there is misrepresentation of inventory value in the financial statements, the core business system being manipulated involves the accounting for the inventory. That doesn't mean other business systems aren't involve as well; however, when management is involved, then we have to look at financial reporting misstatements and the actual concealment techniques involving the counting of the inventory.

Fraudulent Financial Reporting of Inventory

In addition to the actual theft and misuse of inventories, many fraud scenarios involve the misstatement of inventories in the financial reporting. This misstatement occurs with the action of higher-level management as opposite to the actual theft by an employee or outside agent. Similar to our discussion of revenue recognition fraud, the involvement of management in these schemes means that the pressures element of the fraud triangle comes into play rather than just opportunity. We have to ask, then, what are the motivating factors for management to overstate or understate inventory? The auditor must understand both the external and internal pressures facing management in order to properly assess the likelihood of inventory misstatement. The reasons may vary, but the outcome will be the same—the key is finding out if there are reasons at all.

Some typical reasons for understating inventory are:

- Reducing income.
- The company has achieved its goals.

- Reducing the value of the business.
- New management team in place.

Some reasons why management would overstate inventory are:

- To overstate income.
- To achieve goals.
- To increase the company's value.
- To meet bank covenants.
- To hide poor operational performance.
- For management compensation.
- To affect future acquisitions or sale of the business.
- To hide the theft of inventory.

Inventory Concealment Techniques

False inventory counting methods are indicative of the misstatement of inventory in the financial reporting, specifically, the management team records improper counts. Such schemes are likely to occur with inventory perceived to be less likely of being counted or with a planned reason for the false count. The hope is that the auditor will view the false count as an error versus an intentional plan to misstate the inventory. Therefore, the auditor needs to ensure that management has no record of the test counts. Certain types of inventory counts are more susceptible to being false, such as:

- **Periodic inventory.** This particular inventory is susceptible to false counting because the auditor has no inventory reports to determine what the inventory should have been prior to the count.
- **Perpetual inventory.** Variances or in-transit items are often used as an explanation for the deviations.
- **Multiple inventory locations.** The non-tested sites are susceptible to false counts because the auditor is not performing procedures at those locations. Management may also use other schemes in conjunction with the false-count fraud schemes.

Data Analysis

There are several key analyses that a fraud audit program can include to detect inventory fraud, whether it involves the actual theft of inventory items or is the misstatement of inventory value in the financial reporting process. The standard data mining routines to determine real or false vendors can be used in this situation also, so we won't bore you by rehashing them. However, we have to note that any data mining search routine should, in regard to theft and misuse, focus on searching for "ship to" addresses that aren't the company's real location.

So, we will start our discussion with the auditor's determining the type of assets in the inventory that would have a significant resale value or personal use value. We are talking significant here, not paper clips. If you are solely interested in petty theft, that type of inventory theft is usually easier to identify through traditional audit procedures. For the fraud audit, the auditor should search for significant variance or frequent use. A logic analysis should be developed to determine if the consumption or use of the asset correlated to the anticipated consumption or usage. Another analysis to find consumption irregularities involves performing a trend analysis on the use or consumption of an asset. Note that when the pattern of use can be benchmarked to data independent of the fraud, the variances tend to be dramatic. Using the accounting system can also identify the likelihood of theft through the review of the fixed asset ledger to identify those assets that would be prone to misuse, personal conversion, or resale.

For financial reporting misstatement of inventory, the data analysis should entail several comparisons. The following is a list of these analyses:

- The beginning inventory balances should be compared to the ending inventory balances, whereby the auditor is looking for changes consistent with fraudulent over- or understatement of inventory.
- Unit purchases should be compared to unit sales in order to correlate the variances to any change in inventory. The procedure requires drilling down to the lowest data element possible.
- Compare dollar purchases to dollar sales. This analysis is a variation on the unit comparison described above.
- Compute the number of inventory locations (bins) prior to the physical count.
- Compare beginning inventory to the ending inventory for new or deleted items.
- Compare inventory balances before and after the physical counts.
- Identify the largest physical counts.
- For multiple locations, compare total beginning inventory to total ending inventory. For those locations experiencing deviations that would indicate

fraudulent activity coinciding with the identified fraud scheme, perform data mining search routines on the inventory items.

- Determine which inventory items have had stock outages during the year.
- Through inquiry with the sales force, determine which items have had stock outages during the year.
- Compare inventory balances at the end of the third quarter to the inventory balances at the end-of-year.
- Identify inventory variances by stock item.
- Examine internal sales forecasts for sales projections consistent with representations on inventory movement.

 ## AUDIT PROCEDURES

Inventory is a different type of asset to handle within the context of fraud. It makes one wonder: how can such a large asset be the target of so many variations of fraud schemes? Maybe the very fact that inventories are comprised of so many items and types of items provides the reason why there are so many opportunities to steal or misuse it.

Inventory Examination

The same characteristics that make inventories the target of fraud—namely, that there are typically comprised of large amounts and variety of items—makes inventories so accessible as well. How many people handle inventory items in a given business on any given day? However, it is this very tangibility that can aid the auditor in detecting fraud involving inventories. Simply, inventories can be examined. Sure, you say that cash can be counted and fixed assets like buildings can be seen for what they are, so what makes inventories different from these asset types? It is that we have to use this ability to examine inventory to our advantage in identifying any fraudulent acts involving the asset. The audit approaches to examining inventory include:

- Examining inventory tags for evidence of changes.
- Examining inventory tags for evidence of tags being included or excluded.
- Comparing the number of inventory tags to the number of inventory locations.
- Establishing an inventory variance percentage and examining those inventory items exceeding the range.

- Computing inventory items by square footage of the warehouse and comparing beginning and ending square footage calculations.
- Performing inventory counts at locations not known to management.
- Based on the data analyses performed, the auditor may need to determine additional procedures to determine the reasonability of the data analyses results.

Inventory Fraud Schemes

The inherent schemes used by management are fundamentally simple to understand. How management conceals the truth from their auditor becomes the challenge. The audit process, whether the brainstorming or building the audit response, should include the following inherent schemes.

Fictitious Inventory

There are several situations where the examination of the inventory is critical in detecting fraud; one of these is when fictitious inventory is created. Specifically, management will use the business environment to create the illusion of inventory by placing empty boxes in the warehouse or creating a reason why inventory cannot be physically inspected. The reasons will vary; however, the intent is always the same. Management will need to inhibit the auditor's ability to physically inspect the items. In such schemes, the items do not exist, they are incomplete, or they are substituted with other products or items that will be represented as the inventory. The same data analysis that is performed for false counting can also be performed for fictitious inventory schemes. The audit procedures include:

- Examining the inventory item critically to ensure the physical existence of the item.
- Performing a testing procedure to ensure the item functions in a manner consistent with that described in the sales catalog.
- Considering using an outside expert to validate the item.
- Developing a logic test to determine the reasonability of the inventory.

Partially Fictitious Inventory

In this situation, the auditor is presented some item that provides the illusion that the inventory does indeed exist. The complexity of the item makes it difficult to determine whether it is in fact the correct item and not fictitious or a substitute. Again, the data analysis performed for false inventory counts can apply in this situation. The audit procedures should include:

- Examining the inventory items critically to ensure physical existence of the item.
- Performing a testing procedure to ensure the item functions in a manner consistent with that described in the sales catalog.
- Considering using an outside expert to validate the item.

False Certifications

In these schemes, management creates documents certifying inventory balances by altering the original documents, providing copies or drafts, or having an outside expert provide false documents supporting the inventory item. Inventory stored at remote locations, independent warehouses, engineering estimates, ore and minerals, and percentage-of-completion are all areas susceptible to this scheme. The data analysis performed for the false inventory count will also provide information for the scheme for items of a unit nature. The audit procedures include:

- Examining the documents critically to ensure they are original and not altered.
- Confirming directly with the source of the authenticity of the documents.
- Confirming the valid existence of the source or the outside expert.
- Performing an on-site inspection of the inventory.
- Confirming the existence of the inventory at the location with some other source within the company.
- Interviewing operations staff about their knowledge of the inventory amount.
- Reviewing vendor invoices to ensure cost elements of the project have reasonably occurred.

Alterations

By alterations we are referring to the altering of inventory counts after the physical counts have taken place. The audit procedures include the following:

- Prior to the physical inventory count, the auditor should obtain a report or a data file confirming inventory balances prior to taking a physical count.
- The auditor should compare the inventory report obtained above with the final physical inventory report.

Multiple Locations

These schemes involve inventory at locations not counted being moved to locations that are being counted in order to hide the overstatement of the inventory. The data analysis should consist of searching for inventory transfer documentation between locations. The audit procedures involve the following:

- The consideration of doing an unannounced physical inventory count.
- Prior to the inventory count, examine shipping documents, transfer documents, or other related source documents involving the transfer of inventory.
- Interview operations management at inventory locations to determine if any unusual inventory movement occurred around the same time of the physical inventory.

Timing

These schemes involve inventory's being recorded in the wrong reporting period. Key areas to focus on include inventory received at year-end, hidden purchases, goods in transit, title transfer of inventory, sales returns, and the recording of sales without inventory's being updated. The data analysis consists of performing two specific data mining search routines, one for inventory transfers between operating locations and the other for purchases recorded after year-end reporting. The audit procedures include:

- Matching shipping documents to inventory movement.
- Examining purchase returns and credits for any indication of false purchases.
- For purchases recorded after year-end reporting, examining the shipping documents to ascertain the date of receipt.
- Examining shipping records after year-end reporting for evidence of the passage of "risk of loss" from seller to buyer.

Hiding Inventory

You are probably getting a good laugh out of this section title if you are thinking about inventory made up of really large objects. However, there are schemes out there that involve the hiding of slow-moving inventory. Particular to these schemes is altering the inventory or sales reports in some manner to indicate inventory movement. Management may create fictitious sales to indicate the product is moving. The sold inventory could then be used as part of a false count scheme. The detection of this type of scheme is data analysis intensive. Specifically, the auditor needs to compute the sales history of an inventory item in terms of units and dollars, and compare the sales history for a minimum of one year in order to recognize any patterns or anomalies. Then the auditor computes the inventory amount from the previous quarter and compares it to ending inventory amount to determine reasonableness. Data mining searches need to be performed to search for ship-to addresses that are company-owned properties, sales with no commissions attached, and returns with no adjustments. There is only one recommended audit procedure, that being to perform interviews with sales management to validate explanations regarding the marketability of the inventory.

Misstatement of Marketability

When we state misstatement in this context, we are not referring to financial reporting misstatement, but rather the situation where management provides the auditor with explanations or documents that indicate pending or future sales. The data analysis to be used is the same as with slow-moving inventory. Also similar is the one-audit procedure, but in this case, the auditor needs to confirm the explanations with sources outside the financial systems.

Improper Costing

These schemes involve improper costs being assigned to the inventory. As you probably are well aware, this entails the costing of an inventory item and the cost-flow assumption, such as, Frist In Frist Out, Last In Frist Out, weighted average, or specific identification being used. The key to detecting this fraudulent act is to have sufficient knowledge of the business and how it "costs" its inventory. The data analysis that needs to be performed is to search for updates to cost items in the last quarter, and then to compare last quarter cost elements to year-end cost elements. The audit procedures are:

- Matching cost elements to original supporting documentation, verifying unit prices and the proper usage of the inventory costing method.
- Confirming that cost composition elements agree with operation blueprints or other like plans.
- Comparing ending unit costs to beginning unit costs. The lowest component cost possible will provide the best results.

Year-End Journal Entries

These schemes involve management's altering inventory balances through journal entry. This altering can occur through documentation supporting the entry, the volume of the entries, and whether the entries are part of the normal course of business. The data analysis includes performing data mining search routines to determine the year-end journal entries that affect ending inventory and to search for year-end journal entries that indicate the transfer of inventory from various locations. Two audit procedures are indicated:

- Validating the explanations provided.
- Determining if similar entries were made during the year or in prior years.

Report Alteration

These schemes involve the alteration of year-end inventory reports. To detect such alteration, the auditor must match the year-end inventory report to the financial statements. The purpose of this matching is to identify erroneous calculations or totals. The nature of the scheme doesn't really lend itself to any specific data analysis. The audit procedure would be to recalculate the inventory report.

Other Audit Procedures

There are several other audit procedures that can be used in detecting inventory fraud scenarios. These include:

- Reviewing the statement of cash flows and asking whether the increases and decreases in cash make sense in relation to the inventory account balances and changes.
- Computing the inventory turnover ratio and days-to-sell ratio. Do these ratios make sense in relation to what the auditor has verified regarding the physical aspects of the inventory?
- Computing the percentage of gross profit and the related percentage of the cost of goods sold, and then trend to look for understatement of the cost of goods sold percentage.
- Ensuring there is a consistent use of the inventory cost flow assumption. For example, the use of FIFO gives a higher net income in an inflationary environment.

- For complex inventory methods, such as dollar value LIFO, verifying the assumptions and methodology used to cost inventory. This procedure usually involves the use of an expert.
- For manufacturing environments, ensuring that product/period costs are properly classified.

SUMMARY

It is typically the large number of items that comprise a given inventory that make it such a target for fraud. Theft and misuse are the actions of choice when it comes to inventory fraud. The rationale typically is: "Who is going to miss a few hundred widgets in an inventory of thousands, perhaps millions?" The size of inventory as a percentage of the amount of total assets also makes it an easy target for management-initiated financial reporting misstatement. Having two types of fraudulent acts ganging up on inventories, the auditor doesn't want to waste time going down the wrong path, so it's very important to determine the which fraudulent act is likely occurring. Any discussion of fraud likelihood involves the concepts of concealment, conversion, and opportunity. So, in addition to "how" the inventory fraud took place, other questions need to be addressed, such as: How sophisticated is the concealment strategy? Who has the most benefit to gain by the theft, misuse, or misstatement of inventories? Who has and where are the opportunities to divert inventories? These are the questions that need to be answered by the auditor, and fortunately, the tools and knowledge are available to achieve the right answers when faced with situations of inventory fraud.

CHAPTER FIFTEEN

Journal Entry Fraud

A FTER READING THE TITLE of this chapter, you're probably thinking that journal entries aren't a core business system. Sure, they are part of the accounting process, but a system unto itself? Let us explain. As with any daunting task, we have to break things down into sizes we can work with, and sometimes that is the rawest of the raw data. Financial reporting and statements can be thought of as the first and topmost level of journal entry fraud because financial reporting misstatement implicates the organization as a whole. With this starting point in mind, the answers to our usual question of "who," "when," and "how" such fraud is committed are pretty obvious.

Typically, it is executive management that benefits from financial statement manipulation. For example, a company has a sizable loan with certain financial covenants that must be met or there would be a default. One such covenant could concern something as simple as a working capital ratio that has to be maintained at 2:1 per the loan agreement. If management realizes that the covenant will not be met during a specified financial reporting period, then account balances could be inflated or deflated through fraudulent journal entries to meet the covenant. This type of fraud doesn't always occur at the CEO level—for example, a sales department may inflate the number of sales

251

completed in a reporting period in order to meet quotas or, in the case of an individual salesperson, perhaps to receive a large bonus.

Through these examples, we can ascertain that the answer to the question of "who" initiates financial misstatements is clearly management-oriented. "The "why" of such fraud's occurring relates to the elements of the fraud triangle: opportunity, rationalization, and pressures. Management has the *opportunity* through control authorizations, and the typical *pressures* are derived by the need to present the organization in a positive light for the board of directors, investors, banks, employees, and so on. The rationalization that the organization has survived and jobs are intact because of the fraudulent act completes the triangle. "How" the fraud occurs is through manipulation of journal entries resulting in misstatement of financial reporting.

 FRAUD RISK STRUCTURE

Even though this type of fraud can be considered organization-wide, it typically occurs at the business-system level through the manipulation of journal entries. On the surface, you may ask which is more important in the detection of this type of fraud: the journal entries or the controls of those processes involving journal entries? The answer is both.

As previously done with other types of fraud, the first step is to perform a risk assessment that would focus on the action element of the inherent scheme. Given the organizational level where this fraud typically originates, assessing the controls associated with the core business process is critical. Therefore, the action element is the point at which business system controls are absent, flawed, or overridden, resulting in the opportunity for fraudulent journal entries to be made. The actual misstatement of financial reporting, of the financial statements, or internal financial reporting systems typically involves fictitious or sham transactions; improper recognition; improper measurement in regard to estimates, calculations, or assumptions; improper disclosure or omission; and misapplication of generally accepted accounting principles (GAAP).

SAS 99 and Manipulation in Financial Reporting

SAS 99 identifies two key areas often involved when there is manipulation in financial reporting. Specifically, the recording of inappropriate or unauthorized journal entries throughout the year or at period-end or making adjustments to amounts reported in the financial statements that are not reflected in formal journal entries (e.g., adjustments and reclassifications). To detect fraud in these two target areas, an auditor needs to obtain an understanding of an entity's financial reporting process and the controls in place. Additionally, an auditor per SAS 99 needs to be able to identify "the type, number, and monetary value of journal entries and other adjustments that are typically made in preparing the financial statements."

Transactions and Journal Entries

Establishing a fraud risk structure is the starting point for identifying the fraud scenarios that can occur through manipulation of journal entries. In other words, how schemes are structured within an entity's accounting system. Given that we are focused on journal entries, the lifeblood of accounting systems, the determination of fraud seems to be a layup. How could an auditor not know how accounting systems work and, therefore, be manipulated? However, you have to remember the concealment strategy employed with fraudulent behavior. Also, remember that the risk structure, when talking about a specific business process, in this case accounting, depends on the size and type of the entity. A large manufacturing firm with many subsidiaries will have different transactions than a regional not-for-profit charity; however, whatever transactions comprise an entity's manner of doing business, all transactions can be categorized as one of three types, according to the Public Company Accounting Oversight Board (PCAOB) Audit Standards. The three types of transactions are:

1. Routine transactions: Recurring financial activities reflected in the accounting records in the normal course of business.
2. Nonroutine transactions: Activities that occur only periodically (e.g., taking a physical inventory, calculating depreciation expense, adjusting for foreign currency exchange rates). A distinguishing feature of nonroutine transactions is that the data involved is generally not a part of the routine flow of transactions.
3. Estimation transactions: Activities that involve management judgments in formulating account balances in absence of a precise means of measurement.

Control Points for Journal Entries

Each transaction type can be broken down further in terms of journal entries. Accounting systems are designed to ensure that a transaction is processed from origination to the final recording in the general ledger. Internal controls are built into the system to minimize both unintentional errors and intentional ones. In reality, not all transactions adhere to the controls in the same manner. Not only are the transactions handled differently, but often the controls are applied differently. Therefore, the goal is to identify those transactions that may be more prone to fraud because of inherent control weaknesses. An understanding of the control points for journal entries is critical. These control points occur:

- At origination: A control that creates a basis for a journal entry, including criteria, rate calculations, identification of transactions, and estimates.
- With authorization: The approval process in place for the processing, recording, and documentation of a journal entry.
- Through processing: The steps from initiation through recording of the journal entry.
- When recording: Posting of the journal entry into the general ledger.
- Documentation: Creating and retaining documentation supporting a journal entry.

Types of Journal Entries

Understanding the control points means nothing if there is little to no understanding of the types of journal entries being used within a specific entity. Correlating the type of journal entries and the control points is a necessary step in developing a risk structure. The following list describes the types of journal entries and their correlating fraud risks:

- Recording: Entries entailing routine transactions and routine accounting journals. Although source journals are properly posted to the general ledger, the source journal could contain fictitious transactions or contain arithmetic inaccuracies.
- Adjusting: Entries that are designed to change, alter, or adjust an original transaction or change an estimate of a transaction. Fraud can be concealed in the assumptions of the adjustments (e.g., who involved in the business process would gain from such a deception?)
- Reclassification: Entries designed to transfer a transaction from one account to another one. The amount is not changed, just the account. As with adjustments, we go back to the fraud triangle and determine who had the opportunity to make or authorize such a change, how can

such a change be rationalized, and what pressures exist to lead to such a change?

■ Consolidating or combination: Entries that are designed to adjust inter-company accounts. The fraud risk involves related party activity or management override. Whenever consolidation occurs, an opportunity for concealment is presented (e.g., what is a routine journal entry for one company, may be handled differently within the related company's system).

■ Reversal: Entries that are designed to reverse a period-end adjusting entry. Be aware of adjustments that create a zero balance and are reversed, thereby creating new balance after the reporting period.

Data Analysis

SAS 99 provides guidelines for identifying journal entries for testing. Incorporating these guidelines into a determined fraud risk structure allows for an effective audit process. Therefore, the auditor should consider several key areas, such as the auditor's assessment of fraud risk, the effectiveness of controls, the financial reporting process, the characteristics of fraudulent entries, the nature and complexity of accounts, and journal entries processed outside the normal course of business.

Although dealing with journal entry fraud, the auditor needs to assess the fraud risk at a business-process level. This assessment involves linking specific internal control procedures to the fraud risk inherent to the process. Therefore, the auditor's overall objective is to develop an audit program that mitigates the inherent risk. So, a determination of management's risk tolerance is needed. In light of management's risk tolerance, the auditor needs to answer the question of just how extensive the control testing of processes involving journal entries has to be. This is the point where the auditor's risk assessment acts as a tool to help management arrive at an informed decision regarding the cost of managing fraud risk. Remember, one purpose of the fraud risk assessment is to know the inherent fraud schemes associated with an organization in an effort to identify the fraud scenario taking place. Therefore, the types of journal entries found in the inherent fraud schemes may identify the specific classes of journal entries to analyze and the extent of that analysis.

The difference between testing of journal entries and testing the controls of journal entries may sound like a case of semantics; however, fraud might be occurring even with controls operating effectively. Remember concealment strategy goes hand-in-hand with fraudulent behavior. Therefore, matching controls to the specific journal entries is needed. What is the intent of the control? Is a journal entry control override, or misuse of such, concealing the fraud scheme? Are there control exceptions, whereby certain journal entries are excluded? Are controls missing? Is there an override of a control? Has the control been in place for so long that no one knows its intended purpose or cares, for that matter?

Using data mining search routines can be effective in searching for fraudulent journal entries comprising the financial reporting process except when there's an element of manual entry. When data mining transactional data, the areas to look at include control numbers, account activity, amounts, correlation of various controls, and errors. Is the financial reporting supported by the appropriate processing of journal entries? Do other journal entries exist outside of the automated system? Does the processing of transactions involve a combination of manual and automated procedures? Such a mix of methods can result in controls that are effective only with one method and not the other. The data searches should be made to recognize types of patterns, such as:

- Anomalies, extreme deviations from the norm.
- Unusual or abnormal, irregular or uncommon.
- Illogical, contrary to what seems reasonable.
- Frequency, increasing number of same transaction.
- Changes, in control or amounts.
- Errors, in arithmetic or information.

Outside of the aforementioned patterns, there are characteristics of fraudulent journal entries that can be identified in conjunction with a data search routine. Some of these characteristics can be found by asking: Are the entries unrelated to routine business transactions, are they unusual, or do they involve seldom-used accounts? Are they made by individuals whose job responsibilities do not include working with journal entries? Are they not described or do they have little explanation included, when made at the end of a reporting period or postclosing. Are account numbers missing? Are the numbers containing rounded or a consistent ending number?

Another consideration in analyzing journal entries concerns the complexity of the accounts. It is a matter for an auditor's judgment to consider the level of complexity, because it can take on many forms in regard to journal entries. Is there a pattern of errors from one reporting period to the next? Is there an abnormal amount of estimate use? Are there numerous irreconcilable differences or differences not reconciled on a timely basis? Are there intercompany transactions and how complex or possibly vague are they?

As with transactions occurring in off periods, journal entries or other adjustments processed outside the normal course of business have a high fraud-predictability factor because they are probably not subjected to controls that are in place for routinely occurring transactions.

Characteristics of Fraudulent Entries or Adjustments

There are various characteristics found with fraudulent journal entries or adjustments, and knowing them can aid the auditor in building an effective fraud audit program. Although as previously discussed, the cost of finding all fraudulent entries is unrealistic, so you have to determine management's tolerance for fraud and proceed from there. These characteristics include:

- Movement of asset, liability, equity, revenue, or expense accounts in terms of over- or understatement. Income can be overstated by omitting items, such as purchase returns or fictitious reductions of expenses, and liabilities can take place to conceal losses.
- Timing of when the entry is recorded. Was the entry made during an off-period? Was the entry made at the end of a reporting period?
- Manual entries or nonroutine entries. Manual entries lend themselves to lax security measures.
- End-of-quarter or end-of-year entries. Management is pressured to meet analysts' forecasts for earnings and so fictitiously inflate profits with end-of-period entries or adjustments.
- Entries initiated or recorded by senior financial management, thereby circumventing the controls.
- Round or even amount entries. Data mining searches can effectively isolate such irregularities.
- Entries recorded after the closing of routine journals. May be performed in an attempt to conceal fictitious, routine entries by reversing them after close.
- Reversal entries that cause an account balance to have a material change. Data search for identical entries having a material effect.
- Journal entry number or range of numbers out of sequence with standard numbering. A visual scan of journal numbers will denote out-of-sequence entries.

- Journal entry references containing numbers, letters, or symbols not consistent with standard identification. Data searches sorting reference numbers can isolate such inconsistencies.
- Manual reversal of journal entry.
- Journal entries between operating entities and affiliates. Examine notation of due/to, due/from entries.
- Journal entries transferred through more than the account or company. Tracking entries from raw data to general ledger is necessary.
- Journal entries not posted to the general ledger. The entry is posted solely for financial statement preparation.
- Journal entries to accounts affecting the below net operating income amounts. Comparison to prior years' statements to examine whether this is a standard procedure or if it is an uncommon practice.
- Revenue entries with other side of entry to unusual accounts. Unusual accounts may appear to manipulate balances used in financial reporting. The concealment strategy is the eventual burying of the unusual account when like accounts are consolidated for the financial report.

Characteristics of Accounts Containing Fraudulent Journal Entries

Although some of the same characteristics as found with fraudulent journal entries and adjustments apply to fraudulent accounts, the audit procedure for fraudulent accounts provides a second level of examination after detecting inconsistencies with the journal entries and adjustments. Do the same patterns for manipulation appear with the accounts, as found with the journal entries and adjustments? Here's where to look for the answer:

- Accounts without entries from standard transaction journals.
- Accounts used solely for period-end adjustments.
- Accounts for reserves.
- Accounts for intercompany transactions.
- Accounts adjusted to a zero balance.
- Accounts with a significant year-end change.
- Irreconcilable accounts.
- Accounts where the opposite side of the entry is nonstandard or unusual by the nature of the entry.
- Accounts whose net movement is consistent with fraud theory.
- New general ledger account numbers containing journal entries.

- Accounts with zero or insignificant account balances resulting from journal entries.
- Accounts having an unusual activity-level below control thresholds.
- Accounts having multiple manual entries on successive dates or times.
- Accounts having multiple manual entries initiated by same individual.
- Accounts comprised of only manual journal entries.
- Accounts containing manual entries and no subsequent reversal.

Examples of Fraudulent Journal Entries

The following examples involve the nature of journal entries and the methods by which they can be fraudulently manipulated. These examples pertain to most organizations; however, in small companies with no accounting staff, journal entries may not exist in the general ledger, except as proposed by a CPA performing a year-end audit for the company. In those cases, the auditor should document that no entries were posted and that no additional audit work is necessary. We have identified the following 10 areas of fraudulent journal entries.

1. **Recurring automated entries from integrated standard journals.** Typically, recurring automated journal entries are not a source of fraudulent activity. Fraud in the standard journals tends to take the form of sham transactions or the improper recognition of transactions. The method to detect such fraudulent activity would consist of tracking of the journal entries from the source documents to the general ledger.

2. **Recurring automated entries from nonintegrated standard journals.** The fraudulent act in this case is when there is altering or changing of the totals in a nonintegrated standard journal that leads to a misstating of revenue. The totals may be misstated through computer program code manipulation, substituting altered total pages, and journal entries not matching standard journal totals. Detecting the fraudulent entries once again involves tracking the entries from source documents to the general ledger. A data mining routine can be performed to validate the totals on the source journal.

3. **Recurring entries from a manual original source journal.** The totals may be misstated by substituting altered total pages, intentional arithmetic errors, and journal entries not matched to standard journal totals. Again, tracking the entries from source to the general ledger and validating the totals on the source journal is necessary. However, due to

the manual nature of the journal, automated data extraction cannot be performed.

4. **Recurring automated journal entries.** These entries occur when the business system has the ability to initiate journal entries without human intervention. Tests need to be performed that would focus on the criteria for the entry.

5. **Recurring manual journal entries.** Recurring journal entries that are manually entered are entries that are initiated by an individual on a regular periodic basis. The individual initiating the entry controls the documentation and support. Manual entries, by their nature, indicate that an individual posted the entry; therefore, fraud detection should focus on determining who has the opportunity and/or is under enough pressure to commit entering fraudulent entries and what event prompted the creation of such entries.

6. **Nonrecurring manual journal entries.** These entries are ones that are initiated by an individual on a non-routine basis. The individual initiating the entry controls the documentation and support. The purpose is to adjust actual events versus estimates. These entries tend to occur at the end of a reporting period, and history has shown that entries at the end of a reporting period are most often associated with fraudulent misstatement. Therefore, by their very nature, year-end entries should garner a closer scrutiny.

7. **Journal entries that are made to adjust estimates.** Fraudulent financial reporting is often accomplished through intentional misstatement of accounting estimates. The fraud risk should be ascertained by the intent found in the direction of misstatement. It is necessary to test the assumption or criteria used to make the adjustment. The use of the retrospective review of significant estimates described in SAS 99 can be a valuable tool. Specifically, the pertinent paragraph states: "The auditor also should perform a retrospective review of significant accounting estimates reflected in the financial statements of the prior year to determine whether management judgments and assumptions relating to the estimates indicate a possible bias. . . . With the benefit of hindsight, a retrospective review should provide the auditor with additional information about whether there may be a possible bias on the part of management in making the current-year estimates. This review, however, is not intended to call into question the auditor's professional judgments made in the prior year that were based on information available at the time."

8. **Reclassification entries.** Typically, no change occurs to the original transaction other than the account in which the transaction is recorded. Again, the direction of misstatement and the accounts should be noted. Also noted are entries that change the reporting of a transaction on the financial statement, for example, expense items reclassified to a current asset or a nonoperating income item to operating revenue.

9. **Top-sided journal entries.** Top-sided entries are entries that do not occur in a company's general ledger. Typically, the error occurs at a corporate level for the purpose of adjusting, reclassifying, combining, or consolidating transactions. Since such entries are often associated with senior management, they should be closely scrutinized. As an overall response to the risk of fraud, a more senior member of the audit team should consider examining these entries.

10. **Journal entries initiated by senior financial management.** The inquiry should focus on verbal instructions given by management and the actual creation and recording of an entry consistent with those instructions. Entries that are directly or indirectly initiated by senior management should be more closely scrutinized.

AUDIT PROCEDURES

Given that journal entry fraud exists on a core business-system level within a real organization, there is less emphasis on determining whether an entity is real or false. The focus is on the credibility of the financial reporting and how the company is reflected in the financial reports to the outside world. With the emphasis on the financial reports, the audit procedures need to focus on what comprises these reports and what outside influences can affect them. Remember, fraud audit procedures, in general, are to be designed to determine the true nature of a business transaction. A fraud audit procedure does not test the existence of the internal controls or rely on management representations as with traditional audit procedures, nor do procedures assume the falsity of the transactions. The procedures are designed to focus on the concealment strategy and associated red flags. Therefore, the auditor needs to know the characteristics of fraudulent entries or adjustments. By being familiar with the characteristics, the influence of management, especially those with override authority can be closely examined in terms of concealment strategies. When dealing with transactions, both the journal entries and the accounts associated with the inherent fraud scheme need attention in order to determine a falsity.

Steps to Identifying Fraudulent Journal Entries

Although elements such as the size of the business (e.g., existence of subsidiaries), kind of business system (e.g., manual versus automated data entry), and type of goods and services provided (e.g., not-for-profit charity, large equipment manufacturer, grocery store) all need to be considered, there are general steps that an auditor can take when examining journal entries for fraud. These steps are:

1. Include the fraud triangle. The fraud triangle prescribes that for fraud to occur, there must be opportunity, pressures, and rationalization. For financial reporting fraud, the opportunity is associated with the control environment because controls are typically in place with senior management approval. The organization-wide nature of this type of fraud lends itself to examination of pressures and rationalization on senior management or the business owner. Is the CEO under pressure from investors to show a sizable profit this quarter? Is the business owner, who is unable to distinguish his business from himself, rationalizing that misstating the company's financial reports to evade taxes will allow his company (i.e., himself) to survive?

2. Identify material accounts balances and assertions in the financial statements. Where is the best hiding place for fraudulent entries, such as accounts with immaterial or material balances? Manipulating which account balances has the greatest impact? As applies to data mining, start large and drill down.

3. Link fraud theory to material account balances and financial statement assertions.

4. Based on key external and internal operating statistics, identify material account balances and assertions in the financial statements. Does the amount of widgets (the ones with high profit margins) manufactured translate into material balances? Did a sizable number of new chain stores indicate a proportional increase in balances?

5. Determine the extent of an account balance created through journal entries. Does the number of journal entries account for the actual balance or are entries missing, reclassified, and so on?

6. Determine the impact of adjusting entries on material account balances. Are an unusual number of adjusting entries being used?

7. Determine accounts that are primarily based on estimates. Are there many such accounts? Are the estimates reasonable?

8. Consider both the qualitative and quantitative impact of journal entries on account balances. Simply put, do the entries make any sense? Are there too many of a questionable nature being made? Can they be tracked back to the appropriate raw data?

9. Identify year-end adjusting entries as to:
   - Accruals to record activity in the proper period.
   - Adjustments based on estimates.
   - Reclassifications between major segments of the financial statements.

10. Interview regarding journal entries:
   - Determine individuals responsible for initiating the basis for the journal entry.
   - Determine the control environment with regard to authorization.
   - Determine the extent of influence senior management has regarding the basis of the entry and the recording of a journal entry.

11. Consider the characteristics of fraudulent journal entries or accounts.

12. Implement professional skepticism:
   - How fraud would be concealed through the misrepresentations.
   - Know the characteristics of fraudulent journal entries or accounts.
   - Linking journal entries in accounts from nonroutine sources to the inherent fraud scheme.
   - Predictability factor: Are the elements of the fraud triangle evident?
   - The frequency of journal entries is not expected with the type of business or with the amount of business being done.
   - The dollar amounts of specific entry-types are not expected to be that high or low considering the type of business or with the amount of business being done.
   - Amounts appearing are suspicious because they are rounded dollar figures.
   - Change: Have systems been converted from manual entry to automated? Are entries being made differently than in previous reporting periods? Have new controls been put in place? Have control authorizations changed? Denote any changes and find out the reasons for them.

Fraud Audit Procedures for Journal Entries and Accounts

The procedures are straightforward with journal entries, although the number of them can seem overwhelming. That is why determining the risk structure is so important. Having targeted schemes reduces the amount of journal entries under consideration. The first step is to obtain the supporting documentation, then recalculate the entry, trace to the general ledger, determine the logic of the entry, and determine the sufficiency of the documentation. If entries are found to be fraudulent, further inquiries are needed to determine their true economic substance. Specifically:

- **Unrecorded transactions.** Is the reason for the transaction not being recorded normal within the business operation? If so, validate that the transaction occurred in the later period. If not, what changed in the organization and corroborate the reason to a source other than the originator of the reason. Validate that the transaction occurred.
- **Adjustment for criteria or rate.** Compare to prior year. Is the change or lack of change consistent with expectations? Corroborate rate to a source independent of the originator.
- **Estimates.** Perform a retrospective analysis of last year's adjustments.
- **Cutoff adjustments.** What other accounts could be impacted by a cutoff issue? How does the cutoff issue impact other performance measures in the company?

Examples of Fraud Schemes Involving Journal Entries

The following examples are broken up into two types: financial reporting schemes involving journal entries and specific examples. The former is a list that generally defines the schemes, while the latter provides examples of some of these general types.

There are general categories of financial reporting schemes involving journal entry manipulation. These categories include the following:

- Overstated assets: Estimates of inventory are adjusted in order to inflate assets on the financial reports.
- Overvalued assets: Assets that are recorded in excess of their worth to support financing that is then redirected.
- Understatement of liabilities: By understating liabilities, financial ratios that are used as loan covenants may be misrepresented.
- Omitted liabilities: Typically done to enhance financial statements in order to satisfy analyst or investor expectations.
- Overstated revenues: Can be performed by eliminating journal entries that lower revenues (e.g., purchase returns and allowances).
- Revenue recognition: Profit may be falsely inflated to include sales that are in process.

- Income reduction: Often performed to avoid paying taxes. Schemes can also be performed by inflating expenses or a combination of both.
- Understatement of expenses: Increases to expense accounts outside the normal course of doing business may be concealing misclassification of expenses incurred for nonbusiness activities.

Examples of Journal Entry Fraud Schemes

The following examples also include a discussion concerning estimate bias, which may be helpful in addressing the detection of fraudulent journal entry schemes.

Overstated Assets

Inventory is overstated due to obsolete inventory related to a change in product mix. Inventories are stated at the lower of cost or market. Cost is determined by the average cost method. Inquiries regarding the obsolete inventory corroborate that finished goods are stated at the lower of cost or market. Since the overstatement is a fraudulent attempt to misstate financials, no response is necessary.

Revenue Recognition

Yes, we gave you an entire chapter on revenue recognition fraud, but now we are discussing it within the context of the role of journal entries. For example, a construction company's revenues from cost-plus-fee contracts are recognized on the basis of costs incurred during the period plus the fee earned. Revenues from fixed-price and modified fixed-price construction contracts are recognized on the percentage of completion method (e.g., the percentage of costs incurred to date to estimated total costs for each contract). Upon interviewing the project manager, it was found out the weather impacted road jobs this year with roadwork completion dates being delayed by as much as 60 days.

The fraud occurs when costs are misapplied or transferred to other contracts to avoid disclosure of the losses. Consequently, the percentage-of-completion is overstated to offset completed contract losses associated with the weather delays. Searches need to be performed for journal entries that reclassify costs between projects. Also a review of the allocation of owned-equipment charges to projects is needed. Finally, examination of year-end adjustments for open projects is required.

Another area of key importance concerns the use of estimates. In reviewing the adjusting entries for open contracts, the calculation for the percentage-of-completion is the targeted risk area, not the journal entry itself, because the entry is simply the method of recording the misstatement.

There is a mini-decision tree that can be used when reviewing accounting estimates for bias.

The first decision is to determine whether the prior-year estimate reflected the actual results that occurred by using actual data recorded in the current year. If so, determine that the current year estimate was calculated based on a similar methodology. If that condition is met, then conclude that the current methodology is appropriate for the current year business environment.

Some areas where estimates are abused include construction, inventory obsolescence, sales returns, pension accounts, and oil/gas reserves. The two examples described above involve these areas of abuse, specifically, construction and inventory obsolescence. However, in the inventory example, finished goods were found to be stated at the lower of cost or market and that the cost was determined by the average cost method. If we applied our decision tree to the construction example, the first decision point would result in detection of a difference between current year and prior year, resulting in examination of the journal entries that were used to record the misstatement.

Expense Allocations

The program manager of a not-for-profit has been informed by the social services agency that provides the majority of funding for the not-for-profit's programs that there will be no funding increases for programs in the next two years. The program manager is under pressure to increase administration expenses because of the cost of living increases mandated within employee contracts. Given that other sources of program funding will increase direct expenses based on inflation, the inherent fraud scheme involves the reclassification of entries between administration and direct expenses in consideration that administrative costs could be allocated to direct expenses for the program. Searching for reclassification entries between administrative categories and direct expenses should result in detection of administrative expenses being misallocated to direct expenses.

 SUMMARY

Reflecting on the information outlined in this chapter, an important conclusion is made: A fraud auditor must question how many financial statements have been falsely altered via journal entries. The easy answer is that too many misstatements have been made. Journal entries are one of the easiest ways to record false entries into financial statements. With that being said, an auditor's response to the risk of journal entry fraud is also easy.

The spirit of the fraud audit approach provides the answer in how to respond to the "presumed risk" associated with journal entries. First, through the planning process, the auditors need to understand the most logical place for misstatement to occur in the financial statements. Using data mining the auditor should search for entries that meet the fraud data profile. Using fraud audit procedures, the auditor should verify the authenticity of the management representations. I know that real-life auditing is more challenging than a simple and easy statement in a book. However, I also know that our profession can and must respond to financial statement fraud with the vigor of fraud auditing techniques.

CHAPTER SIXTEEN

Program Management Fraud

W HEN WE SPEAK OF programs, we are not focused on core business systems per se; rather, we are referring to projects that are not funded through the sale of a product or service, but projects that obtain outside funding via the government, charitable grants, or donations to achieve a specific outcome. These outcomes can be any of a variety of things, from a scientific research study to find a cure for a catastrophic illness or federally legislated programs to provide health care to the indigent and elderly, as with the Medicaid and Medicare programs, respectively; or a not-for-profit charity that provides several programs, each funded from different sources, but all providing services to the elderly such as delivered meals, community center operations, adult daycare, and wellness programs. Typically, these outcomes are of a social benefit. Some of these programs are of a specific duration, while others are renewed on a periodic basis depending on continued funding and the successful management of the program to achieve the desired outcomes. So, you may ask, with such a variety of objectives, funding mechanisms, and organizational configurations, how can there be one-size-fits-all inherent fraud schemes to build our fraud risk structure?

The projects or programs themselves are not the object of our search for fraud; it's the management of the programs. Managers are engaged to operate such programs consistent with their scope and budget. The opportunity for fraud in these programs will vary in three specific aspects: by the independence provided to the program manager, by organizational structure of the program, and by the level of oversight by the funding source. These three elements make the conducting of a fraud audit with regard to program management different from that of auditing for fraud in the typical core business functions found in businesses like manufacturing or retail stores. Of course, the fraud schemes may sound similar because of the primary fraud classifications that apply to almost all organizations, but the key is how they are adapted by the program management.

Problems arise because there is a tendency to think of such programs as just mini-businesses and treat the parts as a sum of the whole, especially when there are numerous programs comprising an organization. Sure, you could claim the similarities are there and we are just talking smaller apples to apples rather than the standard apples to oranges. Examples abound to support this way of thinking, too. The request to fund a program is similar to defective pricing schemes found in the procurement functions. Also, the financial reporting schemes for a program are similar to fraud schemes for a financial statement misstatement. However, there are these underlying differences that present opportunities for fraud that are unique to program management, and it is these differences that are at the center of our discussion of program management fraud.

FRAUD RISK STRUCTURE

Before we can build a fraud risk structure for program management, we better know just what a program is. A program can be thought of as a project with a defined purpose, for example, it may be one that is conducted on a worldwide basis involving developing science or technology. Often, the subject matter is so specific that an auditor will feel like the proverbial fish out of water, which causes a challenge on its own. In keeping with our water-themed analogies, the key when you're feeling in over your head is to just focus on "the "how" and not the "what"—specifically, how the program is being operated so that its objectives can be carried out. The problem resulting from technical aspects being beyond the understanding of the auditor can be alleviated through use of consultants who are knowledgeable about the program's objectives. Such consultants may also be used to provide a scope disclaimer or to disclose the qualitative aspects of the evidence in regard to the degree of certainty.

The three primary classifications of fraud that are most pronounced with regard to fraudulent opportunities in program management are asset misappropriation, corruption, and financial statement reporting. Now, don't turn the page, because the following discussion is not a rehashing of previous chapters. No, this discussion goes straight to how these fraud types occur in programs and if it sounds familiar, then we ask you to read a little more closely to catch the subtle nuances, while keeping in mind the entire time that we are talking about programs.

Asset Misappropriation

When we speak of asset misappropriation, the fraudulent action involved is embezzlement. Why embezzlement and not, say, theft of funds? While they are both criminal actions, embezzlement is particular in its meaning. *Black's Law Dictionary* states it best: "the fraudulent taking of personal property with which one has been entrusted, esp. as a fiduciary." Now, if you want to be picky, it really is a matter of intent. Having cleared the air with regard to embezzlement, let's give some inherent fraud schemes and descriptions of how these schemes are carried out within a program.

False Expenditures

Unlike our decision of whether a company is real or false, we need to dig a little with any falsity regarding programs and that usually involves looking for falsity surrounding expenditures. For example:

- The program is not being conducted, but funds are being expended. This sounds like our old shell company scam, except we are talking about a program. What's the difference? you ask. The difference is simple—a program by itself is legitimate, but it is the intent of management that makes it false.
- The program is not performed to its completion; however, the funds are fully expended. The decision to be made is whether the intent was to embezzle funds throughout the program or if there are other underlying reasons as to why the program wasn't completed that resulted in the funds being embezzled.
- The program budget does not allow for program completion. Is this a case of bad budgeting or the use of budgeting with the intent to embezzle?
- The work plan is fictitious. This scheme seems too obvious. Can there really be an easier method of detecting fraud? You have to remember that some

programs involve work that is so technologically or scientifically driven that it is difficult to understand just what the objective is.

Overbilling

Unlike false expenditures, overbilling with regard to programs is more of a means to commit the fraudulent act of embezzlement within the program's functions versus the overall program as found with false expenditures. Specifically, overbilling schemes are found in staffing misuse or with expenditures not used in an approved manner. For example:

- Staff members are performing nonprogram duties. Often, personnel are pulled from one program to work on another. There are many reasons for why this decision is made, but we have to ask, Was the funding for that amount of personnel intentionally requested with the purpose of using personnel on another program that would not receive the funding for the additional staff members?
- Staff members are misrepresenting the performance of the program. Often, staff will show the project to be operating on a level that seemingly requires more resources. In reality, the project is operating on a lower level of resources, and whoever has the authority uses that responsibility to overbill.
- Staff members are hired who are not qualified to perform program duties. Many times, often with large grant monies involved, the program manager hires friends or relatives, or perhaps there is such a strict time frame involved with the funding that management will hire a warm body just to fill the approved item. In both cases, proper vetting procedures should be in place, even though the granting authority may not require them.
- As with staffing, funds are often redirected to other programs for similar reasons.
- Funds expended are not consistent with the proposed budget. You have to ask why the budget is out of line with expenditures. Is the budget actually in use, or was it just prepared as window-dressing for a grant proposal?
- Funds are expended that are not consistent with the governing cost principles. The classic example is the outrageous amounts the military spends on commonly used items, like the $5,000 toilet seat.
- The program is not completed, but the funding has been expended. Yes, this is the same inherent scheme we talked about under asset misappropriation. You have to remember that embezzlement can occur within the framework of asset misappropriation or overbilling, but because

programs can differ in their objectives to large degrees, the opportunity for fraudulent action may be more susceptible to say asset misappropriation rather than overbilling or vice versa.

Disguised Purchases

Again we focus on the procurement process, but in the case of disguised purchases, we have to look for transactions that either stand out because they are atypical of the purchases being made or are of a sizable amount that is inconsistent with items approved for purchase by the funder.

Income Skimming

There are four fraud schemes inherent to programs that involve income skimming. The first occurs when funds awarded in the name of an organization are diverted. In this case, we have to ask whether the donor(s) of these funds are known or unknown.

Another scheme involves the diversion of project-created income. Although it often seems like we are talking about not-for-profit charity-type organizations when discussing programs, we have to remember that not-for-profits can and do make profits. This fact creates headaches for auditors because some program managers become masters at hiding profit. Of course, most of this hiding is perfectly legit under the conditions of the funding, but as auditors, we have to find out under what conditions fraudulent behavior is going on. Similar conditions apply when other program income is included in a different program. Many times programs are only reimbursed for what they expend and any profits are taken out of the next year's funding. Yes, it sounds cruel, and what results is the diverting of those program profits to another program.

The last scheme involving income skimming that we will discuss involves the depositing of funds into an unauthorized bank account. This scheme seems pretty simple; however, if you have an organization with many programs, some of the funds may end up being commingled, resulting in an opportunity for fraud to occur. Which funds belong to which program—it's like untangling strings of holiday lights.

Corruption

Favored-status and conflict-of-interest schemes can be inherent to many types of organizations, but with program fraud they tend to be found in the funding-proposal process.

Favored Status

These types of schemes are operated through an implementing partner in several ways. For example:

- An implementing partner submits false credentials.
- An award of funding is managed through an unauthorized entity.
- A shadow entity is used disguising the implementing partner.

Conflict of Interest

These types of schemes are similar to the favored-status ones with the variation being some sort of relationship existing between those managing the program and those providing the funding.

Reporting Manipulation

We've broken up our primary fraud classification of financial reporting manipulation into two parts in consideration of the fact that we are discussing program fraud. The first part concerns financial reporting manipulation, and the second involves the overall program reporting.

Financial Reporting

There are three areas to be concerned with when financial reporting is manipulated concerning programs rather than the entire organization. The objective in committing these types of schemes is clearly to show that the program is operating successfully, thereby reflecting positively on the program management. Often, it is not so much in the desire of program management to save their hides as it were, but these manipulations are often performed to ensure that grant funding will be renewed. Here are some common examples:

Fictitious or Missing Transactions
Examples include:

- Program results and/or statistics are falsified with the intent to mislead.
- There is false reporting of line items for revenues and/or expenditures.
- There is a failure to report incurred liabilities.

Improper Recognition As with most financial reporting manipulation, whether it is the reporting for the entire organization or just a single program within a large organization, things can be made to look positive by simply recognizing revenue and/or expenditures in the improper period.

Manipulation of Budgets Since many programs are grant funded, budgets are a key element in the granting of monies. Whether the budget has to be strictly followed is another story. It's like the mom who gives her kid an allowance that is intended for the purchase of pens and pencils for school. However, when the dad returns with the kid from the store, she finds crayons, colored chalk, and a bunch of candy bar wrappers in the shopping bag. While our mom has only to look at the incriminating evidence of chocolate around the mouths of the dad and kid to detect, in this case, allowance manipulation, the auditor has to work a little harder to detect the manipulation of budget data in a program. Here are some examples of how budgets are manipulated by program managers.

- Program benchmarks are falsified. Budgets dealing with programs provide benchmarks that need to be met for program renewals. Therefore, managers will manipulate their financial reporting to meet these benchmarks.
- Program measurement techniques are false. How a program is measured to determine successful performance in reaching the program objectives is through measurement techniques that can be thought of as sales goals in a car dealership. A program manager may manipulate the data to fit the techniques employed or use techniques, if that opinion is available, to frame the program in the best light.
- Often the budget data is manipulated from the beginning to ensure positive program results. This is not to say that the program manager conservatively budgeted or underbudgeted. Instead, the budget data was manipulated to show that the program was successful in order to hide fraudulent behavior.

Program Reporting

In an effort to be as clear as possible, financial reporting and program reporting are two different things. Financial reporting can be a component of program reporting, but not the other way around. Many funded projects have strict guidelines on how to report project performance. For example, when you go to your general practitioner for an annual checkup, someone weighs you, takes your BP, taps your knees, listens to your heart race, and so on, but do these required checks find all the illnesses that can occur? Similar to a disease that goes undetected because everything checked out in the physical exam, fraudulently behaving program managers find ways to misrepresent performance, either to hide misuse of funds or just to indicate program success when there's none. The following are some examples:

■ The project status is falsely reported. This type of program reporting misstatement is typically done to give the illusion that the project's objectives will be met in order to continue funding streams.

■ The program results are falsely reported. The difference between project status and program results may not be apparent at first glance. The motivation is the same in that both are done to hide fraud. However, whereas falsely reporting program status is typically done to keep funds ongoing throughout the project, falsifying program results is typically done to ensure renewal of funding for another year or period of years. The project type indicates the likelihood of which false reporting is occurring.

■ Improper criteria are used to measure performance. Remember, this is overall performance, not financial performance. Given that funded projects can be difficult to understand considering the level of technology being used or the scientific nature of the research being performed, performance-measuring criteria could be manipulated because of the complex nature of the project. No one understands the project, so how could anyone know whether it's succeeding or not? This deception is especially true if the project is divided into so many subparts that no one person, except the project manager, knows how it is proceeding.

■ Program accomplishments are falsely reported. How many times have you heard organizations state that their program provided such and such a service to such and such an amount of indigent, homeless, children, the elderly, and so on? How do we know if the program goal and subsequent funding was to provide services to three times that amount of people in need? The auditor should find out because something is certainly amiss.

■ Operating statistics are manipulated to provide false results. Remember, these are operating statistics, not financial ones. An example would be a program that provides meals to the homebound elderly. An amount of payment by those receiving the meals is suggested. However, the government reimbursement for those meals deducts any amount contributed by the elderly being served. The project manager may manipulate the statistics to weight more heavily on the fixed-income, city-dwelling elderly it services, because they, in all likelihood, are unable to pay anything for their delivered meals.

 **AUDIT APPROACH**

The overall audit approach should start with obtaining an understanding of the program objectives. The goal of a fraud audit is not to question the legitimacy of the program's objectives, but rather to obtain an understanding of how to measure performance in reaching those objectives.

Measuring Program Performance

How does an auditor know a program is successful? Does she use the same criteria as perhaps given by the funding authority or maybe those criteria established by the program manager? It really depended on just how much oversight is in place. So, to rely on the funding authority or the program management would not be helpful in detecting fraudulent activity because the former may not have established meaningful criteria and the latter may be falsifying performance, thereby using false criteria. With so many types of funded programs existing, the auditor must develop his or her own criteria specific to the program objectives. If these objectives are too complex, then reliance on an outside consultant will be necessary.

Once the criteria for measuring program objectives are established and understood by the project team, the focus of the fraud audit turns to the data comprising these criteria. Specifically, the fraud audit should focus on the process for collecting and summarizing data. Were generally accepted practices for collecting the data used? Did the process ensure the integrity of the data collected? Did the method of collecting the data have an inherent basis?

Most importantly, is the data authentic? Do the source documents appear authentic or were they altered or created, or are they missing in an effort to hide the fraudulent behavior? Can the information provided on the authenticated documents be collaborated to an independent source? The challenge for the auditor is determining between false and misleading data. Whereas false data is obvious, misleading data can be unclear.

False Data

By false data, we are referring to false reporting schemes highlighted in the Fraud Risk Structure section of this chapter.

False and Misleading Reporting

False reporting occurs when the underlying supporting data is false, incorrect, or missing. The audit approach to detect false reporting is to examine the data for authenticity. Misleading reporting tends to occur with how the data is interpreted in the context of the program's objectives. Anytime there is interpretation, there are judgments to be made. With this in mind, the audit approach is to obtain standards of measurement for such a program. Are there benchmarks established as standards for such programs? Benchmarks are common with programs that have been in existence for some time. Their longevity also indicates a soundness of the benchmarks. However, if a research study is new or groundbreaking, then benchmarks specific to the research will be difficult to find. Therefore, researching similar studies may have to be performed. In researching published studies, the following guidelines should be considered.

- Is the study on point with the program under audit?
- Is the data used in the study on point with the program under audit?
- What are the fundamental differences between the study and the program under audit?
- Is the study current?
- Has the study been updated?
- Are there conflicting opinions in various studies?
- Is the source a recognized authority?
- Are the results of the study recognized by the applicable professional community?

Use of Improper Criteria

The audit approach for detecting the use of improper criteria is hampered when determining what criteria should have been used. A challenge exists to establish a basis upon which any impropriety can be measured. Remember, the audit report must disclose the reasons for challenging the criteria used and disclose the reasons given by the program management.

Falsely Reported Program Accomplishments

A program states an accomplishment achieved. The auditor must ask if there are factual data supporting the statement. Also, the auditor must ask if the interpretation of the data is consistent with generally accepted criteria. With regard to interpretation, the following questions need to be addressed:

- Is all the data included in the interpretation?
- Is the data properly summarized?

- Is the data included in the proper categories?
- Are the operating statistics correct as stated?
- Is the data consistent with the criteria used in the performance measurements?
- Are the criteria used consistent with authoritative literature?

Falsely Reported Project Status

By project status, we want to know if the project will accomplish its objectives within a stipulated time frame. The fraud audit approach should consider the following:

- Is a project status report issued in a timely manner?
- Is the project status reporting factually correct?
- Is the project forecast consistent with the timeline of the actual performance?
- Have all the deliverables been considered in the project forecast?
- Is the project forecast based on optimized or hard data?

Program Fraud Audits

The methodology for conducting fraud audits for programs is the same methodology used for conducting fraud audits for detecting asset misappropriation, errors in financial reporting, or corruption. However, the fraud risk structure at the inherent scheme level is not as defined as in, for example, a disbursement system audit. The inherent schemes need to be developed around the program objectives. Therefore, the fraud auditor will need to have a definitive idea about the inherent scheme within the planning phase of the fraud audit. The fraud scenarios will evolve from understanding how the project is managed and the associated program objectives. With all these factors in mind, the fraud audit can be developed around the four distinct areas of questioning.

1. **Have the desired results or benefits been derived or accomplished?** The funding source is expecting a successful outcome to occur from the project funding it is providing. The funding recipient is expecting to continue receiving funding. Given these two perspectives, the fraud audit needs to determine if the funding is being used to its desired purpose. Keep it simple. Just match the inherent fraud scheme to the structure of the program with regard to funding, purpose, and requirements. Specifically,

we are searching to determine if the program-declared results are a product of false or misleading reporting, use of improper criteria to measure performance, false reporting of program accomplishments, or false reporting of project status.

2. **Has the program complied with the applicable terms and conditions of the funding and the laws and regulations associated with the program?** As with detecting contract fraud, the first step is to identify the pertinent terms and conditions that apply with the funding. Think of the funding as a loan that doesn't bear interest, charges, fees, or repayment. Yes, it sounds like science fiction, but the point is that such funding typically does have some form of conditions, stipulations, guidelines, and so on. It depends on the funding source, and we know there are a variety of sources. A personal example of this variety is in the conducting of a fraud audit for a training program that your author performed. Although the training was administered at a local level, the program was administered by a university, and it received funding through the state and federal governments. The federal government funding was through a grant that was initially established through public legislation. Identifying all the pertinent terms and conditions and establishing the priority of funders required more time than the actual audit. However, without that exhaustive research, the audit would have missed a significant overbilling scheme.

In developing the working papers, the auditor should document the pertinent terms by source and contract reference. The terms and conditions should correlate to the program objectives. Since a contract is a legal document, the auditor should consult with attorneys to ensure a full understanding of the terms and conditions. Some particular points of this understanding include:

- "Whereas clauses" often refer to other documents that are embodied in the contract by reference.
- Legislation often contains terms that have different meanings than those found in common usage. For example, in a court case involving property tax assessments for commercial property, the law indicated that the municipality had the right to audit the petitioner's books and records to validate the profitability of the commercial property. The term *audit* was not defined in the legislation, nor were there any references to auditing standards. The opposing attorney argued that the audit report exceeded the audit standards because it contained proposed adjustments to the petitioner's income statement for purpose of the legal

action. While the court ruled in favor of the fraud audit findings, extensive filings were required to override the objection. Clearly, the meaning of *audit* became the point of difference.

▪ Understand the definition of terms within the contract. Many contracts have a terms section; however, the auditor must know that his or her professional definition is consistent with the legal interpretation of audit. Similarly, the term *cost* has many connotations, for example, if expenditures occur with a related party, is the cost what the program actually paid or is the cost what the program paid less the profit inured by related party?

▪ Read clauses for what the language actually states and not what you want it to state. Going back to the term *cost*, what if the related vendor charge was at fair market value? Is the cost the fair market value or the amount the program paid less the profit?

3. **Is the financial management of the project conducted in an effective manner?** Cost effectiveness in general is a relative phrase. From the perspective of a fraud audit, it comes down to a single question, that being, Were the expenditures made associated with the program?

4. **Are expenditures consistent with the program's scope and objectives?** We have to test for relatedness, whereby we have to ask if the expenditure benefitted the program. From a fraud audit perspective, fictitious expenses obviously have no benefit; however, actual expenditures can be disguised in varying ways, including the following:

▪ The expenditure was clearly not associated with the program (e.g., when office supplies are used for nonprogram purposes). Think back to our kid, whose whole allowance was to be spent on pens and pencils. However, after giving in to the temptation of candy bars, there was with no more allowance to buy the needed pens and pencils. So, his accomplice, aka Dad, thought he would help out by raiding his office's supply cabinet.

▪ The full value of the expenditure did not relate to the program (e.g., an employee's full salary was charged to the program); however, the employee had a portion of her time spent on tasks unrelated to the program.

▪ Timing of the expenditure did not provide full value for the program. For example, an office furniture purchase was allowed for in the budget, but the purchase was made at the end of the program period.

▪ Expenditures are inflated. For example, the program paid gross value for an item and the resulting refunds were applied to other programs.

 **SUMMARY**

Program management fraud isn't the variety of fraud found in core business systems, and therefore, shouldn't be approached in the same manner. That doesn't mean fraud can't be detected through the fraud audit methods outlined in this book. The primary classifications of fraud, such as corruption and asset misappropriation, aren't going to change because we are dealing with program management. The building of a risk structure still applies. Inherent fraud schemes exist. So, why devote an entire chapter to program management fraud if it's already been covered in the previous chapters, you ask?

If you are to take away one thought from this discussion, it is that the programs themselves are not typically fraudulent, meaning we don't have to start our audit program with the determination of whether the entity is real or false. Fraud is committed by people, not programs or business systems; they are the tools of fraud. You could argue that the funding sources are people, too, but in reality those sources are entities, such as the federal government or charitable corporations. Sure, those entities function through the work of people, but we have to remember we are operating on a specific program level in this instance and funding sources are just one aspect, albeit an important one. Moreover, it is the complexity of these funding streams that add to the challenge. Monies coming into a program from various directions can easily be unintentionally commingled or misdirected, especially if the financial management of the program isn't the most highly qualified. How many small not-for-profits have a staff of CPAs? So, the auditor's job becomes one of ultimately determining intent. Is it just a matter of bad management, or is it fraudulently behaving management?

It is not only the sometimes vast amount of funding monies that flow to programs that present the justification for making an effort to detect fraud in not-for-profits' management. Programs that rely on funding are typically not-for-profit entities that are established to provide a public benefit; to fill in the gaps for services and products not provided through any other means. So when fraud occurs in these programs, no matter the size, it becomes an especially heinous act because of the loss of social benefit that results. For that reason alone, the fraud auditing of program management is greatly needed.

CHAPTER SEVENTEEN

Quantifying Fraud

MPACT! YES, WE ARE using the term *impact* and not *effect* or *affect*, not because we don't know when to use which of the latter words, but because the cost of fraud is a force-like blow on an organization in both monetary and nonmonetary terms. The focus of this chapter is how to incorporate the fraud conversion point of the fraud scenario into the fraud audit. The following discussion will not consider the intent of the person committing the fraudulent act or attempt to establish a responsible party. Also, there won't be any legal treatise on how to present loss calculations in an expert witness report. No "what," "where," or "who," just "how," as in how to link the economic gain to the employee and how to calculate the loss from a fraud scenario. Think of it as the time you went to the auto repair shop for just an oil change and tire rotation. An hour later, the manager comes to you and proceeds to give you a seemingly endless list of things that are wrong. Finally, unable to hear anymore, you say: "Just how much is this going to cost me?"

In looking at the primary classifications of fraud from Chapter 3, asset misappropriation and corruption schemes result in dollar loss amounts that can be calculated, while with avoidance strategies there are the fines or penalties that can be identified with the fraud. With the other primary classifications, it is more difficult to calculate an actual number. For example, what would be the dollar impact associated with a financial statement fraud scheme? Would it be the difference in the company's stock value from before it was learned that the organization overstated revenue by 20% due to improper revenue recognition to afterwards? Then there is the issue of how you determine if the loss in value is temporary versus permanent.

 ## CONVEYING THE IMPACT TO MANAGEMENT

Impact is the name of the game in communicating a fraud scenario to management. Calculating the impact gives the scenario life. The red flags become more than a series of anomalies, they represent real money. Once the fraud has been identified, resulting in creditable evidence of a fraud scenario's occurring, the loss calculation (i.e., giving the impact a reality) becomes the last step for the auditor before communicating the findings to management.

Using the Fraud Audit Report

In the end, the fraud audit report becomes a valuable tool for management to use in decision making concerning the appropriate course of action to take. While there are many considerations in this decision-making process, the cost of the fraud should be known and understood by management. Therefore, the fraud audit report by design should:

- Offer opinions whether creditable evidence exists that a fraud scenario has occurred.
- Provide the facts that support the fraud scenario opinion.
- Communicate the documents or actions that are required to gather the necessary records and information to perform an investigation of the fraud scenario.
- Describe the financial impact that the fraud scenario has on the organization.
- Describe what economic benefit the employee received from committing the fraud scenario.

Loss to the Company versus Employee Economic Benefit

It is difficult to believe, but not all fraud scenarios cause losses to an organization. It is possible that a vendor could bribe an employee and the company still receives the best price. This is an important concept for the auditor to get his or her head around because it concerns perspective. The following two situations illustrate what we mean.

Situation one: A company employee receives World Series tickets at Yankee Stadium. From the vendor perspective, the ticket cost is a customer goodwill expense that is absorbed as part of the vendor's cost of doing business. From the company perspective, the receipt of the gift, while viewed as perhaps unethical, doesn't entail a dollar loss to the company.

Situation two: The same as situation one with the employee receiving World Series tickets (perhaps this time at Wrigley Field), but this time, the vendor, instead of absorbing the cost of the tickets, increases the price charged to the company for products in order to cover the cost of the gift. Clearly, the gift did cost the company in terms of higher product charges, while at the same time the employee received an economic benefit at the company's expense, literally and figuratively.

The point of both of these situations is that the fraud audit report needs to distinguish between the difference between an employee's receiving a benefit and the financial impact, if any, to the organization. The starting point to making this distinction is to understand how the fraud conversion occurs for each fraud scenario.

Fraud Conversion and the Fraud Scenario

Identification of a fraud scenario lends a predictability to how an employee benefits and the amount of loss incurred by his or her actions. Here are some examples of what we mean.

Example 1: A payroll fraud scheme involving overstated hours. The employee receives the economic benefit of the scheme through her paycheck. The fraud auditor can establish with certainty that the employee received the benefit, and the loss can be calculated to be the amount of false overtime paid.

Example 2: A controller overstates revenue through false journal entries. Since the company achieved its profitability goal, the controller received a bonus. The controller receives the actual economic benefit when the company deposits the bonus into the controller's bank account through the payroll direct deposit process. The loss amount is the amount of the bonus.

Example 3: This scheme uses false billing through a fictitious vendor. A company wires funds to the fictitious company's bank account. The fraud audit can establish, with certainty, where the money was wired; however, without access to the banking records of the fictitious vendor, the fraud audit cannot establish, with certainty, who received the funds. The loss is the amount of funds wired to the false vendor.

Example 4: A vendor and employee operate in collusion to rig a bid. The vendor wires funds to the employee's secret personal bank account. Since the fraud auditor has no access to either the vendor's book or the employee's personal bank account, he can't establish, with any degree of certainty, that the employee received an economic benefit. The loss calculated is the difference between the price paid and the fair market price.

In the first two examples, the fraud auditor can establish, with a reasonable degree of certainty, that the employee did receive the economic benefit. In the third example, the fraud auditor has creditable evidence that a loss has occurred, but does not know who received the benefit. In the fourth example, the fraud auditor can observe the red flags of bid rigging, but cannot determine with a reasonable degree of certainty the loss amount or whether even the employee received a bribe.

So, why is this being able to determine "with a degree of certainty" so important? Do auditors have to be lawyers, too? Well, in many instances, when management and auditors talk about the audit, statements like these are heard: "I know he is guilty, I just can't prove it" or "What does that red flag prove?" Worse yet is when the auditor continues to analyze a situation, but is just spinning her wheels because she still can't obtain sufficient evidence. The auditor needs to understand just what can be proved and what can't be proved in performing a fraud audit. To aid with this understanding, the following questions must be answered:

- Did the employee receive an economic gain from the fraud scenario?
- Do we have access to the necessary books and records to link the economic gain to the employee?
- Is there sufficient evidence to establish with a reasonable degree of certainty that the employee did receive the funds?
- Did the company suffer a loss from the scenario?

Fraud Conversion and the Loss Calculation

The loss calculation is the process of assigning a dollar amount to the fraud conversion point of a fraud scenario. To calculate a loss amount, there is an underlying premise that the fraud auditor has access to the necessary records. With this assumption in mind, the process of identifying the impact requires answers to the following questions:

- Is there a loss?
- Did an employee receive an economic benefit?
- Is the loss monetary, intangible, or both?
- If a loss has occurred, what is the extent of the loss? (Please note that our discussion concerns only tangible losses and not intangible losses or administrative costs.)
- If a loss has occurred, what methodology is used to calculate the extent of the loss?
- What assumptions are required in the calculation of the loss amount?
- Can those assumptions be supported by authoritative studies?
- How and where can the evidence be obtained to calculate the loss amount?
- Can the loss be determined in the fraud audit stage or will a fraud investigation become necessary?
- What evidence is necessary to cause management to react to the situation?
- What is the intended outcome: administrative, civil, or criminal proceedings?

 ## ROLE OF EVIDENCE IN CALCULATING A FRAUD LOSS

A loss calculation is based on the fraud scenario and the type of available evidence. The types of evidence are discussed in the following sections.

Direct Evidence

Direct evidence is proof that tends to show existence of a fact in question without the intervention of the proof of any other fact. Direct evidence includes testimony and documents that tend to prove or disprove a fact or issue directly. Sorry to get all legal on you, but that's the point we are at in this fraud discussion. To make it up to you, here is an example of the use of direct evidence from a fraud auditing perspective: A fraudulent financial transaction is recorded in the accounting records of an organization. The transaction is direct evidence, so the dollar value assigned to the transaction becomes the basis for the loss calculation. Depending on the type of fraud scenario, the recorded cost amount can be either a starting point or ending point of the calculation. In an overbilling scheme, the cost is the starting point, whereas in a false billing scheme involving a fictitious vendor, the cost is the ending point.

Schemes indicated through direct evidence involve what we call "on-the-book" loss calculations. The nature of the scheme allows for the specific identification of the financial transactions forming the basis for the calculation. Company credit cards, travel expenses, and false billing scenarios are examples of fraud scenarios that typically use direct evidence in calculating loss.

Circumstantial Evidence

As *Black's Law Dictionary* states, circumstantial evidence is "evidence based on inference and not on personal knowledge or observation." The expression "it is more probable than not" applies when calculating loss with circumstantial evidence present.

Loss calculations for schemes involving circumstantial evidence are typically referred to as "off-the-book" because the nature of the loss calculation requires the use of assumptions. The assumptions should not be mere guesses, but ones supported by authoritative sources that lend a creditability. Remember, it is based on inference and not intuition, or going with your gut, as it were. When discussing loss calculations and circumstantial evidence, there are two types of loss calculations: no direct evidence loss calculations and fair market loss calculations.

No Direct Evidence Loss Calculations

In many fraud cases, the direct evidence is not there. Often, the necessary records are not available because an individual destroyed them or management failed to either create or maintain the records. The mechanics of the fraud scenario also influences the availability of records. For example, a revenue-skimming fraud scenario occurs, whereby the diversion of revenue before the sales transaction is recorded. Therefore, the loss occurs with through the diversion of monetary funds or diversion of a tangible asset before the revenue transaction is recorded in the accounting records. Since the transaction is not recorded, the financial loss must be estimated based on records other than the sales records.

When the records are not available, the acceptability of the estimating technique often relates to why the records are not available. For the interest of the reader, there are a sufficient number of court cases that indicate when the lack of records is directly attributable to the actions of the perpetrator; the courts have allowed reasonable estimating techniques to calculate the loss amount. Obviously, discussing such a situation with legal counsel is a good idea before an auditor starts any loss calculation. Please note, though, that if the records are not available due to management's failure, the courts have been less inclined to allow estimating techniques.

Another obstacle occurs when the necessary records to calculate the loss are located within an external organization. In this case, the auditor will need the cooperation from the third party in order to calculate the loss. Going back to the skimming example, let's assume the theft and resale of scrap inventory occurred. Since the scrap was sold to a scrap dealer, the scrap dealer becomes the external party. The loss calculation becomes the price paid by the scrap dealer. In this variation of a revenue scenario, the loss calculation is arrived at using direct evidence through an external party rather than circumstantial evidence realized internally.

Fair Market Loss Calculations

Fair market value is what a knowledgeable individual would probably pay for a product or service in an unpressured business environment. Therefore, a loss calculation would consider the difference between the price paid and the fair market value. Corruption schemes are examples of fraud scenarios that would require a fair market value loss calculation.

The fair market calculation requires the fraud auditor to perform research in the marketplace to ascertain the fair market price. To be assured, the effort requires more than an Internet search, although that may be a good starting point. Challenges in this task are associated with understanding the product and determining its fair market price at a historical point in time. Clearly, obtaining current fair market value is easier than obtaining historical fair market value.

For example, in dealing with a pass-through scheme involving equipment rental, it was necessary for the auditors to visit actual equipment rental companies in the geographically local marketplace on the pretext of being real, ready, and willingly buyers. Five different, but similar, equipment rental companies were visited in order to obtain pricing information on various models and purchasing situations. The current fair market pricing information was then compared to the historical expenditures associated with vendors in the same industry. Using all this gathered information, the calculated loss amount exceeded one million dollars.

 IMPACT ON THE FRAUD AUDIT

From the fraud audit perspective, understanding how to calculate the loss is a valuable tool in planning the audit methodology. Calculations involving direct evidence do not typically require an intricate process to determine the loss and thus are easy to perform, whereas calculations involving circumstantial evidence tend to require a process based on a series of assumptions. Let's look at how the loss calculation occurs with schemes related to the two types of primary fraud classifications: asset misappropriation and corruption.

Loss Calculations for Asset Misappropriation Schemes

The fraud risk structure for asset misappropriation has six categories, and the categories have inherent schemes that are associated with each of the categories.

Category 1: Embezzlement of Funds

Remember that the embezzlement of funds is the act of taking monetary or monetary equivalent funds entrusted to one's care. So, in false billing fraud scenarios, the loss calculation is direct because it entails the totaling of funds disbursed to the false company. To the contrary, a pass-through fraud scenario or an overbilling scenario would entail a loss calculation based on fair market determinations.

Category 2: Theft of Tangible Assets

The theft of tangible assets is the act of taking tangible property of an organization for personal use or resale on the open market. The first step is to develop a methodology to identify which missing assets are attributable to the individual that allegedly committed the fraud scenario. As to the loss calculation, there are three methods as follows:

- Missing assets that are recorded in the accounting records with specific identification numbers. The first step is to determine which assets are missing due to the actions of the individual. The cost of the missing asset is then determined by the cost assigned in the financial records. It may also be necessary to estimate the replacement cost of the asset. Fixed assets and inventory records on a perpetual basis are examples of assets whose loss can be calculated in this manner.
- Missing assets that are not recorded in the financial records will require estimating techniques to determine the quantity of missing assets attributable to the fraud scenario. If you must estimate the cost of the missing assets, historical records can provide a basis for calculating the loss.

Supplies that have no inventory records are examples of assets that are calculated in this manner.

▪ Personal use of the asset provides direct evidence if the individual permanently retains the asset. In temporary-use schemes, the associated fair market value for the temporary-use period is the basis for the calculation.

Category 3: Misuse of Assets

When there is the conversion of the organization's assets for personal or nonbusiness use without theft of the asset, the loss is calculated based on the fair market value of like-kind assets for the time period associated with the personal use.

Category 4: Lack of Business Purpose

Lack of business purpose pertains to when organizational funds are used to acquire assets that are not intended to benefit an organization. The loss calculation is specific identification using the amount paid for the asset.

Category 5: Conflict of Interest

A conflict of interest is an undisclosed legal ownership or beneficial interest in a related entity of an organization, such as a vendor, a customer, or an employee. It has to be determined if the organization has suffered a loss in terms of fair market value. Therefore, the loss calculation is predicated on the difference between the costs paid by the organization versus the cost of procuring the item in a competitive marketplace.

Category 6: Unauthorized Asset Disposal/Acquisition

Remember, it is just not unauthorized asset disposal/acquisition, but such actions that are below or above fair market value respectively. In either situation, a relationship often exists between the seller and the buyer where each will benefit by the fair market difference.

Loss Calculations for Corruption Schemes

The loss exposure calculation needed for corruption schemes differs from those needed for asset misappropriation schemes because of the nature of the corrupt act. In addition to the loss, the organization may also face fines, penalties, or civil and criminal remedies. For example, the loss calculation for most vendor bidding schemes is based on some form of a fair market value calculation; however, the corrupt act could also have fines and penalties as associated with the Foreign Corrupt Practices Act. In the case of discriminatory practices, the scheme could result in civil penalties. Therefore, corruption scenarios can have a double impact, one associated with the loss incurred by the transaction and one pertaining to the legal remedies.

Another facet of most procurement corruption schemes is the presence of some form of a bribe or kickback. At first glance, the loss calculation would appear to be at least the amount of the bribe or kickback. However, in reality, the bribe or kickback may not have a direct relationship to the loss calculation amount. Specifically, the bribe is what induces the employee into the action and the loss is the difference between fair market value and the cost paid in procuring the goods or services.

 ## OPTIONS FOR MANAGEMENT

There are remedies available' to an organization to recover losses through fraudulent behavior. There are three options in particular: administrative, civil, and criminal. Note that these issues need to be discussed and agreed upon by management. A fraud response policy would address the issues and provide the necessary direction for the fraud auditor.

Administrative

When there is creditable evidence to suggest that the scenario did occur, management can reprimand, transfer, or terminate the employee. These are referred to as administrative actions. If this is the expected outcome, calculating the loss amount is less critical in relation to establishing that the employee was a party to the scenario occurring. Also, without cooperation from the parties, the fraud auditor is limited to using direct evidence of the fraud scenarios occurring.

Civil

If there is creditable evidence to suggest that the scenario did occur, and management wishes to recover the lost funds, then calculation of the loss amount is essential. The fraud auditor will need to start at the beginning of the fraud scenario, and assuming cooperation of the parties or with the assistance of the discovery process in a legal action, link the economic benefit to the individual and then calculate the loss amount.

Criminal

When there is creditable evidence to suggest that the fraud scenario did occur and the legal authorities are interested in the case, the amount of loss is less critical to the linking of the financial transaction to the fraud scenario. Similar to the civil remedies, the fraud auditor would need to have access to the necessary records.

CASE STUDIES

Two case studies involving the topics discussed are included in the following sections. The first one illustrates the use of direct evidence to calculate the loss and the second the use of circumstantial evidence.

Case 1

The following case study is based on an actual court case in which the controller of a company was committing a false billing scenario by issuing checks to his benefit. The loss calculation is shown in Table 17.1. The first column for line number is included for easy reference to each item, and the column for the "Check # Ref" indicates the tab number for the evidence binder. The column titled "Payee on Check" shows which checks were directly attributable to the controller and those checks that required an explanation as to why the check was attributable to the controller. The column titled "Check Memo" provides the explanation if one exists.

Case 2

The following case study is based on an actual court case in which the court agreed with our loss calculation. The actual report was over 50 pages. No, we won't present the entire 50 pages here, but offer a brief synopsis instead.

Background: The perpetrator of the crime was the general manager of a retail center that sold home heating oil, gasoline, heating equipment, and

TABLE 17.1 Loss Calculation for John Doe

Line #	Check # Ref	Check #	Check Date	Payee on Check	Check Memo	Amount
1	10	1002	7/2/2009	John Doe	None	10,000.00
2	7	1019	7/19/2009	John Doe	None	12,500.00
3	9	1024	7/24/2009	John Doe	None	19,000.00
4	8	1029	7/29/2008	John Doe	None	15,000.00
5	2	1034	8/2/2009	John Doe	None	23,445.00
				Calculated Total		79,945.00
6	1	1044	8/12/2009	American Express	1234 123456 12345	24,190.00
7	3	1055	9/12/2009	American Express	1235 123456 12345	7,334.00
8	4	1040	8/2/2009	ABC Company	Inv # 4465	12,345.00
9	5	1007	7/4/2009	John Doe	Advance of Funds	10,000.00
10	6	1008	7/10/2009	John Doe	Advance of Funds	15,000.00
				Calculated Total		68,869.00

heating service to retail and wholesale customers. The allegations of the case were that he diverted incoming revenue before the transaction was recorded. The case showed that the accounting records were either not available or were in such poor condition or incomplete that it was not possible to calculate the exact amount of the loss.

The fundamental scheme in play was to skim the revenue and conceal the fraud through poor record keeping. It was discovered by the holding company through a tip from an employee. The general manager of the operating location skimmed over $450,000 of revenue within a three-year time period. During this time period, he diverted funds from each revenue source, with the exception of home heating oil. The following sections of the report have been extracted to illustrate how the loss is calculated based on circumstantial evidence (see Table 17.2). It can truly be stated that in looking at this extraction, the one picture is worth a thousand words.

The loss calculation was the difference between the overall gross profit of the organization and the gross profit of the operating subsidiary during the

TABLE 17.2 Partial Income Statement

Revenue	Net Sales	Cost of Goods Sold	Gross Profit	Gross Profit %	Pre - Management Gross Profit
Kerosene & Heating Oil	$2,351,100	$1,846,405	$504,695	21.0	22.5
Gasoline & Diesel Fuel	$ 365,907	$ 524,416	($158,509)	Loss	12.7
Motor Oil	$ 5,028	$ 7,865	($ 2,837)	Loss	1.6
Coal	$ 34,685	$ 42,001	($ 7,316)	Loss	25.4
Service	$ 94,826	$ 89,411	$ 5,415	5.7	60.3
Installations	$ 33,871	$ 40,903	($ 8,032)	Loss	60.3
Total	$2,884,417	$2,551,001	$333,416	11.6	

management period of the individual committing the fraud scenario. The loss calculation used the operating subsidiaries cost of sales because the perpetrator had no control over the cost accounting records.

The following equations illustrate how the loss was calculated:

Cost of the inventory assigned to the location	$2,551,001
Plus estimated gross profit based on Cost of Goods sold (see 1 through 3 below)	$ 790,810
Equals estimated total sales at location	$3,341,811
Less actual sales reported by the defendant During the management period	($2,884,417)
Equals lost sales attributable to the defendant During the management period	$ 457,394

1. Calculation of Estimated Gross Profit:

Cost of goods sold on corporate accounting records	$2,551,001
Gross profit rate used to estimate gross profit	24 percent
Gross profit rate based on Cost of Goods Sold	31 percent
Estimated gross profit based on Cost of Goods Sold	$790,810

2. Gross Profit Rate Based on Cost of Goods Sold:
    The 24% gross profit rate was converted to a comparable rate based on the Cost of Goods Sold.

3. Estimated Gross Profit:
    The Cost of goods sold on corporate accounting records, $2,551,001 multiplied by 31% equals $790,810 in estimated gross profit.

SUMMARY

Until this chapter, our focus has been upon fraud in the core business systems, particularly where it occurs and how it occurs. We briefly may have used the term *fraud conversion point*, but only with the reference that the understanding of fraud conversion is critical to the fraud investigation. Since we have discussed the fraud risk assessment and building a fraud audit program from almost all aspects of the core business systems, the only remaining component to discuss is the fraud investigation. We didn't leave it for last because it is an unimportant task for the fraud auditor. Hopefully, you have realized just how important it is just by the number of high-profile court cases held in recent years involving fraudulent behaviour.

The fraud conversion is the economic benefit received by one committing the fraudulent act. When there is benefit for a party, then it has to be at another party's expense, which is why the majority of our discussion entailed the reaction of management to a fraudulent occurrence. The auditor's task is to determine if a loss has occurred and to calculate said loss. How the loss is calculated depends largely on the type of evidence found. The questions of if the loss can be determined in the fraud audit or will a fraud investigation be necessary have to be answered. Last, there is the question of what outcomes are available for management to pursue: administrative, civil, or criminal. These are all important questions that require very purposeful answers.

Appendixes

THE FOLLOWING APPENDIXES CONTAIN fraud audit programs that are intended to illustrate how to use the techniques identified throughout the book:

Appendix A: Fraud Audit Program: Payroll—Illustrates a complete fraud audit program, including the definition of terms, fraud risk structure, and the red flag decision tree.

Appendix B: Fraud Audit Program: Disbursements—Illustrates the red flag approach and the associated fraud audit steps.

Appendix C: Fraud Audit Program: Procurement—Illustrates the red flag approach and the associated fraud audit steps.

Appendix D: Fraud Audit Program: Inventory—Illustrates the linking of the data mining and audit procedures to the fraud scenarios.

Appendix E: Fraud Audit Planning Program: Revenue Recognition—Illustrates a fraud audit planning program for revenue recognition audit programs.

Appendix F: Checklist of Inherent Scheme Structure—Easy reference of the inherent fraud schemes listed in the book.

Appendix G: Fraud Audit Matrix—Document used to link the fraud scenario to the audit program.

Recognizing diverse approaches, these documents are intentionally designed utilizing different formats and styles.

Fraud Audit Program: Payroll

 ## BACKGROUND

The audit approach is based on a combination of testing procedures from a random sample and data mining for events that create the appearance of ghost employees or avoiding, circumventing, or exploiting the policy or the intent of the policy.

The traditional testing will focus on red flags that could be indicative of fraud in the payroll process.

The data mining will focus on the attributes of a ghost employee or the circumvention, avoidance, or exploitation of the payroll process by searching for frequencies and patterns of specific schemes.

The fraud risk structure is composed of the inherent fraud schemes. These inherent fraud schemes in conjunction with an assessment of internal controls may result in mitigation of some inherent fraud schemes. This assessment should be done at the audited entity level.

This document is a general guideline for auditing for fraud in the payroll process. The red flags and fraud audit procedures may need to be customized by the auditor for the specific audited site processes and characteristics.

 ## KEY TERMS

1. Ghost employees—individuals listed in the payroll register who are not providing services, but who are receiving a payroll check.
   a. Terminated ghost employee—a company employee that exists at the time of hire, but terminates without notifying human resources. The supervisor falsifies the time report and diverts the company employee's payment. At the time of the audit the company employee may be:
      i. Terminated in the system by the supervisor or at the supervisor's request after the supervisor has decided to stop perpetrating the scheme.
      ii. Not terminated in the system and still being used to perpetrate scheme.
   b. Fictitious ghost employee—a nonexistent company employee placed on payroll, allowing the supervisor to falsify time reporting and divert the company employee's payment.
   c. No-show ghost employee—a company employee who is a real person who provides no actual services to the company. Many times this company employee is in collusion with the supervisor.
   d. Temporary ghost employee—a type of company employee who bypasses the normal hiring procedures due to the nature of being temporary. The supervisor diverts the company employee's payment.
   e. Family ghost employee—a family member placed on payroll who provides no actual services to the company.
   f. Rehire ghost employee—a company employee who has been terminated and at a later date is placed back on payroll as a current company employee. The supervisor falsifies the time report and diverts the company employee's payment.
   g. Preemployment ghost employee—a company employee that the supervisor places on payroll one pay period prior to the commencement of work. The supervisor diverts the company employee's payment.
2. Payroll adjustments—changes to the database fields or subsystems in the payroll function that allow for changes to compensation.

a. Salary adjustment field—a field allowing a manually calculated lump-sum adjustment to payroll.

b. Other salary adjustment field—a field allowing payments to company employees for various reimbursements.

c. Other compensation fields—various data fields influencing retirement, health benefits, and personal leave calculations.

3. Overtime reporting fraud—company employee falsifies the hours worked, or due to a breakdown in the time card approval process.

FRAUD SCHEME STRUCTURE

Major Type: Asset Misappropriation

1. Embezzlement
   a. Ghost employee
      i. Terminated ghost employee.
      ii. Fictitious ghost employee.
      iii. No-show ghost employee.
      iv. Rehire ghost employee.
      v. Family ghost employee.
      vi. Temporary ghost employee.
      vii. Preemployment ghost employee.
   b. Payroll adjustments
      i. Additional compensation (through bypass of policy)
         (a) Incentive bonus.
         (b) Allowance programs.
      ii. Unauthorized adjustments
         (a) Salary adjustments.
         (b) Reimbursements.
         (c) Manual payroll check.
   c. Overtime
      i. Lack of review of time by supervisor.
      ii. Lack of knowledge of company employee's workday by supervisor.
      iii. Collusion with another company employee or supervisor.
      iv. Avoidance of review of time by forged approval.
      v. Overstating hours post approval.
      vi. Use of overtime as additional compensation.
      vii. Overtime being claimed on days not worked, e.g., annual or sick leave.

OVERALL AUDIT APPROACH

1. Decision

The overall audit approach is the fraud audit red flag approach. This approach entails the following two standard decisions.

DECISION 1: Is there a TRIGGER RED FLAG*?

If there is no trigger red flag, STOP.

If there is a trigger red flag, PERFORM FRAUD AUDIT PROCEDURES and CONTINUE.

DECISION 2: Is the red flag resolved by the FRAUD AUDIT PROCEDURES?

If the fraud audit procedures resolve the existence of the red flag, STOP.

If the fraud audits procedures do not resolve the existence of the red flag, INCLUDE TRANSACTION IN AUDIT REPORT.

 RED FLAGS

1. Ghost employee

  a. Trigger events

    i. Changes to wiring information

      (a) Terminated—in the last four pay periods prior to termination.

      (b) Preemployment—after the first pay period prior to the second pay period.

      (c) Rehire—at the start of the rehire period.

    ii. Fictitious or no-show—highest allowable exemptions.

    iii. Temporary—temporary employment status.

    iv. Family—bank account number same as another (key) company employee (routing number as basis).

  b. Awareness

    i. Nonparticipation in benefit program.

    ii. Missing documentation.

    iii. Similar handwriting to supervisor.

    iv. No personal, sick, or vacation time.

---

* Note: Trigger red flag in the decision process refers to:

A. A specific red flag associated with a fraud scenario with sufficient weight to cause the auditor to perform additional fraud audit procedures

B. The totality of all awareness red flags associated with the fraud scenario that the auditor judges are sufficient to perform additional fraud audit procedures.

       v. No company telephone number.

      vi. No company computer login ID.

     vii. No security access records.

    viii. Use of a common name.

     ix. No physical address.

      x. Missing company employee information.

     xi. Invalid social security number.

    xii. Last name and city of origin same as another (key) company employee.

   xiii. Address same as another (key) company employee (zip code or city as basis).

   xiv. Telephone number same as another (key) company employee.

    xv. Lack of work log or evidence of performance.

2. Payroll adjustment

  a. Trigger events

     i. Abnormal frequency of adjustment.

    ii. Abnormal amount of adjustment.

   iii. No original source documentation for adjustment.

  b. Awareness:

     i. Pattern of use of adjustments by one department or manager.

3. Overtime

  a. Trigger events

     i. Changes to time card

       (a) Post submission.

       (b) Post approval.

    ii. Missing time card.

   iii. Hours using computer do not align with hours reported.

   iv. Hours in and out in security system do not align with hours reported.

    v. Hours using machinery or equipment do not align with hours reported.

   vi. Hours match a day where the company employee took sick, annual, or holiday leave or a weekend.

  b. Awareness

     i. Alteration of time card.

    ii. Forged approval.

   iii. Consistency in overtime hours reported.

   iv. Increase in hours reported.

    v. Lack of firsthand knowledge by supervisor of hours worked.

DATA MINING

1. Ghost employees

  a. Terminated ghost employee

    i. Company employee terminated in the system by the supervisor or at the supervisor's request after the supervisor has decided to stop perpetrating the scheme

      (a) Understand the population of terminated company employees

        (1) Search for company employees with a status of terminated.

        (2) Sort company employees by logical classification groupings, e.g., location international, national, shift, job classification. These groups will have the same attributes as the payroll and termination process.

        (3) Interview personnel to identify the process for termination of company employees in the payroll systems. This may be management for the specific group, human resources, payroll, etc.

        (4) Create reports to analyze the population of terminated company employees.

        (5) For each classification group, create a report for the period of all terminated company employees

          (I) Include company employee name, number, job title, and birth date in the report.

          (II) Include termination date and hire date.

        (6) For each terminated company employee, create a report including the hours/days for the last four pay periods and the first four pay periods in the job title

          (I) Compare last four pay periods with first four pay periods.

          (II) Search for consistency or under pattern in hours/days in last four pay periods.

        (7) For each terminated company employee, create a report including changes to the bank information and address information in the last four pay periods

          (I) Include the change date and ID used to change the record.

          (II) Search for change in bank information or address information in last four pay periods.

        (8) Create reports to identify company employees whose calculated age is greater than life expectancy and/or

retirement age as some terminated ghosts may be on the payroll past these guidelines

(I) Create a report for company employees who, based on the date of birth, are greater than 75 (life expectancy) or 62 (retirement age) years old.

(II) Create a report for company employees who, based on the hire date and the average age of employment, are greater than 75 or 62 years old.

ii. Company employee not terminated in the system and still being used to perpetrate scheme

(a) Understand the population of terminated company employees

(1) Search for company employees with a status of active.

(2) Sort company employees by logical classification groupings, e.g., location international, national, shift, job classification. These groups will have the same attributes as the payroll and termination process.

(3) Interview personnel to identify the process for termination of company employees in the payroll systems. This may be management for the specific group, human resources, payroll, etc.

(b) Create reports to analyze the population of active company employees

(1) For each active company employee, create a report including changes to the bank information and address information in the last four pay periods

(I) Include the change date and ID used to change the record.

(II) Search for change in bank information or address information in last four pay periods.

(2) Create reports to identify company employees whose calculated age is greater than life expectancy and/or retirement age as some terminated ghosts may be on the payroll past these guidelines

(I) Create a report for company employees who, based on the date of birth, are greater than 75 (life expectancy) or 62 (retirement age) years old.

(II) Create a report for company employees who, based on the hire date and the average age of employment, are greater than 75 or 62 years old.

b. Fictitious ghost employee

   i. Understand the population of company employees

     (a) Sort company employees by logical classification groupings, i.e., location, shift, job classification. These groups will have the same attributes as the payroll process.

     (b) Interview personnel to identify the process for paying of company employees in the payroll systems and the standard earnings, benefits, exemptions, and deductions. This may be management for the specific group, human resources, payroll, etc.

   ii. Create reports by classification group to analyze the population of company employees for fictitious ghost employees

     (a) Create a report for those company employees with high withholding exemptions, i.e., low tax withholdings. (The type of exemptions or if exemptions are applicable will depend on the audited entity.)

     (b) Create a report of company employees who do not have voluntary deductions, such as health insurance or retirement deductions.

     (c) Create a report for company employees who have not used vacation/sick/personal time.

     (d) Create a report for company employees who have not received salary adjustments, merit adjustments, or promotions.

     (e) Create a report for company employees who are paid by direct deposit and have duplicate bank account numbers.

     (f) Create a report for company employees who are paid by check and have duplicate addresses.

     (g) Create a report for company employees who have no record in security access system, computer access, or telephone records.

c. No-show ghost employee

   i. Understand the population of company employees

     (a) Sort company employees by logical classification groupings, i.e., location, shift, job classification. These groups will have the same attributes as the payroll process.

     (b) Interview personnel to identify the process for paying company employees in the payroll systems and the standard earnings, benefits, exemptions, and deductions. This may be management for the specific group, human resources, payroll, etc.

ii. Create reports by classification group to analyze the population of company employees for no-show ghost employees

(a) Create reports for areas (locations, managers, jobs, shifts) where this scheme is more likely to occur.

(b) Look to the data mining for fictitious ghost employees (no-show and fictitious ghost employees are similar in the data mining techniques).

d. Temporary ghost employee

i. Understand the population of temporary company employees

(a) Search for company employees with a temporary status.

(b) Sort company employees by logical classification groupings, i.e., location, shift, job classification. These groups will have the same attributes as the payroll process.

(c) Interview personnel to identify the process for paying of company employees in the payroll systems and the standard earnings, benefits, exemptions, and deductions. This may be management for the specific group, human resources, payroll, etc.

ii. Create reports by classification group to analyze the population of company employees for temporary ghost employees

(a) Analyze for frequency and length of employment.

e. Family ghost employee

i. Understand the population of family company employees

(a) Interview personnel to identify the policy regarding hiring and payroll for family members of current company employees. This may be management for the specific group, human resources, payroll, etc.

ii. Create reports to analyze the population of company employees for family ghost employees

(a) Create a report for company employees with the same last name and same city of origin.

(b) Create a report for company employees with the same address (using the city or zip code as the basis).

(c) Create a report for company employees who are dependents of other company employees.

(d) Create a report for company employees who have the same dependents.

(e) Create a report for company employees with the same bank account numbers (using the routing number as the basis).

f. Rehired ghost employee
  i. Understand the population of rehire company employees
     (a) Search for company employees with a rehire status.
     (b) Sort company employees by logical classification groupings, i.e., location, shift, job classification. These groups will have the same attributes as the payroll process.
     (c) Interview personnel to identify the process for rehiring company employees. This may be management for the specific group, human resources, payroll, etc.
  ii. Create reports by classification group to analyze the population of company employees for rehire ghost employees
     (a) Create a report for company employees with short periods of rehire employment.
     (b) Create a report for company employees who made or will make less than $3,000. (The amount will vary based on the governing rules and regulations at the audited site. This amount example is based on United States income tax reporting guidelines.)
     (c) Create a report for a change in the bank account number at the point of rehire.
g. Preemployment ghost employee
  i. Understand the population of new hire company employees
     (a) Search for company employees with a start date in the previous year.
     (b) Sort company employees by logical classification groupings, i.e. location, shift, job classification. These groups will have the same attributes as the payroll process.
     (c) Interview personnel to identify the process for paying company employees in the payroll systems. This may be management for the specific group, human resources, payroll, etc.
  ii. Create reports by classification group to analyze the population of company employees for temporary pre-employment company employees
     (a) Search for inconsistency in hours/days for first pay period to other pay periods.
2. Payroll adjustments
  a. Understand the population of company employees and payroll adjustments

     i. Sort company employees into classification groups by location, international, national, shift, job classification, etc. These groups will have the same attributes as the payroll adjustments that should occur.

     ii. Interview personnel to identify the norm for adjustments in each classification group. This may be management for the specific group, human resources, payroll, etc.

  b. Create reports to analyze the population of company employees and payroll adjustments

     i. For each classification group, create a report for the calendar year by company employee detailing all fields calculating net pay

       (a) Include both compensation and non-compensation fields in the report.

       (b) Include company employee number and job title in the report.

     ii. Identify anomalies in the frequencies of each adjustment. The anomalies would have been identified when you interviewed the personnel as to the norm.

     iii. Identify anomalies in the amount of the adjustment.

3. Overtime

  a. Understand the population of temporary company employees

     i. Search for company employees with overtime paid.

     ii. Sort company employees by logical classification groupings, i.e., location, shift, job classification. These groups will have the same attributes as the payroll process.

     iii. Interview personnel to identify the process for paying of overtime to company employees in the payroll systems. This may be management for the specific group, human resources, payroll, etc.

  b. Create reports by classification group to analyze the population of overtime transactions for company employees

     i. Create a report for the calendar year by company employee, by hours reported per period the hours are entered (daily, weekly, etc.)

       (a) Identify anomalies in the hours reported as to the department, shift, location, job classification, etc.

       (b) Identify increases in the hours reported over time.

       (c) Identify part-time company employees with over 30 hours reported.

FRAUD AUDIT PROCEDURES

1. Ghost employee
  a. Verify work performance
    i. Compare days/hours worked to security access systems.
    ii. Compare days/hours worked to computer terminal access.
    iii. Compare days/hours worked to telephone records.
    iv. Compare days/hours worked to use of equipment or machinery used in the company employee's job function.
    v. Compare days/hours worked to documented record of meetings or other work product (base the documentation reviewed on the company employee's specific job functions).
  b. Verify physical existence
    i. Coworker recollection of company employees
      (a) Speak with audit management regarding the ability to interview coworkers as to recollection of company employees.
      (b) Request an interview with coworker or request that investigation personnel interview coworker.
      (c) If an interview is granted, request the following information:
        (1) Termination date.
        (2) Start date.
        (3) Knowledge of work performance.
        (4) Rehire date.
    ii. Company employee (or former company employee)
      (a) Speak with audit management regarding the ability to interview the company employee (or former company employee).
      (b) Request an interview with the company employee (or former company employee) or request that investigation personnel interview the company employee (of former company employee).
      (c) If an interview is granted, request the following information:
        (1) Review government photo identification.
        (2) Termination date.
        (3) Start date.
        (4) Rehire date.
2. Payroll adjustment
  a. Verify validity
    i. Review the original source documents.
    ii. Independently verify the reason for the adjustment.

    b. Verify amount
       i. Compare the adjustment amount to the original source documents.
      ii. Recalculate the adjustment amount.
3. Overtime
    a. Verify work performance
        i. Compare days/hours worked to security access systems.
       ii. Compare days/hours worked to computer terminal access.
      iii. Compare days/hours worked to telephone records.
      iv. Compare days/hours worked to use of equipment or machinery used in the company employee's job function.
       v. Compare days/hours worked to documented record of meetings or other work product (base the documentation reviewed on the company employee's specific job functions).
    b. Verify physical existence
       i. Coworkers in the department or job function that did not receive overtime regarding department or job function work schedules
        (a) Speak with audit management regarding the ability to interview the coworkers in the department or job function who did not receive overtime regarding department or job function work schedules.
        (b) Request an interview with the specific company employees(s) or request that investigation personnel interview the specific company employees(s).
      ii. Inspection
        (a) Speak with audit management regarding the ability to perform a surprise inspection of work areas and examine reported hours on that day.
        (b) Perform a surprise inspection of work areas and examine reported hours on that day or request that investigation personnel perform the surprise inspection.
      iii. Surveillance
        (a) Speak with audit management regarding the ability to perform surveillance of suspected departments or company employees.
        (b) Set up surveillance of suspected departments or company employees or request that investigation personnel set up surveillance.

APPENDIX

Fraud Audit Program: Disbursements

 RED FLAGS

1. Shell corporation
   a. Invoice general information
      i. Trigger red flags
         (a) Invoice numbers are illogical given the amount of business the vendor provides. For even a small business that works with other customers, it would be considered normal that the invoices received by the organization would have gaps in invoice numbers where the invoice numbers were used for other customers. It would not be considered logical for the organization to receive sequential invoice numbers.
         (b) The product or service description on the invoice is nonexistent or vague as to specification on the products or services provided. It would be considered normal for a service provider to provide a description with details on what tasks were completed and include hour work, even the people working on the

tasks. It would not be considered logical for a service provider to provide a description of "for services performed" without any additional detail.

(c) The product number(s) included on the invoice are illogical or nonexistent. For example, electrical component product numbers tend to be at least eight digits, so it would be considered illogical for an electrical component to have a two-digit product number.

(d) The invoice was created or entered on off periods, i.e., weekends, holidays, or after hours in a regular duty station. Although it would not be illogical for a three-shift, seven-day-a-week organization to have invoices created or entered on what normally are considered off periods, every organization does have off periods. An analysis on when invoices tend to be created or entered can give information on when would be considered the off periods.

ii. Awareness red flags

(a) Invoice number is illogical given the amount of time the vendor has been in business. It would be considered normal for a well-established vendor to have invoice numbers with three or more digits. Many vendors do not start their first invoice with the number 1, more likely they start with 100 or 1,000.

(b) The invoice does not list a purchase order number. Since a purchase order number is an agreement between the purchaser and the vendor for the purchase of goods or services, if a purchase order is available, the vendor may put this information on the invoice.

(c) There is a single purchase order number that is associated with multiple invoices and payments to the vendor. Although there are legitimate reasons for using one purchase order for multiple purchases (bulk purchase orders), it would not be considered normal for a single purchase order to be used for multiple unrelated purchases or purchases all received at the same time.

(d) The invoice does not list a customer number. Many companies assign numbers to their customers for easier tracking in their accounting systems and tend to put this information on the invoice so that they can track the customer activity.

(e) There are errors in arithmetic on the invoice. For example, the tax percentage is stated on the invoice as 8% but when the tax amount is recalculated, it is listed at 10% of the total.

(f) The invoice line items have illogical units of measure. There are standard units of measure that are used for certain types of goods. It would be considered normal for drums of chemicals to be measured by drums, gallons, or liters, but it would be considered illogical for the drums to be measured in pounds or buckets.

(g) The invoice quantity of goods or time of service is illogical based on the needs of the organization. For example, it would be considered illogical for a small organization of 20 people to have a need for 60 computers.

(h) The invoice lacks information considered standard for the industry or the country, i.e., railcar numbers on railcar repair cards.

(i) The method of payment used to pay the vendor is illogical for the particular vendor or based on normal operating procedures for the organization. For example, the invoice is paid in currency where the vendor traditionally pays by a wire payment.

b. Invoice vendor information
   i. Trigger red flags
     (a) The invoice lacks a telephone number for the vendor. A telephone number on an invoice is standard in most industries and countries as a means of contact for questions and concerns regarding the billing.
     (b) The invoice lacks an address for the vendor. An address on an invoice is standard in most industries and countries as a location for payment to be sent.
   ii. Awareness red flags
     (a) The phone number provided for the vendor on the invoice is a mobile telephone number. Most midsized to large established vendors will have a land line in an office as a contact phone number. A mobile number as the only means of contact is an indicator of a small business, individual contractor, or a scheme.

(b) There is no contact person listed on the invoice. A contact person on an invoice, although not always standard, provides information on the vendor as well as whom the organization works through from the vendor.

(c) There is no web site address listed on the invoice. A web site is a marketing means that many vendors put on their invoices as a means to get the organization to know more about the vendor or to make additional purchases.

(d) There is no e-mail address listed on the invoice. An e-mail address on an invoice, although not always standard, provides another means of contact for the organization.

(e) There is no logo included on the invoice, or the logo is illogical for the invoice or vendor. It would be considered illogical for a logo to be blurry on an invoice or for a car dealership to have a pencil as the logo.

(f) The logo on the invoice appears to be cut and paste from a standard media source. Examples of signs of cut and paste include discrepancies in the spacing of lines, differences in font, sharp lines around images, etc.

(g) The invoice is on false company letterhead. For example, a copy of a company logo is used on falsely created word processed document.

c. Propriety of supporting documents
    i. Trigger red flags
        (a) Supporting documents for the transaction do not provide adequate details concerning goods or services purchased. For example, the packing slip does not give a delivery address or a delivered from location, which is standard on most packing slips.
        (b) Supporting documents for the transaction include handwritten or illegible information. Handwritten documents or notes are easier to alter or in and of themselves could be alterations to the documents.
        (c) Supporting documents for the transaction do not include verification or receipt and inspection reports for the items received. These documents provide additional information about what was actually provided to the organization.
        (d) Supporting documents for the transaction do not include the signature of the recipient of goods or services or another

authorized official. Missing signatures may not only be a control issue, but also may be an indicator of a scheme.

(e) Supporting documents for the transaction include copies retained by different departments which differ in the information included when compared to each other.

d. Information change
  i. Trigger red flags
    (a) If the vendor is paid by check, there is a change to the vendor payment address information. Although it is not considered illogical for a vendor to change its address, it is not common.

    (b) If the vendor is paid by wire, there is a change to the vendor financial institution payment information. Although it is not considered illogical for a vendor to change its banking information, it is not common.

    (c) A vendor has been dormant with respect to doing business with the organization for greater than one year, and the vendor then becomes active again with the organization.

e. Invoice condition
  i. Awareness red flags
    (a) The invoice is handwritten in whole, in part, or there are updates that are handwritten. Handwritten invoices or notes are easier to alter or in and of themselves could be alterations to the invoice.

    (b) The invoice is a photocopy, fax, electronic, or draft version, and an original invoice cannot be located. Any substitute for an original invoice may have been altered or may not be the most current version.

    (c) The invoice age (based on the appearance of the document) is illogical given the invoice date on the document. It would be considered normal for an invoice that is dated 07/19/2010 to be wrinkled, discolored, have finger marks or stains, or even be torn, but if the invoice is on crisp, stark white paper and the date on the invoice is 07/19/2010, this would be considered illogical.

    (d) The paper stock used for the invoice is illogical given the other invoices in the vendor file and/or the type of paper that is customarily used by companies of similar size, i.e., the invoice is on card stock when all other invoices are on copy paper.

(e) The font type is illogically varied on the invoice. Although it would be considered normal to have different font types for the invoice heading and the line items on the invoice, it would be considered illogical to have different font types for each line item on the invoice.

(f) The font size is illogically varied on the invoice. Although it would be considered normal to have different font sizes for the logo and the line items on the invoice, it would be considered illogical to have different font sizes for each line item on the invoice.

(g) The invoice has signs of cut and paste of information. Examples of signs of cut and paste include discrepancies in the spacing of lines, differences in font, sharp lines around images, etc.

(h) The information on the invoice is misaligned either horizontally or vertically. Misalignment can be an indicator of cut and paste or alteration of scanned or copied documents.

(i) The invoice has signs of white-out tape or liquid use. For example, there is white-out over part of description or an amount, which alters the invoice.

(j) The invoice was received through the mail, but folds do not exist on the document. Although a vendor may send letter size invoices in flat letter size envelopes, it is not common.

(k) The invoice has illogical spots, stains, or marks. Spots, stains, or marks could be strategically placed to hide information or alter information on the invoice.

(l) The invoice is ripped or torn. Rips or tears could be strategically placed to hide information or alter information on the invoice.

   f. Business usage of vendor
      i. Awareness red flags
         (a) The vendor is used only by one manager or department. If the vendor is the best vendor providing the goods or services, it would seem logical that all managers or departments would use the vendor.

2. False billing
   a. Trigger red flag
      i. One employee has a high degree of control over the selection and acceptance of the service or goods. This employee has an opportunity to manipulate the process at these control points.

b. Awareness red flags

   i. The same red flags are applicable for false billing as those of a front company (listed above).

3. Pass-through billing

  a. Trigger red flags

   i. The product description or number does not appear to be logical, focusing on the number of integers, special symbols, or references to other numbers. It would be considered illogical for an invoice to have a description of "carton of paper" versus "HammerMill ® Fore MP Premium Multi-Function Paper, $8^1/_2$" × 11", Case."

   ii. The goods were shipped directly to the customer from a company other than the vendor invoicing for the goods. If the vendor is an actual provider of the goods, the vendor would logically have a warehouse to store the goods and ship the goods from its own location.

  b. Awareness red flags

   i. The same red flags are applicable for pass through billing as those of a front company (listed above).

4. Temporary holding

  a. Trigger red flag

   i. Payment is made to the vendor within 10 days or less of the invoice date. If the standard payment time is 30 days or more, it would be considered illogical that a vendor be paid sooner.

  b. Awareness red flag

   i. There are complaints by a real vendor on the delay of payments received. If the organization records show payment within 10 days or less of the invoice date, then it would be illogical that the vendor did not receive the payment in a timely manner.

5. Overbilling

  a. Trigger red flags

   i. The invoice dollar amount exceeds the purchase order amount by more than 5 percent. Although invoices at times do exceed the purchase order amount, many organizations will adjust the purchase order with appropriate approval for the additional amount.

   ii. A duplicate payment where the invoice is a nonoriginal, duplicate invoice number, or duplicate date. Mistakes may be made by a vendor where a duplicate invoice is sent, but it could be an indicator of a scheme, especially if there is a pattern of duplicate invoices.

iii. The fee exceeds original contract pricing. Although goods or services at time do exceed the original pricing for reason, many organizations will adjust the contract or create an amendment to the contract with the appropriate approval for the additional amount.

b. Awareness red flags

  i. Overbilling on price

   (a) The unit pricing exceeds original contract pricing. Although unit pricing can change, especially if there is a time delay between the original contract and the purchase of the units, many organizations will adjust the contract or create an amendment to the contract with the appropriate approval for the additional amount.

   (b) The invoice includes add-on charges not part of original purchase order or contract. It would be considered illogical for a vendor to put additional items on the invoice not discussed in the contract or purchase order agreement process.

  ii. Overbilling on quantity

   (a) The invoice is unclear as to the quantity of the goods received or the amount of services provided. It would be considered normal for a vendor to detail the hours worked for a consulting project per person. It would be considered illogical for a vendor to only put "for services provided" with a total amount on the invoice.

   (b) The items are received directly by the employee that either ordered the item or uses the item. This employee has an opportunity to manipulate the process at these control points.

  iii. Overbilling on quality.

   (a) The invoice contains a vague or unclear description of types of goods received or services provided. It would be considered normal for a service provider to provide a description with detail on what tasks were completed and include hour work, even the people working on the tasks. It would not be considered logical for a service provider to provide a description of "for services performed" without any additional detail.

   (b) The quality of specifications of item(s) exceeds apparent needs of the location. For example: It would be illogical for an employee in the accounting department to require an Apple computer with programs for art and design which would be better suited for an employee in the marketing department.

6. Disguised purchases
   a. Trigger red flags
      i. The nature of goods or services procured has no logical connection to department for which the goods or services are being procured. For example, the accounting department is purchasing sweatshirts and jackets.
      ii. The goods procured are reportedly stored offsite when usually or customarily stored on site. For example, a purchase of laptops is shipped to an offsite location when normally they are sent to the IT department.
   b. Awareness red flags
      i. The goods or services that are procured are of a nature that would be of personal benefit to an individual directly or allow for ease of personal conversion. Common goods that fit this category are gift cards (used by the organization as employee awards) and computer supplies. Common services that fit this category are lawn care and cleaning services.
      ii. There was an excess amount of goods or services supplied. It would be common at the beginning of a project to purchase a large amount of goods or services, but at the end of a project we would not expect large purchases.
      iii. A manager is defensive when the auditor inquires about goods or services that were procured. This manager may have an opportunity to manipulate the process at key control points.
7. Conflict of interest
   a. Trigger red flags
      i. The auditor receives a tip or learns of rumor concerning a manager's close relationship with a vendor. It is important to note a distinction between a good working relationship and excessive contact or relationship.
      ii. The name of an employee is found on documents related to the vendor showing an interest in the vendor. An employee's name may show on documentation as a contact at the organization, but should not show with any interest in the vendor unless the interest has been disclosed.
   b. Awareness red flags
      i. A manager insists on the organization's use of a specific vendor. If the manager is unable to give reasoning as to why the specific vendor should be used, the indicator is heightened.

ii. The same red flags apply to a conflict of interest as with a front company. Many times there is a conflict of interest when a front company scheme exists.

 FRAUD AUDIT PROCEDURES

1. Shell corporation
   a. Verify legal formation/existence
      i. Review registrations and/or incorporation documents
         (a) Compare the registration/incorporation date to the first date the vendor had provided goods or services to the organization and determine if the length of time is reasonable.
            (1) Generally, this period would be greater than 90 days. A lesser activity period would indicate formation for the sole purpose of perpetrating a false billing or pass-through billing scheme.
         (b) Domestic companies—use the LexisNexis search engine to identify whether the vendor is registered with the appropriate government entity (is legally incorporated)
            (1) Determine if the vendor has any other logical government recordings, e.g.,
               (I) Secured debt through a UCC filing.
               (II) Tax registrations.
               (III) Fictitious business names (dba).
               (IV) Judgments and liens.
               (V) Motor vehicle registrations.
               (VI) Assessment records.
                  The presence of these records lends to the legitimacy of the business.
         (c) Canadian companies—use the specific territories registry office to identify whether the vendor is registered with the appropriate government entity (is legally incorporated).
         (d) Other international companies—each country varies in its registration process. Some countries' files may not be accessible. If this is the case, review other sources to identify the existence.

    ii. Review other sources to identify the existence

        (a) If the country's legal registry files are not accessible or the registry files do not resolve the red flags, look for other sources such as:

            (1) Trade and business associations for the industry or region

            (2) Public advertising

                (I) Conduct a Web search to identify if the company has a web site. Review the web site to see if the information is consistent with the vendor invoice information.

                (II) Look for other Web presences such as Internet listings or recent articles about the company or including mention of the company.

            (3) Proof of insurance; this could be on file or may need to be requested of the vendor.

        The presence of these sources lends to the legitimacy of the company.

b. Verify physical existence

    i. Locate the physical business using a satellite mapping tool such as Google Maps

        (a) Identify if the location is commercial versus residential and if a suitable building is located at the location.

    ii. Conduct a site visit to confirm the location is occupied by the vendor.

c. Verify that the vendor has the capacity to conduct business

    i. Phone inquiry

        (a) Identify if the manner in which the phone is answered is professional and adequate given the industry of the vendor.

        (b) Identify if there is a pattern of answering calls via a telephone service or answering machine/voicemail.

        (c) Request information regarding the phone numbers, addresses, and Web presence of the company.

    ii. Internet

        (a) If the vendor has a web site, identify that the type of business being conducted is consistent with the invoice.

        (b) Identify if the company does business through the Internet.

    iii. Item numbers

        (a) For vendors of tangible goods, search the product number via the Internet.

    iv. Trade or business associations

       (a) Identify and contact appropriate trade or business associations to determine if the vendor holds membership.

  d. Verify goods or services receipt

    i. Services

       (a) Interview two individuals independent of the procurement officer, ᵗequestor, or certifying/approving officer to verify the services were actually provided by the vendor. Look for evidence of the services being performed

          (1) If there is no recall, record, or evidence of the services being performed, this is an indicator of false billing.

          (2) If there is recall, record, or evidence of the services being performed, verify the services were performed by the listed vendor. If the services were not performed by the listed vendor, this is an indicator of pass-through billing.

    ii. Goods

       (a) Determine if a packing slip exists for the goods that were provided by the vendor

          (1) If there is no packing slip, this is an indicator of false billing.

       (b) Review the packing slip for information regarding the location from where the goods were provided and determine appropriateness

          (1) If there is a packing slip that includes information of another company outside of the vendor, or the packing slip does not have logical information required, this is an indicator of pass-through billing.

  e. Verify bank account

    i. Contact the vendor to verify the invoices are from the listed vendor

       (a) If the invoices are not from the listed vendor, this is an indicator of false billing.

    ii. Contact the vendor to determine if the bank account the funds are being deposited in is an appropriate bank account

       (a) If the bank account is not an appropriate bank account but the vendor has received payment, this is an indicator of a temporary holding scheme.

2. Overbilling

  a. Interview the requestor of the goods or services and obtain reasons for the higher than expected billing

      i. The lack of information provided, as well as documentation, is an indicator the overbilling could be occurring.

  b. Corroborate the requestor's representations through at least one independent source

      i. This could include looking at market trends, looking at immediate needs at the time of the purchase, and other means.

  c. Determine which type of overbilling could be occurring based on the analysis of the invoice(s)

      i. Overbilling on invoice total (on each item on the invoice)

        (a) Look at market pricing trends or investigate with other vendors selling the same goods or services as to pricing.

      ii. Overbilling on add-on charges

        (a) Independently verify that the add-on charge is part of the original contract.

        (b) If the add-on is a tax, determine why the tax is being charged and if it is appropriate to charge the tax.

     iii. Overbilling on quantity

        (a) Inventory item

          (1) Trace quantity of the item on the invoice to the available inventory records for that item as close to the purchase as possible.

          (2) Determine when the last physical inventory was performed and obtain the physical inventory records to compare on-hand quantities.

          (3) Determine if any shortages have occurred for the item in the scope period.

          (4) Perform a physical count of the item quantity on hand and compare to inventory records.

          (5) Perform a usage calculation for the item for the scope period and compare to inventory records.

        (b) Supply item

          (1) Perform a usage calculation for the item for the scope period.

          (2) Determine if any shortages have occurred for the item in the scope period.

     iv. Overbilling based on product substitution (providing inferior or lesser quality goods or services than were procured)

        (a) Perform a physical inspection of the item and compare to the description on the invoice or packing slip.

(b) If the nature of the item does not allow for physical inspection, use an outside expert to validate the quality of the item.

(c) Interview users of the item, independent of the requestor or asset manager, to determine if the product performs at the required level or meets the anticipated specifications.

    v. Determine the frequency, percentage, and amount of the potential overbilling in the scope period.

3. Disguised procurement

    a. Determine if the goods or services were received at an organization facility and used at that facility

      i. This verification procedure should be independent of discussions with the staff member primarily responsible for the approval or the primary user of the goods or services.

    b. Determine if the goods or services were not needed by the organization.

4. Conflict of interest

    a. Registration

      i. Based on the government registration information, determine if any names on government documents for the vendor match organization employee names or other known family relationships

        (a) Family member names may be found through beneficiary information.

    b. Tax returns

      i. If the vendor entity is a limited liability company, request and inspect copies of the tax returns for the company. Look for names that match organization employee names or other known family members.

    c. Shareholders

      i. If the vendor entity is a corporation, request and inspect stock records (for review of shareholders) of the corporation. Look for names that match organization employee names or other known family members.

      ii. Request that counsel for the vendor provides confirmation of the entity's owners/shareholders. Look for names that match organization employee names or other known family members.

APPENDIX

Fraud Audit Program: Procurement

KEY TERMS

1. Favored status—the vendor selection process favors a vendor without proper disclosure and approval. The favored status may have occurred by the virtue of a personal relationship with the vendor, company employee's prior employment, or an extended business relationship with the company. The scheme occurs with the knowledge of management.

2. Bid avoidance—structuring the procurement process to circumvent or avoid standard bidding requirements

   a. Structured purchasing—the process of issuing multiple purchase orders to the same or related vendor; each order is individually below the bid threshold level with the purchase orders exceeding the control threshold in the aggregate.

   b. Split bids—the process of awarding two vendors a purchase order for the same product to avoid the control threshold.

   c. Contract amendment—the process of awarding the vendor additional work assignments without following the competitive bid process.

    d. Sole source—the process of procuring goods or services without using the normal, competitive bidding process. The sole-source nature of the process implies that there is only one vendor that can provide the goods or services needed and that, in the end, competitive bidding would yield the same result.

    e. Exigency purchase—the process of using an "exigency" condition(s) to bypass control thresholds and competitive bidding procedures.

3. Advance communication of information—the procurement officer provides information to one vendor to the detriment of other vendors.

4. Favoring of key control points

    a. Establishment of a need—submitting purchase order at "peak demand times" or under "'exigency conditions" in order to increase the probability of paying a higher price for goods or services, thereby increasing vendor margins.

    b. Specification setting—designing product/service specifications so as to ensure that only one vendor can be awarded the contract.

    c. Identifying the vendor pool—structuring the bidding process so as to exclude qualified vendors that would otherwise be ready, willing, and able to offer competitive pricing.

5. False statements—creating false bid documents. The scheme occurs by using false or real company names on the bid documents. By having real companies participate in the scheme by knowingly submitting inflated amounts or falsifying vendor qualifications.

6. Management override—management intentionally authorizes the selection of a vendor and bypasses control procedures.

7. Vendor bid rigging is a scheme perpetrated by the vendors without the knowledge of management. The scheme occurs by intentional unresponsive bids, bid suppression, bid rotation, and market division strategies.

8. Vendor nepotism or discrimination—the selection of a vendor that favors or discriminates based on country, region, family, or other characteristics.

9. Conflict of interest—employee or relative of the employee has an undisclosed legal or beneficial interest in a vendor.

10. Bribery—a prize, reward, gift, or favor bestowed or promised to pervert the judgment of or influence the action of a person in the position of trust.

11. Kickback—a return of a portion of a monetary sum received for the false administration of a contracted service or delivery of a good. Typically associated with vendor overbilling schemes.

12. Defective pricing—the intentional understatement of costs by the vendor for the sole purpose of winning the contract, generally with the intent of later increasing the costs through change orders.

13. Progress payment fraud—the contractor applies for payment during the course of a contract, fraudulently certifying that the costs eligible for reimbursement have been incurred at a pace faster than actually incurred.

14. Nonconforming material or services—the contractor provides materials or services that do not conform to the contract requirements.

15. Cost mischarging—the contract is charged for costs not allowable under the contract or for costs relating to a separate contract.

 ## FRAUD SCHEME STRUCTURE

Procurement Cycle

Major Type: Corruption

1. Favored status.
2. Vendor nepotism/discrimination.
3. Conflict of interest.
4. Bribery/kickback/extortion.
5. Vendor bid rigging.

Contract Administration

Major Type: Asset Misappropriation

1. Embezzlement
   a. Defective pricing.
   b. Progress payment.
   c. Overbilling—see Disbursements Audit Guidelines for overbilling
      i. Nonconforming materials or services.
      ii. Cost mischarging.

 ## OVERALL AUDIT APPROACH

1. Decision
   The overall audit approach is the fraud audit red flag approach. This approach entails the following two standard decisions.

DECISION 1: Is there a TRIGGER RED FLAG*?
If there is no trigger red flag, STOP.
If there is a trigger red flag, PERFORM FRAUD AUDIT PROCEDURES and CONTINUE.

DECISION 2: Is the red flag resolved by the FRAUD AUDIT PROCEDURES?
If the fraud audit procedures resolve the existence of the red flag, STOP.
If the fraud audits procedures do not resolve the existence of the red flag, INCLUDE TRANSACTION IN AUDIT REPORT.

 RED FLAGS

Procurement Cycle

1. Favored status
   a. Trigger red flags
      i. Bid avoidance
         (a) Purchase orders issued within ___ days of a bid threshold.
         (b) Sole source award above or just below competitive bidding limits.
         (c) Requisitioning department bypasses procurement.
      ii. Advance communication of information
         (a) Pattern of low bid award followed by change orders that increase the price of the contract.
         (b) Pattern of low bid award followed by change orders that increase the scope of the contract.
         (c) Significant changes to the financial proposal during contract negotiations.
         (d) Original contract was short term and second or more contracts issued to vendor without bidding.
      iii. False statements
         (a) Vendor provides false test or quality assurance certificates

---

* Note: Trigger red flag in the decision process refers to:

C. A specific red flag associated with a fraud scenario with sufficient weight to cause the auditor to perform additional fraud audit procedures.
D. The totality of all awareness red flags associated with the fraud scenario that the auditor judges are sufficient to perform additional fraud audit procedures.

iv. Management override

    (a) No justification or documentation for noncompetitive awards.

    (b) Identical ranking of the same bidders upon rebidding when original bids were rejected as being too far over the company estimate.

v. Control avoidance

    (a) Purchase specifications—acquisition planning specification

        (1) Vague contract specifications.

        (2) Vague contract specifications followed by change orders.

    (b) Vendor identification—sourcing

        (1) Failure of bidders from previous projects to bid.

        (2) Failure of original bidders in a rebid situation to send a bid.

        (3) Allowing unusually short time for bidding process.

    (c) Vendor selection solicitation and evaluation of bids

        (1) A qualified bidder is disqualified for "questionable reasons" or reasons that cannot be substantiated.

        (2) High number of competitive awards to one vendor.

        (3) High number of sole source awards to one vendor.

        (4) Ex post facto procurements.

    (d) Buyer focus

        (1) Unexplained or unusual change orders for a specific contractor approved by same staff member.

        (2) Numerous change orders for a specific contractor approved by same staff member.

    (e) Bid opening procedures

        (1) Different versions of bid documents provided to vendors.

        (2) Acceptance of bids after close date.

    (f) Bid evaluation procedures

        (1) No technical evaluation team.

        (2) Develop technical evaluation criteria after bid opening.

        (3) Technical evaluation team members without the required skills being driven by a dominant team member.

    (g) Lack of required documentation in the file.

    (h) Post award indicators

        (1) Significant changes within 60 days (period based on audited entity and process) of award date.

        (2) Requisitioning unit approves changes and bypasses procurement.

     (i) Contract awarding and administration
       (1) Continual extending of existing contract that was placed to bid or vendor selected.
       (2) Contract amendments issued within 60 days (period based on audited entity and process) of the original contract, which adversely affect the company.
       (3) Contract violates restrictions on hiring former company employee.
  b. Awareness red flags
    i. Bid avoidance
     (a) Inadequate publication of requests for bids, e.g., using only local publications or complete failure to publicize.
     (b) Adopting or use of unreasonable "prequalification" procedures.
     (c) Unjustified separation of procurement, e.g., separate contracts for labor and materials, each of which is below competitive bidding limits, but when combined are over such limits.
     (d) Two or more similar procurements from the same vendor in amounts just under competitive bidding or upper level review limits.
    ii. Advance communication of information
     (a) Multiple awards for similar work are given to the same contractor.
     (b) Winning bid amount "just under" next lowest bid.
     (c) Significant discrepancy between bid projection and actual purchases.
     (d) High consistency of vendor bid to internal cost estimates.
    iii. False statements
     (a) Unusual degree of commonality of the vendor bids. Focus on bid layout, bid language, paper type, font style and size.
    iv. Management override
     (a) Previously competitive procurements changed to non-competitive.
     (b) Winning bid is voided for "errors" in contract specifications and the job is rebid.
     (c) Bids won by vendors in offshore countries and territories.
     (d) Winning vendor has bank and office in different countries and either or both are offshore.
     (e) Requisitioning office purchases goods/services directly without use of purchasing department.

(f) Staff member at a higher level injects self in the process.

(g) Staff member cancels bid despite technically compliant vendor.

(h) Bid due date extended without sufficient reason.

(i) Winning bidder participated in drafting contract specifications.

v. Control avoidance

(a) Purchase specifications—acquisition planning specification

(1) Incomplete or "preliminary" specifications subject to change based on later engineering studies, etc.

(2) Brand name used in requests for bids, e.g., without words such as "or equivalent."

(3) Requirements are inconsistent with industry standards.

(4) Specifications are significantly narrower or broader than similar previous requests for bids.

(5) Unreasonably narrow contract specifications.

(6) Vendor prepares the specifications.

(b) Vendor identification—sourcing

(1) Bid prices appear to drop whenever a new or infrequent bidder submits a bid (indicating old vendor was inflating prices).

(2) A significant number of known qualified bidders fail to bid.

(3) Dissimilar vendors bid.

(c) Vendor selection solicitation and evaluation of bids

(1) Winning bid too high/low compared to costs estimates.

(2) Winning bid too high/low compared to published price lists.

(3) Winning bid too high/low compared to similar jobs.

(4) Winning bid too high/low compared to industry averages.

(5) Late bidder is the winning bidder.

(6) Last bid received is the winning bid.

(7) Winning bid is NOT the lowest bid.

(8) Vendor selection criteria favor one vendor.

(9) Contract contains an unfavorable clause, i.e., restricts company's ability to monitor or verify vendor delivery.

(10) Errors in the evaluation criteria documents.

(11) Requests for clarification after bid opening.

(12) Pricing significantly above market prices.

(d) Buyer focus

(1) Reluctance to take annual leave.

(2) Reluctance to rotate out of position.

(3) Vendor insists on working with one buyer.

    (e) Bid opening procedures
        (1) Improper communication between staff and vendors.
        (2) Bid opening was not transparent.
        (3) No documentation that vendors were invited to bid opening.
        (4) Uninvited vendors submit bids.
        (5) Pricing information provided prior to completion of technical evaluation report.
        (6) Changes to vendors' bids after opening.
    (f) Bid evaluation procedures
        (1) Multiple evaluations.
        (2) Inclusion of technically noncompliant vendor in pricing evaluation.
    (g) Postaward indicators
        (1) Added charges that were not originally included in the contract.
        (2) Favorable payment terms.
        (3) Suspicious payment terms: advance payments, payment directed to a third party, or paid in cash unnecessarily.
        (4) Failure to obtain credits for returns or damaged goods.
        (5) Company provides goods, services, or space that should have been part of original contract.
    (h) Contract awarding and administration
        (1) Voiding of bid selection process on technical grounds.
        (2) Change of terms and conditions from previous contract regarding payment terms, contract fulfillment, contractor obligations, and unique terms relevant to the actual purchase.
        (3) Interpretation of contract clauses that have unfavorable results for the company.
2. Management preference
   a. Trigger red flags
      i. The decision for the selection of the vendor is disclosed to the company as based on preference or standing relationships.
   b. Awareness red flags
      i. The decision for the selection of the vendor is not disclosed.
     ii. The decision for the selection of the vendor is controlled by a local team.

3. Nepotism/discrimination
   a. Trigger red flags
      i. The ethnicity, religion, tribal affiliation, etc. is consistent with that of the local management team.
      ii. The name, address, or telephone number of the vendor or parties of the vendor are consistent with a staff member.
4. Bribery/extortion/kickbacks—guidelines for overbilling fraud audit procedures
   a. Awareness red flags
      i. Strained relationship between vendor and company employee.
      ii. Change in relationship between vendor and company employee.
5. Conflict of interest
   a. Trigger red flags
      i. Apparent connections between vendor and a company employee: common name, telephone numbers, fax numbers, addresses, bank accounts.
      ii. Auditor receives tip or learns of rumor concerning manager's close relationship with a vendor.
   b. Awareness red flag
      i. Manager insists on the company's use of a specific vendor.
6. Vendor bid rigging
   a. Trigger red flags
      i. Losing bidders hired as subcontractors.
      ii. Identical bid amounts on a [service] contract line item by two or more contractors.
   b. Awareness red flags
      i. Unusual bid pattern, the bids are round numbers.
      ii. Unusual bid patterns, the bids are too consistent.
      iii. Unusual bid patterns, the bids are too far apart.
      iv. Unusual bid patterns, the bids are identical or similar to prior or other bid.
      v. Unusual bid patterns, the bids are too close together.
      vi. Unusual bid patterns, the bids are too high.
      vii. Unusual bid patterns, the bids are incomplete.
      viii. Certain contractors always bidding against each other.
      ix. Bidders that ship their product a short distance bid more than those who must incur greater expense by shipping their product long distances.

Contract Administration

1. Defective pricing
   a. Trigger red flags
      i. There are change orders to contract pricing greater than XX.OO%.
   b. Awareness red flags
      i. Contract pricing is significantly less than other bidding companies.
2. Progress payment
   a. Trigger red flag
      i. Progress payments are requested without appropriate documentation.
   b. Awareness red flag
      i. Progress payments are requested ahead of contract schedule.
3. Overbilling
   a. Nonconforming materials or services
      i. Product substitution.

 ## COST MISCHARGING

Data Mining

Procurement Cycle

1. Favored status
   a. See Disbursements Fraud Audit Guidelines for information on data mining for disbursements for the selection of false vendors.
   b. Using commodity code field create report by commodity code, by vendor, and by purchase order.
   c. Using the bid code field, create report by bid code, by buyer, by commodity code, and by purchase order.
   d. Using the invoice sequence report, search for vendors that have a sequential pattern of invoices or whose invoice range appears illogical for the total vendor expenditures in relation to the date range.
   e. Bid avoidance
      i. Using the data summarization field, create report by vendor summarizing the number of invoices/purchase orders; total dollars; maximum, minimum, and average invoice amount; or purchase order amount.
      ii. Using the monthly average report, search for evidence of structuring, i.e., multiple purchase orders to the same or related vendor,

with each order individually below the bid threshold level but exceeding the control threshold in the aggregate.

2. Vendor nepotism/discrimination
   a. Based on the company's entity policies and procedures regarding nepotism and discrimination, identify vendors who fit the criteria of nepotism or discrimination at the audited entity.
   b. Obtain key statistics on the key vendors who fit the criteria of nepotism or discrimination at the audited entity, e.g., geographic location, common name, nationality.
3. Conflict of interest
   a. Search for vendors with common address or banking information as a vendor.
   b. Search for vendors with members (employees, officers, registering agents, shareholders, etc.) that are staff members of the audited company.
   c. Search for vendors with a favored status (see 1 above).
4. Bribery/kickback/extortion
   a. Search for vendors with a favored status (see 1 above).
   b. Search for vendors with data profiles of overbilling (see 2c under Contract Billing).
   c. Search for vendors with sole source status.
   d. Search for vendors with continual changes to purchase order or contract.
5. Vendor bid rigging
   a. Search for bids with lower turnout than expected.
   b. Search for bids that were awarded the contract priced above the industry norm.
   c. Search for predictable patterns in the vendors being awarded the contract.
   d. Search for vendors using other bidders as subcontractors.

Contract Administration

Major Type: Asset Misappropriation

1. Embezzlement
   a. Defective pricing
      i. Search for contracts with excessive change orders (based on the type of contract and the audited entity).
      ii. Search for contracts that were awarded to the lowest bidder.

b. Progress payment
   i. Search for contracts that are ahead of schedule for payments.
c. Overbilling—see Disbursements Fraud Audit Guidelines for information on data mining for overbilling.

 FRAUD AUDIT PROCEDURES

1. Management preference
   a. Verify there existed full disclosure to management of the management preference prior to commencement of the business relationship.
   b. Verify management assessed appropriateness of the management preference prior to commencement of the business relationship.
2. Nepotism/discrimination
   a. Establish the basis of the nepotism/discrimination.
   b. Determine that the vendor was not the appropriate selection based on the criteria for vendor selection; there was a false representation, etc.
   c. Establish whether the internal staff knew the representation was false; by actual knowledge, circumstantial knowledge, or the individual should have known based on his or her job responsibilities.
   d. Establish the type of influence
      i. Overt influence—directly impacts procurement process or documentation.
      ii. Covert influence—provided information to the advantage of one vendor.
      iii. Indirect influence—uses management position or personal integrity to influence other to award purchase to vendor.
   e. Economic damages to the company (adverse publicity vs. economic damages) do not need to exist.
3. Bribery/extortion/kickbacks
   a. Determine if and how the contract was overbilled—Disbursements Fraud Audit Guidelines.
   b. Determine whether the vendor was the appropriate selection based on the criteria for vendor selection; was there a false representation, etc.?
   c. Establish whether the internal staff knew the representation was false; by actual knowledge, circumstantial knowledge, or the individual should have known based on his or her job responsibilities.
   d. Establish the type of influence
      i. Overt influence—directly impacts purchase process or documentation.

    ii. Covert influence—provided information to the advantage of one vendor.

    iii. Indirect influence—uses management position or personal integrity to influence other to award purchase to vendor.

  e. Establish the economic damages to the company.

4. Conflict of interest

  a. Conduct a comparison of company employee and vendor contact details, banking information, etc.

  b. Based on the government registration information, determine if any names on government documents for the vendor match to company's staff members' names or other known family relationships.

  c. Limited liability vendors

    i. Speak with audit management regarding the ability to request and access limited liability company information.

    ii. Request from the vendor and inspect copies of the tax return to identify partners or request that investigation personnel perform these steps.

  d. Incorporated vendors

    i. Speak with audit management regarding the ability to request and access incorporation information.

    ii. Request and inspect stock records from the vendor or registering state and review to identify shareholders or request that investigation personnel perform these steps.

    iii. Request counsel for the vendor entity to provide confirmation of the entity's owners/shareholders or request that investigation personnel perform these steps.

5. Vendor bid rigging

  a. Establish the relationship between the vendors.

  b. Determine the type of bid rigging

    i. Cover bidding—gives the impression of competitive bidding but, in reality, suppliers agree to submit token bids that are usually too high.

    ii. Bid suppression—is an agreement among suppliers either to abstain from bidding or to withdraw bids.

    iii. Bid rotation—is a process whereby the pre-selected supplier submits the lowest bid on a systematic or rotating basis.

    iv. Market division—is an arrangement among suppliers not to compete in designated geographic regions or for specific customers.

  c. Establish the economic damage to the company.

6. Defective pricing
    a. Determine if the costs were overstated for the purposes of overbilling—see Disbursement Fraud Audit Guidelines.
    b. Determine if the original costs were understated at the point in time of the original bid.
    c. Establish if the costs were purposefully understated.
    d. Establish the economic damages to the company.
7. Progress payment
    a. Verify progress of contract
        i. Independently verify that the progress on the project has been completed by visiting the site of the project.
        ii. Independently verify that the progress on the project has been completed by requesting reports or other supporting documentation for services.
8. Overbilling—see, Disbursements Fraud Audit Guidelines for overbilling fraud audit procedures
    f. Nonconforming materials or services
        i. Product substitution.
    g. Cost mischarging.

Fraud Audit Program: Inventory

 INVENTORY CONCEALMENT TECHNIQUES

False counts. The management team records improper counts. If this proce-dure is performed, it is most likely to occur on inventory perceived less likely to be counted or with a planned reason for the false count. In this way, the auditor will view the false count as an intentional error versus an intentional plan to misstate the inventory. The auditor needs to ensure that management has no record of the test counts.

Fictitious inventory. Management will use their business environment to create the illusion of inventory by placing empty boxes in the warehouse or creating a reason why inventory cannot be physically inspected. The reasons will vary; however, the intent is always the same. Manage-ment will need to inhibit the auditor's ability to physically inspect the item.

    In this scheme the item does not exist, the item is incomplete, or some item will be represented as the inventory.

Partially fictitious inventory. The auditor is presented some item to provide the illusion that the inventory does exist. Oftentimes the inventory item will be of a technical nature, which makes it difficult to understand whether the item is in fact a true item.

False certifications. In this scheme, management creates documents certifying inventory balances, alters the original documents, provides copies of documents or draft documents, or has the outside expert provide false documents supporting the inventory item.

Inventory stored at remote locations, independent warehouses, engineering estimates, ore and minerals, and percentage of completion are the type of items that are susceptible to this fraud scheme.

Alteration of inventory counts after the physical counts. The key for management is to know the auditor's test counts. This has occurred through recording the auditor's test counts or obtaining the information after the auditor has completed his or her test counts.

Multiple locations. Inventory at locations not being counted is moved to the planned locations to hide the overstatement of inventory.

Timing issues. With the receipt of inventory at year-end, either through hiding purchases, in-transit goods, title transfer of inventory, sales returns, and recording the sales without inventory update.

Hiding the slow-moving inventory. The inventory or sales reports will be altered in some manner to indicate inventory movement. Management may create fictitious sales to indicate the product is moving. The sold inventory then could be used as part of a false count scheme. The scheme may also be as simple as false explanations from management.

Improper cost assigned to the inventory. How this occurs will depend on the nature of the inventory item. The key is to have a sufficient knowledge of the business.

Data Mining Strategies

▪ Compare the beginning inventory balances to the ending inventory balances. The auditor should be looking for changes consistent with the fraud theory of over- or understatement of inventory.

▪ Compare unit purchases to unit sales. The auditor should correlate the variances to the change in the inventory. The procedure should be performed on the lowest data element possible.

▪ Compare dollar purchases to dollar sales.

Data Analysis

- Compute the number of inventory locations (bins) prior to the physical count.
- Compare beginning inventory to the ending inventory for new or deleted items.
- Compare inventory balances before and after the physical counts.
- Identify the largest physical counts.
- For multiple locations, compare total beginning inventory to total ending inventory. For those locations experiencing deviations consistent with fraud theory, perform searches on the inventory items.
- Determine which inventory items have had stock outages during the year.
- Through inquiry with the sales force, determine which items have had stock outages during the year.
- Compare inventory balances at the end of the third quarter to the inventory balances at the end of the year.
- Identify inventory variances by stock item.
- Examine internal sales forecasts for sales projections consistent with representations on inventory movement.

Audit Procedure

- Examine inventory tags for evidence of changes.
- Examine inventory tags for evidence of tags being included or excluded.
- Compare the number of inventory tags to the number of inventory locations.
- Establish an inventory variance percentage and examine those inventory items exceeding the range.
- Compute inventory items by square footage of the warehouse. Compare beginning and ending square footage calculations.
- Perform inventory counts at locations not known to management.
- Based on the data analysis, the auditor may need to determine additional procedures to determine the reasonability of the data analysis results.

Fictitious inventory. Management will use their business environment to create the illusion of inventory by placing empty boxes in the warehouse or creating a reason why inventory cannot be physically inspected. The reasons will vary; however, the intent is always the same. Management will need to inhibit the auditor's ability to physically inspect the item.

In this scheme, the item does not exist, the item is incomplete, or some item will be represented as the inventory.

Data Analysis

- The data analysis performed for the false count will also provide information for the fictitious inventory scheme.

Audit Procedure

- The inventory item needs to be critically examined to ensure the physical existence of the item.
- Perform a test to ensure the item functions consistent with the sales catalogs.
- Consider the use of an outside expert to validate the item.
- Develop a logic test to determine the reasonability of the inventory amount.

Partially fictitious inventory. The auditor is presented some item to provide the illusion that the inventory does exist. Oftentimes the inventory item will be of a technical nature, which makes it difficult to understand whether the item is in fact a true item.

Data Analysis

- The data analysis performed for the false count will also provide information for the fictitious inventory scheme.

Audit Procedure

- The inventory item needs to be critically examined to ensure the physical existence of the item.
- Perform a test to ensure the item functions consistent with the sales catalogs.
- Consider the use of an outside expert to validate the item.

False certifications. In this scheme management create documents certifying inventory balances, alter the original documents, provide copies of documents or draft documents, or have the outside expert provide false documents supporting the inventory item.

Inventory stored at remote locations, independent warehouses, engineering estimates, ore and minerals, and percentage of completion are the type of items that are susceptible to this fraud scheme.

Data Analysis

- The data analysis performed for the false count will also provide information for the fictitious inventory scheme for items of a unit nature.

Audit Procedure

- The documents should be critically examined to ensure the documents are original and not altered.
- Confirm directly with the source the authenticity of the documents.
- Confirm the valid existence of the source or the outside expert.
- Perform an onsite inspection of the inventory.
- Confirm existence of the inventory at the location with some other source within the company.
- Interview operations staff as to their knowledge of the inventory amount.
- Review vendor invoices to ensure cost elements of the project have reasonably have occurred.

Alteration of inventory counts after the physical counts. The key for management is to know the auditor's test counts. This has occurred through recording the auditor's test counts or obtaining the information after the auditor has completed his or her test counts.

Data Analysis

- The data analysis performed for the false count will also provide information for the fictitious inventory scheme.

Audit Procedure

- Prior to the physical inventory, obtain a report or data file on the inventory balances prior to the physical count.
- Compare retained copy of inventory report to final physical inventory report.

Multiple locations. Inventory at locations not being counted is moved to the planned locations to hide the overstatement of inventory.

Data Analysis

- Search for inventory transfer between operating locations.

Audit Procedure

- Consider conducting an unannounced physical inventory count.
- Prior to the inventory, examine shipping documents, transfer documents, or other source documents indicating transfers.
- Interview operating management at inventory locations to determine if any unusual inventory movement occurred in around the time of the physical inventory.

Timing issues. Search for discrepancies with the receipt of inventory at year-end, either through hiding purchases, in transit goods, title transfer of inventory, sales returns, and recording the sales without inventory update.

Data Analysis

- Search for inventory transfer between operating locations.
- Search for purchases recorded after year-end.

Audit Procedure

- Match shipping documents to inventory movement.
- Examine purchase returns and credits for indicators of false purchases.
- For purchases recorded after year-end, examine the shipping documents to ascertain date of receipt.
- Examine shipping records after year-end for evidence of fraud.

Hiding the slow-moving inventory. The inventory or sales reports will be altered in some manner to indicate inventory movement. Management may create fictitious sales to indicate the product is moving. The sold inventory then could be used as part of a false count scheme. The scheme may also be as simple as false explanations from management.

Data Analysis

- Compute sales history by units and dollars by inventory item. Compare sales history for a minimum of one year.

- Compute inventory from the previous quarter and compare to ending inventory.
- Search for ship-to addresses that are company-owned property.
- Search for sales with no commissions.
- Search for returns with no adjustment to a sales representative.

Audit Procedure

- Perform interviews with sales management to validate explanations regarding the marketability of inventory.

Misstatement regarding the marketability of the inventory. The key is to provide the auditor with explanations or documents that indicate pending or future sales.

Data Analysis

- The procedures would be the same as hiding slow moving inventory.

Audit Procedure

- Confirm explanations with sources outside the financial area.

Improper Cost Assigned to the Inventory. How this occurs will depend on the nature of the inventory item. The key is to have a sufficient knowledge of the business.

Data Analysis

- Search for updates to cost items in the last quarter.
- Compare last quarter cost element to year-end cost elements.

Audit Procedure

- Match cost elements to original supporting documentation.
- Confirm that cost composition elements correlate to operation blueprints or other like plans.
- Compare ending unit costs to beginning unit costs. The lowest component cost possible will provide the best results.

Journal entries at year-end. I call this the easy approach. The management team alters the inventory balance through journal entries. The key is the documentation supporting the entry, the volume of entries, and whether the entries appear to be part of the normal course of business.

Data Analysis

- Search for year-end journal entries affecting ending inventory.
- Search for year-end journal entries transferring inventory from locations.

Audit Procedure

- Validate the explanations provided.
- Determine if similar entries are made during the year or prior years.

Alteration of year-end inventory reports. The auditor will match the year-end inventory report to the financial statements. The key to the concealment technique is to have the all reports provide the same erroneous calculations or totals.

Data Analysis

- The nature of the scheme does not lend itself to a specific data analysis.

Audit Procedure

- Recalculate the inventory report.

APPENDIX

Fraud Audit Planning Program: Revenue Recognition

 FRAUD RISK STRUCTURE: REVENUE RECOGNITION

SAS 99 states that the auditor should ordinarily presume that there is a risk of material statement due to fraud related to revenue recognition.

The search for revenue fraud should start with understanding how management has historically misstated revenue. Revenue fraud can be categorized into four major groups, with each group having several general schemes and several industry-specific fraud schemes.

I. **Management records fictitious revenue through a false billing scheme.** Illusion is the key word in this fraud scheme. Management must provide representations, supported by documentation, that a customer exists, delivery has occurred, or that services have been rendered, and that the revenue transaction has been realized. Documentation will be obtained, created, or altered to support the false assertions. The overall audit approach should search for and critically examine each of the main revenue assertions. The attributes of a false billing scheme are:

A. The revenue transaction is recorded through the billing system.

B. The revenue transaction is recorded through the use of fictitious customers and the use of real customers.

C. Management obtains, creates, or alters documents to provide the illusion that the customer ordered the product or services.

D. The delivery of the product is disguised in one of many methods.

E. The realization of the receivable is concealed.

II. Improper recognition of revenue either because it was recorded prematurely or intentionally delayed to a later period. In this case, the problem relates to:

A. The revenue is not realized and is eventually returned. The audit approach should focus on the realization assertion.

B. The revenue is eventually recognized. This fraud scheme is the most difficult to detect because all the revenue assertions are achieved. The audit should focus on the delivery point of the revenue transaction and the documentation.

C. Improper recognition schemes occur as follows:

- Recognition of revenue on "soft sales" from customers that have not agreed to purchase the item.
- Recognition of revenue on products that is incomplete or flawed.
- Recognition of revenue on partial shipments.
- Recognition of revenue involving multiple deliverables that have not all been satisfied
- Recognition of revenue in the improper period.
- A single revenue transaction.
- Misapplication through timing factors.
- Premature recognition.
- Delayed recognition.
- Disputed sales.

D. Related party transactions are frequently linked to sham transactions and occur as follows:

- Sales activity between two parties, often related by law or industry, where insufficient consideration is given for the sales transaction.
- Seller provides total financing to transfer consideration.
- Below FMV transactions.
- Borrowing or lending on an interest-free basis or at a rate of interest significantly above or below market rates.

- Exchanging property for similar property in a non-monetary transaction.
- Loans with no scheduled terms for when or how the funds will be repaid.
- Loans with interest accruing differently from market rates.
- Loans to parties lacking the capacity to repay.
- Loans advanced for valid business purposes and later written off as noncollectible.
- Nonrecourse loans to shareholders.
- Agreements requiring one party to pay the expenses on the other's behalf.
- Business arrangements where the entity pays or receives payments of amounts at other than market values.
- Consulting arrangements with directors, officers, or other members of management.
- Goods purchased or sent to another party at less than cost.
- Material receivables or payables from/to related parties such as officers, directors, and other employees.

E. **Consignment income.** Transfer of product is based on a consignment contract.

F. **Channel stuffing.** The practice of offering extremely favorable terms to move a sales transaction into a current period. The inducement is so favorable the customer purchases the product in the current period instead of in a later period. Signs of the practice are large discounts, pricing below FMV or cost, extended payment terms, no repayment schedule, or loans to help finance the purchase.

G. **Round tripping.** Sales activity between parties where there is no measurable economic benefit. The main purpose is to increase sales with no measurable benefit to the bottom line. No cash has transferred between the parties.

H. **Barter.** Sales transaction occurs through a swap of products or services.

III. **Creation of revenue through journal entries.** This fraud scheme is easy because none of the revenue assertions need to be achieved. Revenue is misstated simply through one or more journal entries. No customer accounts are impacted. The journal entries maybe recorded in the general ledger or in top-sided journal entries.

IV. **Misapplication of GAAP.** This can be related to:

A. **Misapplication of the fundamental revenue assertions.** Here, the management team intentionally misapplies one of the four key criteria to recognize revenue. The auditor needs to identify the specific criteria and determine how management could manipulate the criteria and then conceal the truth.

- A transaction has to occur entailing an exchange.
- The conversion of income to revenue is essentially complete.
- The price is fixed and determinable.
- Collection is reasonably assured.

B. **Misapplication of industry GAAP.** As stated above, there are a number of specific GAAP pronouncements covering revenue. Here, the management team intentionally misapplies the criteria established under the specific accounting pronouncement. The auditor needs to identify the specific criteria and determine how management could manipulate the criteria and then conceal the truth.

C. **Improper and inadequate disclosures.**

D. **Illustrative of GAAP-specific.** With this transaction, a legitimate sales order is received and executed. However, the terms require the seller to hold the goods until the purchaser is ready to take acceptance. SEC Staff Accounting Bulletin 14 states bill-and-hold transactions can be booked as revenue only after the following criteria are met:

- The risks of ownership must have passed to the buyer.
- The customer must have made a fixed commitment to purchase the goods, preferably in written documentation.
- The buyer, not the seller, must request that the transaction be on a bill-and-hold basis.
- The buyer must have a substantial business purpose for ordering goods on a bill-and-hold basis.
- There must be a fixed schedule for the delivery of goods based on what is customary in the buyer's business.
- The seller must not have retained any specific performance obligations such that the earnings process is not complete.
- The ordered goods must have been segregated from the seller's inventory and not subject to being used to fill other customer orders.
- The products must be complete and ready for shipment.

FRAUD CONCEALMENT STRATEGY

When an individual decides to commit internal fraud, how to conceal the true nature of the transaction is a critical aspect of his or her plan. The goal is to have the business transaction look like a real transaction.

Each fraud scheme has a typical way to conceal it. However, how the individual implements the concealment strategy varies, based on the person's position (opportunity) and the company's internal procedures. The auditor should give consideration to the opportunity list in relation to the system under audit.

Methods to conceal the true nature of the transaction will vary with the business system, employee position, and computerized systems versus manual systems, required documents, internal controls, and corporate governance issues.

In some instances, the individual may use more than one layer of concealment techniques to hide the true nature of the business transaction. The auditor should design an audit approach based on the mechanics of the fraud scheme and the concealment strategy.

1. Fictitious delivery of the product or service. This will occur through the creation of false documentation.
2. Real delivery to false or hidden locations. Here, the company ships product to non-customers for the illusion of sale through the use of freight forwarders, other company warehouses and concealed or false locations, or consignment locations. Or the company ships to distributors without title transfer.
3. Shipment of nonexistent or incomplete product. This occurs through the actual shipment of a container that is either empty, filled for weight purposes, or an incomplete product.
4. Shipment to a real customer that did not order the product. Management ships an actual product to a customer that never ordered the item.
5. Concealment of returns. This requires the delaying of the return after the audit period, recording the return as something other than a return, or a combination of efforts to conceal the return and the adjustment.
6. Subsequent credits or adjustments. Since the fictitious revenue cannot be realized, the receivable must be cleared through credit memos or actual adjusting entries.

7. Disguised customer remittances. The documentation supporting the source of the remittance is altered or created to provide the illusion of realization.
8. Use of company funds to provide illusion of customer remittances. Here, the company uses multiple bank accounts, subsidiary bank accounts, or foreign bank accounts.
9. Lapping scheme to provide illusion of customer remittances. Other customers' remittances or credit balances are applied to the fictitious revenue.
10. Undisclosed terms and conditions. The customer is offered verbal terms or side agreements that are not disclosed to the auditor. Or, the auditor can also be given draft documents, altered copies, or false documents.
11. Right of return not disclosed. The customer is provided the opportunity to return the product through a trial period, approval period, or some other program.
12. Created, altered, or fictitious documentation.
13. No documentation supporting verbal representations.
14. Falsifying company reports to provide an illusion of an event or representation.
15. Control over confirmations. With fictitious customers, the customer addresses are under the control of management. With real customers, the management team must exert some control over the response. In certain industries, obtaining responses can be difficult, so management offers assistance in obtaining the response.
16. There are cases in which the customer conspired against the auditor to falsely respond to the confirmation.
17. Intentional misrepresentation by management.
18. Improper criteria used in estimates.
19. Collusion with outside experts to provide false representations.

 ## PLANNING THE REVENUE AUDIT

During planning, the auditor should consider the following:

1. Structure the brainstorming session to include a discussion of the revenue fraud schemes in relation to the specific client industry and client accounting practices. This discussion should:
   ■ Using the Fraud Risk Structure as a guide, identify how the inherent revenue schemes would occur.

- Using the Fraud Concealment Strategy as a guide, identify how the inherent revenue scheme would be concealed.
- Identify any client practices that may create problems, such as right of return or distributorship arrangements.
- Review industry-specific fraud schemes, such as front-loading for a construction contractor.
- Include any past problems with the client.

2. Using the fraud theory, understand management's motivation for under- or overstatement of revenue. This facilitates where and how to search for the fraud.
3. Understand how the key revenue assertions occur within the company by revenue source.
4. Obtain a thorough understanding of the revenue cycle and types of revenue transactions. The auditor should inquire about:
   - Earnings process in relation to the general rule for revenue recognition; there are four elements:
     - An exchange transaction has taken place.
     - The earnings process is essentially complete.
     - The seller's price to the buyer is fixed and determinable.
     - Collectability is reasonably assured.
5. Discuss how those assertions could be falsified and subsequently concealed.
6. Determine if there are any specific GAAP pronouncements for revenue recognition.
7. Develop global-based analytical analysis around the relevant fraud schemes:
   - Understand the sources of revenue.
   - Differentiate revenue created through the billing system and revenue created through other sources.
   - Differentiate revenue recorded through the sales system and revenue recorded via journal entry.
   - Identify revenue via new customers versus existing customers.
   - Identify revenue recorded at the end of an accounting period.
   - Identify revenue recorded after a significant business event.
   - Identify new customers or new accounts.
   - Identify revenue recorded through noncustomer accounts.
   - Identify revenue by product line. The goal should be a disaggregated analysis at the lowest level practical.
   - Analyze credit activity by customer as to cash, adjustments, or returns.
   - Search for activity by ship-to address.

8. Develop questions for the interviewing of management.
   - Understand how the key revenue assertions occur in the company.
   - Identify which revenue schemes relate to the individual being interviewed.
   - Understand what impact the individual has on the documentation supporting the revenue assertion.
   - Inquire as to negotiation strategies with customers.
   - Identify customers controlled by non-sales force personnel.
9. Discuss improper revenue recognition for the company. Remember the identification of a risk of material misstatement due to fraud involves the application of professional judgment and includes consideration of:
   - The *type* of risk that may exist. As mentioned above, the auditor should consider how management would misstate revenue, first at a top-side level, then at the specific scheme level.
   - The *significance* of the risk; that is, whether it is of a magnitude that could result in a possible <u>material</u> misstatement of the financial statements.
   - The *likelihood* of the risk or scheme's occurring within the industry and organization.
   - The *pervasiveness* of the risk; that is, whether the potential risk is pervasive to the financial statements as a whole or specifically related to a particular assertion, account, or class of transactions.

AUDIT AREAS FOR FALSE BILLING SCHEMES

1. **Customer master file.** False billing schemes require the revenue transaction to be recorded in a customer account.
   - Creation of a fictitious customer.
   - Real customers with no current sales activity.
   - Real customers with multiple accounts.
   - Look-alike customer.
   - Real customer that is not a knowing participant.

   Data Analysis

   - New customers with large sales activity at the end of a reporting period.
   - Dormant customers with large sales activity at the end of a reporting period.
   - Large customers with multiple bill-to addresses.

- House accounts with large sales activity at the end of a reporting period.
- Match customer database to personnel or vendor database for name, address, telephone number, and federal identification number.
- Missing credit terms amounts or large credit terms for new customer.
- Missing key identifying information, such as contact name, identification number, etc.

2. **Sales transaction.** The scheme requires the creation of a sales transaction, such as:

- Sales to fictitious customers.
- Sales to real customers.
- Sales to noncustomer accounts.
- Sales to related parties. Fictitious sales to fictitious customers, real customers, noncustomer accounts, or related parties.
- Incomplete sales.
- Disputed sales.

Data Analysis

- Sales with no commission or assigned to a sales representative or territory.
- Sales to a noncustomer account.
- Missing customer information, i.e., sales order number.
- Search on ship-to address.
- Same address for more than one customer.
- No recorded ship-to address.
- Frequency of sales activity at the end of a reporting period.
  - Large sales transaction at end of reporting period.
  - New customers at end of reporting period.

3. **Realization of revenue.** The scheme requires the illusion of a customer's paying the receivable.

- Credits to a customer's account originating from noncash receipts.
- Deposit of personal funds to provide realization.
- Creation of false documents to provide the illusion of a cash receipt.
- Misapplication of customer cash receipts to provide the illusion of realization.
- Early or false recognition of returns and adjustments.
- Realization through loans.
- Realization through circular transactions.

Data Analysis

- Search for customers with no or limited cash receipts in relation to customer sales.
- Search for returns, adjustments, voids, and write-offs.
- Search for customers with large cash receipts transaction.
- Search for cash receipts transaction missing identifying information.
- Search for cash receipt transaction from nontraditional sources.
- Use of controlled addresses to respond to confirmations or correspondence.
- When lapping is used, consider the following data analyses:
- Search for customer remittances check numbers that do not follow a logical date sequence.
- Search for accounts with frequent credit memos and other credit adjustments to the account.
- Search for account transfers.
- Search for noncustomer accounts.

4. **Fictitious revenue to real customer.** Here the scheme involves:
   - Shipping products to customers that did not order the product.
   - Shipping products to customers that agree to hold the product.

   ### Data Analysis

   - Search for excessive returns, credits, voids after the end of the reporting period.
   - Search for customer accounts with high sales volume and limited cash receipts activity.
   - Search for aged returns and adjustments.

5. **Delivery of product to customer.** Some schemes include:
   - False ship-to address.
   - Creation of a ship-to address.
   - Nondelivery of the product or service.
   - Shipping unfinished products.
   - Distributors and consignment.
   - Trial and evaluation purpose.
   - Bill-and-hold transactions.

   ### Data Analysis

   - Month-by-month comparison of sales to detect "pump up" and reversal of transactions.
   - Inspect shipping documents to see if company employees signed rather than shipping company.

- Inspect shipping documents to see if shipped to warehouse rather than customer's regular shipping address.
- Inspect invoices to see if shipping information is missing.

6. **Other data analysis techniques.** Some to consider are:
- Review past revenue trends to see that they make sense. Consider seasonality, as well as economic changes.
- Compare past revenue trends with similar businesses in the same industry. Investigate large fluctuations.
- Review changes in deferred revenue. A decrease could signal a decrease in business or a release of reserves.
- Compare revenue with physical capacity. Is it possible to have the sales volume recorded with the capacity?
- Compare industry statistics such as revenue per employee, revenue per unit of production, revenue per square foot, revenue for dollar of PP&E.
- Compare receivables to revenue:
  - Rate of change—are receivables increasing with flat or lower sales? In many well-known frauds, the buildup in accounts receivable grew as the revenue recognition policies became more aggressive.
  - Changes in days sales outstanding. Sudden changes up or down may be indicative of fraudulent activities.

7. **Terms and conditions.** As applied to:
- Undisclosed terms and conditions, including terms written in a side letter, verbal terms, or the nonenforcement of written terms.
- Interpretation of the terms and conditions.
- Terms and conditions are not fixed and agreed to by both parties.

8. **False documentation.** Some examples are:
- Create documents.
- Alter or change documents.
- False dating of documents.
- False verbal representations.
- Providing draft documents as the properly executed documents.

AUDIT AREAS FOR IMPROPER RECOGNITION SCHEMES

For improper recognition the audit should focus on the outcome of the revenue transaction versus the occurrence of the transaction. There are two basic outcomes:

1. **The revenue is not realized and is eventually returned.** The audit should focus on events that occur after year-end.

Data Analysis

- Credits to customer accounts resulting from returns and adjustments are indicative of improper recognition.

2. **The revenue is eventually recognized.** The audit should focus on the delivery and terms and conditions of the revenue transactions.

Data Analysis

- Sales order. The documentation should show a clear intent to order the product.
  - Created sales orders.
  - Altered sales orders.
  - Back-dated sales orders.
- Sales terms. The terms and conditions support the recognition of the revenue. Fraud schemes in the past have used undisclosed terms and conditions.
  - Unconditional right to return product.
  - Ease of return of product.
  - Ability to cancel the order.
  - Open payment terms.
  - Extension of payment terms.
  - Negotiation of terms and conditions are open.
  - Future performance terms.
  - Contingent on performance.
- Resale
- Refund for unsold product
- Future performance
  - Delivery of product. The shipment is flawed in some aspect.
    - Deliver incomplete product as final product.
    - Partial shipments represented as complete delivery.
    - Approval, trial, demo sales.
    - Future, trial, demo sales.
    - Future performance of services.
    - Recognizing up-front payments as revenue.
    - Shipments to company-controlled facilities.
    - Shipment before customer finalizes order/contract.
    - Shipments to freight forwarders.
    - Shipments to other company warehouses.

- Manipulation of the closing of the year-end books. Depending on the intent of management, the books are closed early or late. Understanding the fraud risk factors related to the pressure the organization is facing is an indicator of which way the scheme will occur.

3. **Revenue created through recording journal entries.** The starting point is to understand which revenue accounts are impacted by journal entries, other than posting source journals.
   - In the brainstorming session discuss:
     - Characteristics of fraudulent journal entries.
     - Characteristics of misstated revenue accounts.
   - Obtain an understanding of the entity's financial reporting process and controls over journal entries and period ending adjusting entries.
   - Determine the use and the extent of top-sided journal entries.
   - Determine the nature and type of journal entries impacting the account.
   - Determine extent of account balance impacted by adjusting, reclassifying, or consolidating entries.
   - Determine the nature, timing, and extent of auditing procedures.
     - Nature: The type of entry will impact the nature of the audit procedures.
- Adjusting. Validate the assumption of the adjustment
- Reclassifying. Movement of the revenue steam to a different account is consistent with the transaction. Reclassification between operating and nonoperating should be scrutinized.
- Consolidating. Determine whether related party or intercompany revenue is properly reported and disclosed.
     - Extent: The analysis of revenue created by journal entries will be a determining factor.
     - Timing: Revenue misstatement, by its nature occurs at the end of a reporting period.

Checklist of Inherent Scheme Structure

 ENTITY STRUCTURE

False Entity

- Created: entity created for the purpose of committing the fraud scenario.
  - Legally created: Entity created to commit the scheme.
  - Not legally created: Entity that was not legally created.
- Assumed: Taking over the identity of an entity for the purpose of committing the fraud scenario.
  - Internal entity: A real entity already in the internal master file.
  - External entity: A real entity external to the company.

Real Entity

- Complicit: A real entity that is knowingly involved in a fraud scenario.
  - Individual working in the entity.
  - Company/owner.
- Not complicit: A real entity that is unknowingly involved in a fraud scenario.

 **DISBURSEMENT CHAPTER**

False Entity

- False billing:
  - Entity: False entity either created or assumed.
  - Action: Payment for services or an event that did not occur.
- Pass-through billing:
  - Entity: False entity either created or assumed.
  - Action: Payment for services or an event that did occur.

Real Entity

- Overbilling:
  - Entity: A real entity.
  - Action: Overcharging on invoices.
- Speed of disbursement:
  - Entity: A real entity and an internal employee.
  - Action: Funds disbursed after they were entitled.

PAYROLL CHAPTER

False Entity

- Fictitious ghost employee:
  - Entity: A false created employee.
  - Action: Payment for services that did not occur.
- Terminated ghost employee:
  - Entity: A false assumed employee.
  - Action: Payment for services that did not occur.
- Temporary ghost employee:
  - Entity: A false or real employee.
  - Action: Payment for services that did not occur.
- Family ghost employee:
  - Entity: A false or real employee.
  - Action: Payment for services that did not occur or overpaid for services.

Real Entity

- No-show ghost employee:

- Entity: A real employee.
- Action: Payment for services that did not occur.
■ Preemployment ghost employee:
    - Entity: A real employee.
    - Action: Payment for services that did not occur.
■ Overtime and regular hours:
    - Entity: A real employee.
    - Action: Payment for hours not worked.
■ Salary adjustment:
    - Entity: A real employee.
    - Action: Gross salary or net payroll falsely increased.

PROCUREMENT SCHEMES

■ Favored vendor:
    - Entity: A real entity.
    - Action: Procurement decision is corrupted.
■ Vendor bid rigging:
    - Entity: A real entity.
    - Action: Procurement decision is corrupted.
■ Disguised purchases for resale:
    - Entity: A real entity.
    - Action: Theft for resale.
■ Disguised purchases for personal use:
    - Entity: A real entity.
    - Action: Theft for personal use.
■ Conflict of interest:
    - Entity: A real entity.
    - Action: Undisclosed interest in a vendor.

APPENDIX

G

Fraud Audit Matrix

Company Name

Fraud Audit Matrix

Fraud Risk Structure: Primary Category
Fraud Risk Structure: Secondary Category

Inherent Scheme	Fraud Opportunity	Fraud Scenario	Concealment	Red Flags	Conversion

Company Name

Fraud Audit Matrix

Fraud Risk Structure: Primary Category
Fraud Risk Structure: Secondary Category

Fraud Scenario	Sampling Strategy	Data Mining Strategy	Test of Controls Audit Procedure	Fraud Audit Procedure	Fraud Conclusion

About the Author

Leonard W. Vona, CPA, CFE, is a financial investigator with more than 30 years of diversified auditing and forensic accounting experience, including a distinguished 18-year private industry career. His firm advises clients in areas of litigation support, financial investigations, and fraud prevention.

Mr. Vona is the author of *Fraud Risk Assessment: Building a Fraud Audit Program,* published by John Wiley & Sons.

Mr. Vona has successfully conducted more than 100 financial investigations for some of the largest high-profile corporations in the United States. The net result of his efforts has saved clients millions of dollars through recovery or defense strategies. His financial investigation experience includes embezzlement, economic damage, asset theft, bribery, intellectual property, and disbursement schemes. Mr. Vona's trial experience is extensive, including appearances in federal and state courts. He is qualified as an expert witness, as a CPA and a CFE, and is cited in West Law for the successful use of circumstantial evidence.

Mr. Vona lectures nationally and internationally on fraud risk assessments, fraud investigation, fraud prevention and detection, and fraud schemes perpetrated on companies. He regularly speaks at audit conferences and has developed the Fraud Training Curriculum for the MIS Training Institute, an internationally recognized audit training organization. Mr. Vona has provided more than 1,000 days of fraud training to organizations around the world. He is currently on the faculty of the National Association of Fraud Examiners. and is a former faculty member of the Lally School of Management at Rensselaer Polytechnic Institute. He has written the training course on Auditors' Responsibility for Detecting Fraud—SAS 99 used by CPA societies across the country.

His private industry experience includes being recognized by Arthur Andersen as one of the top 25 Audit Directors in North America and conducting a financial investigation as part of a Qui Tam investigation for the U.S. Department of Justice. He led internal audit departments for more than

15 years, and his knowledge of internal controls and fraud prevention theory is vast.

Mr. Vona graduated from Siena College with honors, receiving a bachelor of business administration in accounting. He is a licensed certified public accountant and a certified fraud examiner.

Mr. Vona is a member of the American Institute of Certified Public Accountants, the National Association of Certified Fraud Examiners, and the Institute of Internal Auditors. He was the 1994 president of the New York Capital Chapter of the Association of Government Accountants and the founding president of the Albany Chapter of Certified Fraud Examiners.

Index

Allowance programs, 220
Altered document, 152–153
American Institute of Certified Public
    Accountants (AICPA), 16
    consideration of fraud via SAS 99,
        20–24
American Society for Testing and
    Materials (ASTM) Standard
    E444-09, 149
Asset misappropriation, 32, 36,
        48–49, 105–108,
        271–273, 290–291, 300,
        327, 335–336
    example, 105–108
    in program management fraud,
        271–273
        disguised purchases, 273
        false expenditures, 271–272
        income skimming, 273
        overbilling, 272–273
    loss calculations for, 290–291
Assumed identity entity, 129
Auditing standards, 3, 15–26
    Institute of Internal Auditors (IIA),
        16, 18–20
        guidelines regarding fraud,
            18–20
        recognition of fraud, 20
    international, 25
    SAS 99, 20–24

analytical procedures, 21–22
brainstorming session, 24
communicating with
    management, 23
discrepancies in accounting
    records, 22
interviewing, 21
professional skepticism, 20–21
risk assessment, 21
Yellow Book (GAGAS), 24–25
    "Ethical Principles in
        Government Auditing," 24
    fieldwork and financial reporting
        standards, 25
    "Performance Audits," 25
"The Auditor's Responsibilities
    Relating to Fraud in an
    Audit of Financial
    Statements" (IAASB), 17
Avoidance strategies, 34, 38–39
Awareness Theory Methodology
    (ATM) approach, 2,
    11, 147

Bid rigging, 37, 333, 335, 337
Bidding corruption, 185–187,
        197–199, 325–326,
        334–335
    bid avoidance, 185–186, 197–198,
        325–326, 334–335

Bidding corruption (*Continued*)
  contract amendment, 186, 325
  exigency purchase, 186, 326
  sole source, 186, 326
  split bids, 185, 325
  structured purchasing, 185, 325
  bidding exclusion, 187, 326
  false statements, 186, 198, 326
  favoring of key control points,
      186–187, 198, 326
  management override, 198–199,
      326
Bill-and-hold procedures, 235
Billing schemes, 162
Brainstorming, 24, 53–68
  case study, 59–60
  outcomes from, 66
  purpose of, 54–56
    free-flow approach to, 54–55
    leading the session, 55–56
  red flag matrix, 67–68
  when to brainstorm, 56–58,
      60–65
    establishing audit scope, 56
    fraud audit approach, 58,
        60–65
    fraud scenario boundaries, 57
Bribery, 37, 50, 183–184, 292, 326,
    333, 335, 336–337
Business processes and internal
    controls, 44

Channel stuffing, 236, 349
Classifying fraud, 32–41
  business system considerations, 41
  primary, 32–35
    asset misappropriation, 32
    avoidance strategies, 34
    corruption, 32–33

false program reporting, 35
  financial reporting, 33
  informational manipulation and
      misuse, 34
  management override, 35
  revenue obtained improperly, 33
  technological manipulation and
      misuse, 34–35
secondary, 35–41
  asset misappropriation, 36
  avoidance strategies, 38–39
  corruption, 36–37
  false program reporting, 40–41
  financial reporting, 37
  informational manipulation and
      misuse, 39
  management override, 39–40
  revenue obtained improperly, 38
  technological manipulation and
      misuse, 39
Collusion–corruption–opportunity
    connection, 182–183
Committee of Sponsoring
    Organizations (COSO)
    control model, 76
Concealment strategies, 29, 89–90,
    97–103, 106–107,
    239–240
  effect on audit response, 97–103
    sophistication of, 98–103
    relationship between red flags
        and, 98
  example, 106–107
  identifying, 89–90
  in inventory fraud, 239–240
Conflict of interest, 37, 201, 274,
    291, 326, 333, 335, 337
  hiring schemes, 221
  loss calculations for, 291

in procurement fraud, 333,
335, 337
in program management fraud,
274
Consignment of income, 236, 349
Contract administration, 334,
335–336
Conversion, 29–30
Corruption, 32–33, 36–37, 50,
108–110, 291–292,
325–327. *See also*
Procurement fraud
bidding, 185–187
bid avoidance, 185–186, 325
bidding exclusion, 187, 326
false statements, 186, 326
favoring of key control points,
186–187, 326
example, 108–110
procurement, employee-alone,
191–192, 201–202
in program management fraud,
273–274
conflict of interest, 274
favored status, 274
schemes, loss calculations for,
291–292
vendor, 189–191
collusion, 190–191
vendor-alone, 191
vendors-in-collusion
characteristics, 190
Cost mischarging, 194, 327,
334–336
contract administration,
335–336
data mining, 334–335
Created document, 153–154
Created entity, 128–129

Data analysis
in disbursement fraud, 164–166
master file information,
164–165
off-period transactions, 165
false-entity, 166
in procurement fraud,
184–192
bidding corruption, 185–187
customer directed, 192
employee-alone corruption,
191–192
Foreign Corrupt Practices Act
(FCPA), 192
vendor corruption, 189–191
vendor selection, 187–189
purchase order, 166
vendor invoice, 165
Data mining, 6, 71–72, 85, 88, 101,
103, 106, 111–132,
184–192, 209–212,
227–231, 303–308
assumptions, 114–117
certainty principle, 114
effectiveness, 115–116
number of transactions,
116–117
routines, 114–115
defined, 112–113
detecting internal control
avoidance, 165
fundamentals, 117–129
applying inclusion/exclusion
theory, 119–120
data correlations, 121–128
entity structures and search
routines, 128–129
mapping data fields to fraud
scenario, 118

Data mining (*Continued*)
  type, location, and quantity of
    data, 117–118
  understanding false positives,
    120–121
  understanding integrity of data,
    118–119
  understanding the "norm" of
    data, 121
  limitations of, 131–132
  for payroll fraud, 209–212,
    303–308
  challenges in, 209
  example, 211–212
  planning, 210
  reports, 210–211
  strategies for, 129–131
  off-period transactions,
    129–130
  speed of decision or payment,
    130
  terminology, 113
  using to detect false revenue,
    227–231
  schemes with false customers
    and false revenue,
    229–230
  schemes with real customers
    and false revenue,
    230—231
Decision tree logic, 90, 91–92, 95,
    96, 130, 135, 136
Defective pricing, 200, 327,
    334, 338
Degree of certainty, 86–87
Disbursement fraud, 159–178,
    311–324
  audit approaches, 166–178

schemes involving false entities,
    167–169
schemes involving real entities,
    169–178
fraud risk structure, 159–166
  data analysis, 164–166
  and embezzlement, 163–164
  terminology, 161–162
audit program, 311–324
  audit procedures, 320–324
  red flags, 311–320
Discovery sampling, 7
Discrimination, 37, 183, 221, 333,
    335, 336
  in hiring practices, 221
Disguised compensation
  nonpayroll schemes, 218
  payroll schemes, 217–218
Disguised purchasing, 201, 273
  in program management fraud,
    273
  and resale, 201–201
Document analysis, 147–157
  and fraud audit, 148
  levels of examination, 148–150
  fraud audit document,
    149–150
  questioned document, 149
  red flags, 150–156
  brainstorming sessions and,
    155–156
  document condition and
    existence, 150–154
  document information,
    154–155
  fraud audit program
    and, 156
Drill-down process, 43–44

Duplicate payment scheme,
174–175

Embezzlement, 36, 48, 105–108,
163–164, 271–273, 290,
300, 335–336
example, 105–108
fraud risk structure and,
163–164
loss calculations for, 290
Employee
corruption, 201–202
misuse of, 221–222
reimbursement, 177
Entity verification procedures,
140–144
check references, 143–144
test business capacity, 143
verify legal existence, 141–142
verify physical existence,
142–143
Expense allocations, in journal entry
fraud, 266
Extortion, 37, 177–178, 183–184,
333, 335, 336–337
of vendors, 177–178, 184

False charge scheme, 172–173
False entities, 129, 139–140, 166,
167–168
controlled addresses for, 129
data analysis, 166
schemes involving, 167–169
false billing, 167
illegal activities, 168–169
pass-through billing, 167–168
False program reporting, 35,
40–41

Favored status, 36, 182, 274,
325, 334
in program management fraud,
274
vendor, 182
Financial reporting fraud, 33, 37,
47–48
Foreign Corrupt Practices Act
(FCPA), 192
Fraud
audit, 1–13, 15–26, 83–110,
133–146
Awareness Theory
Methodology (ATM)
approach to, 2
fraud paradigm, 4–5
fraud risk, responding to, 3–4,
12–13, 84–85
procedures, 133–146. *See also*
Procedures, fraud audit
process, four steps of, 5–6
program, building, 83–110
standards, 15–26
traditional audits vs., 6–7
triangle, 8–12
classifying. *See* Classifying fraud
defined, 8, 17
IAASB standard, 17
risk, assessment of, 69–81
preparing, 69–80
scenarios, 27–51, 57, 86–87,
88, 89, 92, 97–98,
106–110
boundaries, 57
classifying fraud, 32–41
concealment, 29, 97–98
conversion, 29–30
examples, 106–110

Fraud (*Continued*)
  fraud audit considerations, 46–50
  identifying, 41–46
  risk structure, 30–31
  scenarios, 29
  inherent fraud schemes, 28–29
Fraud audit program, building,
    83–110
  audit evidence issues, 103–105
  fraud scenario examples,
    106–110
  quality and quantity of evidence,
    103–104
  trier of fact, 104–105
  fraud concealment effect on audit
    response, 97–103
  relationship between
    concealment strategy and
    red flags, 98
  sophistication of concealment
    strategy, 98–103
  key concepts, 86–88
  creditable evidence, 87–88
  degree of certainty, 86–87
  inherent limitations, 86
  linkage, 86
  overt capacity, 88
  purpose, 85–86
  responding to risk of fraud, 84–85
  integrated approach, 85
  steps, 88–89
  testing procedures, 89–97
  fraud audit, 92, 94–97
  red flag, 89–92
  traditional audit vs. fraud audit, 84
Fraud audit matrix, 363–364
Fraud likelihood score, 70–71,
    77–78
  calculating, 77–78

linking audit response to, 80
Fraud-loss exposure score, 70–71
Fraud management program,
    18–19
  ethics policy, 18
  investigating potential fraud, 19
  reviews of audit activity, 19
  risk assessment, 18–19
Fraud opportunity, 45
Fraud theory, 2
Fraud triangle, 2, 8–12
  fear of detection, 11
  opportunity, 9–10
  perpetrators and experience
    levels, categories of, 9–10
  premises, 11–12
  pressure, 10
  rationalization, 11
Front companies, 161–162

GAO. *See* U.S. Government
    Accountability Office
Generally Accepted Audit Standards
    (GAAS) audit, 6
Generally Accepted Government
    Auditing Standards
    (GAGAS), 17, 24–25,
    26, 32
  "Ethical Principles in Government
    Auditing," 24
  fieldwork and financial reporting
    standards, 25
  "Performance Audits," 25
Ghost employees, 207–208,
    213–216, 299, 303–308
  family, 208, 299, 306
  fictitious, 299, 305
  no-show, 214–215, 299,
    305–306

preemployment, 213–214,
299, 307
rehired, 214, 299, 307
temporary, 215–216, 299, 306
terminated, 213, 299, 303–304

Health insurance, payroll schemes
involving, 219–220

Identified fraud risk, 29, 73–75
caveats of, 73–74
models for risk identification,
74–75
core business level (micro level),
74–75
entity-wide level (macro level), 74
fraud penetration risk assessment
model (mega-micro level),
75
Income skimming, in program
management fraud, 273
Informational manipulation and
misuse, 34, 39
Inherent fraud schemes, 28–29, 43,
94, 360–362
structure, checklist of, 360–362
disbursement, 361
entity, 360
payroll, 361–362
procurement, 362
Inherent limitations, 86
Institute of Internal Auditors (IIA),
16, 18–20
guidelines regarding fraud, 18–20
fraud management program,
18–19
International Professional
Practices Framework
(IPPF) standards, 19–20

recognition of fraud, 20
Integrated fraud audit approach,
85
Internal controls, 75–80, 165
categorizing, 76–77
defining, 75–76
detecting avoidance of, 165
linking to fraud scenario,
77–80
International Auditing and
Assurance Standards Board
(IAASB), 16, 17
International Professional Practices
Framework (IPPF)
standards, 19–20
Standard 1210.A2: Proficiency
and Due Professional Care,
19
Standard 1220.A1: Due
Professional Care, 19
Standard 2060: Reporting to
Senior Management and
the Board, 19–20
Standard 2120.A2: Risk
Management, 20
Standard 2210.A2: Engagement
Objectives, 20
International Standards of Auditing
(ISAs), 25
Inventory fraud, 237–249
audit procedures, 243–249
inventory examination,
243–244
inventory fraud schemes,
244–248
fraud risk structure, 238–243
concealment strategies,
239–240
data analysis, 241–243

Inventory fraud (*Continued*)
  identifying inventory theft and
    misuse, 239
  management-derived inventory
    fraud, 240–241
  schemes, 244–248, 339–346
    alterations, 245, 340, 343
    concealment techniques,
      339–346
    false certifications, 245, 340,
      342–343
    fictitious inventory, 244, 339,
      341–342
    hiding inventory, 246–247,
      340, 344–345
    improper costing, 247, 340, 345
    misstatement of marketability,
      247, 345
    multiple locations, 246, 340,
      344
    partially fictitious inventory,
      244–245, 340, 342
    report alteration, 248
    timing, 246, 340
    year-end journal entries, 248,
      345–346

Journal entry fraud, 251–267
  audit procedures, 261–266
    examples of fraud schemes
      involving journal entries,
      264–265
    examples of journal entry fraud
      schemes, 265–266
    for journal entries and accounts,
      263–264
    steps to identifying fraudulent
      journal entries, 262–263

  fraud risk structure, 252–261
    data analysis, 255–261
    SAS 99 and manipulation in
      financial reporting,
      252–253
    transactions and journal entries,
      253–255
Kickbacks, 37, 50, 183–184, 192,
  292, 326, 333, 335,
  336–337

Lack of business purpose, loss
  calculations for, 291
Linkage, 86
Loss exposure, understanding and
  identifying, 78–80

Management override, 35, 39–40
Management-derived inventory
  fraud, 240–241
  fraudulent financial reporting of
    inventory, 240–241
  inventory concealment
    techniques, 241
Missing document, 151–152
Misuse of assets, 49, 291
  loss calculations for, 291
Money trail, 29–30

Nepotism, 36–37, 183, 333,
  335, 336
Nonconforming materials, 193–194,
  327
Nontangible entity items, 144

Overbilling, 169–175, 183,
  272–273, 334, 338
  collusion with vendor employees

after contract/purchase order
issuance, 172–175
prior to purchase orders,
171–172
opportunities created by internal
controls, 169–171
in program management fraud,
272–273
Overstated assets, in journal entry
fraud, 265
Overt capacity, 88
Overtime reporting fraud, 216–217,
300, 308

Pass-through billing, 167–168
Payroll fraud, 205–222, 298–310
audit procedures, 212–222,
309–310
disguised compensation
nonpayroll schemes, 218
disguised compensation payroll
schemes, 217–218
family ghost employee, 208,
299, 306
fictitious ghost employee, 299,
305
no-show ghost employee,
214–215, 299, 305–306
overtime reporting fraud,
216–217, 300, 308
payroll department schemes,
218–219
payroll-related schemes,
219–222
preemployment ghost employee,
213–214, 299, 307
rehired ghost employee, 214,
299, 307

temporary ghost employee,
215–216, 299, 306
terminated ghost employees,
213, 299, 303–304
audit program, 298–310
background, 298–299
data mining, 303–308
fraud scheme structure, 300
key terms, 299–300
overall approach, 301
procedures, 309–310
red flags, 301–302
fraud risk structure, 206–212
data analysis, 208–212
terminology, 207–208
Payroll-related schemes,
219–222
allowance programs, 220
conflict-of-interest hiring, 221
discriminatory hiring practices,
221
health insurance, 219–220
misuse of employees, 221–222
temporary hiring agencies, 219
Permutation analysis, 44–45, 57,
73
Pricing, defective, 200, 327,
334, 338
Procedures, fraud audit, 133–146
basis of, 133–135
design of, 138–145
entity verification, 139–144
linking procedure to scenario,
139
levels of, 135–138
red flag testing procedures
associated with fraud
scenarios, 135–136

Procedures, fraud audit (*Continued*)
  procedures concerning inherent
    fraud schemes residing
    within core business
    system, 136–138
  verifying inherent scheme action,
    144–145
Procurement fraud, 179–203,
  325–338
  audit procedures, 195–202
    approach steps, 195–196
    fraud red flags and, 196–202
  audit program, 325–338
    audit procedures, 336–338
    cost mischarging, 334–336
    fraud scheme structure, 327
    key terms, 325–327
    overall approach, 327–328
    red flags, 328–334
  fraud risk structure, 181–195
    bribery, kickbacks, and
      extortion, 183–184
    collusion–corruption–
      opportunity connection,
      182–183
    contracts, 193–195
    data analysis, 184–192
Product substitution scheme, 173
Program management fraud,
  269–282
  audit approach, 277–281
    false data, 277–279
    measuring program
      performance, 277
    program fraud audits, 279–281
  fraud risk structure, 270–276
    asset misappropriation,
      271–273
    corruption, 273–274

    reporting manipulation,
      274–276
Progress payment fraud, 193, 327,
  334, 338
Purchase order analysis, 166

Quantifying fraud, 283–296
  case studies, 293–295
  conveying impact to management,
    284–287
    fraud conversion and the fraud
      scenario, 285–286
    fraud conversion and the loss
      calculation, 286–287
    loss to the company versus
      employee economic benefit,
      284–285
    using the fraud audit report,
      284
  impact on the fraud audit,
    289–292
    loss calculations for corruption
      schemes, 291–292
    loss calculations for asset
      misappropriation schemes,
      290–291
  options for management, 292–293
    administrative, 292
    civil, 292–293
    criminal, 293
  role of evidence in calculating a
    fraud loss, 287–289
    circumstantial evidence,
      288–289
    direct evidence, 287–288

Real entities, 140, 169–178
  schemes involving, 169–178
    employee reimbursement, 177

extortion of vendors, 177–178
overbilling, 169–175
speed-of-disbursement schemes, 175–176
theft-of-check schemes, 176
treasury department schemes, 176–177
Red flags, 58, 60–65, 67–68, 85, 89–92, 93, 98, 148, 150–155, 196–202, 301–302, 311–320
in disbursement fraud, 311–320
in document analysis, 150–155
document condition and existence, 150–154
defined, 58, 60
development and brainstorming sessions, 64–65
flow chart, 93
four categories of, 60–63
behavioral, 62–63
data, 61
document, 61–62
internal control, 62
matrix, 67–68
in payroll fraud, 301–302
in procurement fraud, 196–202
relationship between concealment strategy and, 98
testing procedures, 85, 89–92, 148
understanding, 58
Reporting manipulation, in program management fraud, 274–276
fictitious or missing transactions, 274–275
improper recognition, 274–275
manipulation of budgets, 275
financial reporting, 274
program reporting, 275–276
Revenue fraud audit program, 347–359
audit areas
for false billing schemes, 354–357
for improper recognition schemes, 357–359
fraud concealment strategy, 351–352
fraud risk structure, 347–350
planning audit, 352–354
Revenue misstatement, 223–236
audit approach, 231–236
documentation, 232
examples of fraud schemes involving revenue recognition, 234–235
Statement of Auditing Standards 99, 232–233
use of real customers, 235–236
fraud risk structure, 224–231
data analysis, 226–227
and revenue misstatement, 224–226
using data mining for detecting false revenue, 227–231
Revenue obtained improperly, 33, 38
Revenue recognition, 265–266, 347–350
in journal entry fraud, 265–266
Revenue-skimming fraud scheme, 5
Risk, assessment of, 69–81, 114
preparing, 69–80
approaches, 71–72

Risk, assessment of (*Continued*)
    fundamental principles, 70–71
    key elements, 72–80
Round tripping, 236, 349
Scenarios, fraud, 27–51, 57, 86–87,
        88, 89, 92, 97–98
    boundaries, 57
    classifying, 32–41
        business system considerations,
            41
        primary, 32–35
        secondary, 35–41
    concealment, 29, 97–98
    conversion, 29–30
    examples, 106–110
    fraud audit considerations,
        46–50
        asset misappropriation, 48–49
        bribery and corruption, 50
        financial reporting, 47–48
    identifying, 41–46
        common mistakes, 46
        decisions, 42
        hints, 43–45
        steps, 42–43
    risk structure, 30–31, 43
    scenarios, 29
    inherent fraud schemes, 28–29
Skimming, 48
Speed-of-disbursement schemes,
        175–176
Standards, professional. *See* Auditing
        standards
Statement of Auditing Standard
        (SAS) 99, 8–9, 12, 16,
        20–24, 26, 29, 32, 70,
        232–233, 252–253,
        260, 347

analytical procedures, 21–22
brainstorming session, 24
communicating with
        management, 23
discrepancies in accounting
        records, 22
interviewing, 21
and manipulation in financial
        reporting, 252–253
professional skepticism,
        20–21
risk assessment, 21
Structuring, 130

Technological manipulation and
        misuse, 34–35, 39
Temporary hiring agencies, schemes
        involving, 219
Theft, 48–49, 238, 290
    loss calculations for, 290–291
Theft-of-check schemes, 176
Treasury department schemes,
        176–177

Unauthorized asset disposal/
        acquisition, loss
        calculations for, 291
U.S. Government Accountability
        Office (GAO), 16, 17

Vendor corruption, 189–191,
        199–201
    advance communication of
        information, 199–200
    collusion
        and bid rigging, 190
        and price fixing, 191
    favored vendors, 200

predetermined pricing, 199
vendor-alone, 191, 200
vendors-in-collusion
    characteristics, 190,
    200
Vendor invoice analysis, 165
Vendor selection, 187–189
  advance communication of
    information, 189

evaluation criteria manipulation,
    188
management override, 189
selection process manipulation,
    188–189

Yellow Book. *See* Generally Accepted
    Government Auditing
    Standards (GAGAS)